To:

From:

Date

Honor Books® is an imprint of
Cook Communications Ministries, Colorado Springs, Colorado 80918
Cook Communications, Paris, Ontario
Kingsway Communications Ltd., Eastbourne, England

Daily Grace for Teens—Devotional Reflections to Nourish Your Soul
2005 by BORDON BOOKS

First printing, 2005
Printed in Canada
2 3 4 5 6 Printing/Year 09 08 07 06 05

Developed by Bordon Books
Manuscript written by Michelle Medlock Adams, Shanna D. Gregor, Todd Hafer, Ronald C. Jordan Sr., and Vicki J. Kuyper. Editing and project management by Shanna D. Gregor in association with Snapdragon Editorial Group, Inc.
Designed by LJ Design

ISBN: 1-56292-400-1

DAILY GRACE FOR TEENS

DEVOTIONAL REFLECTIONS TO NOURISH YOUR SOUL

HONOR HB BOOKS

Inspiration and Motivation for the Seasons of Life

COOK COMMUNICATIONS MINISTRIES
Colorado Springs, Colorado • Paris, Ontario
KINGSWAY COMMUNICATIONS LTD
Eastbourne, England

Grace is love that cares
and stoops and rescues.

JOHN STOTT

Dear Reader:

Daily Grace for Teens: Devotional Reflections to Nourish Your Soul has been written and compiled with much love and care. As you read through these pages in the days, weeks, and months ahead, it is our prayer that the revelation of the riches of God's grace will abound in your heart and mind.

We've designed this book with you in mind, combining the wonderful truth of God's Word with devotional readings relevant to everyday life. A variety of writers were chosen—people from divergent backgrounds and seasons of life—to give each daily reading a fresh, unique perspective. And a "grace principle" has been included so you will have a bit of God's grace to carry with you throughout your day. For the weekend entries, we've taken from the works of classic and modern writers, and added a prayer to help you take hold of these remarkable insights and principles.

We pray that God will bless you as you read, fill your heart with grace and peace, and draw you closer to the God who gave His all to meet your every need.

The Publisher

WRITE THE VISION

The LORD answered me and said: "Write the vision
And make it plain on tablets, That he may run who reads it."

HABAKKUK 2:2 NKJV

Do you have a vision? Has God placed a dream on the inside of you? The Bible tells us in Jeremiah 29:11 that God has a good plan for each one of us. So if you don't know your plan, ask God to reveal it to you today. He will. He desires to share it with you. He wants you to have a sense of purpose and direction. There is nothing quite as exciting as discovering your destiny in Jesus.

GRACE FOR TODAY:

God fills us with potential and fully expects us to achieve our dreams.

Once you have a vision of that plan, it's your job to keep that vision before you. Write the vision. Record it in your journal. Post it on your computer or in your locker. Tape it on your bathroom mirror. Keep a copy in your Bible. You never want to lose sight of what God has for you. It's like keeping your eyes on the ball at all times.

Maybe you haven't thought much about the dream that God has placed in your heart. Maybe it seems too big for you, but nothing is too big for God. He is more than able to help you fulfill every desire He's put on the inside of you. But, you must do your part.

Find out what God says about your vision by locating scriptures that concern it. Talk to God about it every day. Build that dream big in your heart. Ask God if He has anything to add or change in your dream. Usually His plans are greater than we can imagine on our own. Talk about your plans with your Christian friends, mentors, and your family. Imagine yourself fulfilling your destiny. Get excited! You're one day closer to seeing your dream become a reality.

YOUR LIFE COUNTS

Let us praise God for his glorious grace,
for the free gift he gave us in his dear Son!

EPHESIANS 1:6 GNB

G rading a math test is easy. After all, there's only one perfect answer for every problem. There's no "close to" or "almost." There's only right or wrong.

When it comes to God's plan, you are a right answer. You are the only one who is a "perfect fit" for the spot in history God had in mind when He designed you. Without you, there would be something missing in this world, something irreplaceable and immeasurably precious.

Knowing your life counts is key to understanding God's grace. While your life was designed to be a right answer, that doesn't always mean you make the right choices. At times, you may let how you feel overrule what you know is best. You may choose what you want, instead of what God wants for you. When that happens, God offers you the chance to rework the problem, forever erasing the mistakes you've made. That's what grace is all about.

Today, choose to be the right answer God created you to be. Relax in the fact that you're not a "mistake," even though you may make them now and then. Ask God's forgiveness for anything you regret about your past. Then, accept His free gift of grace—free to you because of the price Jesus paid on the cross with His life. Free to you because of how much you matter to God.

God wants to add to your joy, multiply your impact, and subtract your sorrows. He wants you to equate a successful, purpose-filled life with His grace. Take a moment right now to talk to Him about your place in this world and the place His grace should have in your life.

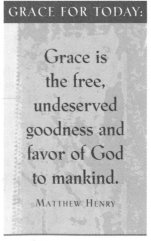

GRACE FOR TODAY:

Grace is the free, undeserved goodness and favor of God to mankind.

MATTHEW HENRY

PURSUE THE GOAL

It is God who arms me with strength and makes my way perfect.

2 SAMUEL 22:33

As a young college athlete, Jackie Joyner-Kersee saw her commitment and hard work pay off after capturing a USA championship and winning the NCAA heptathlon twice. If Joyner had allowed herself to be hindered by physical ailments, her dreams of future success would have been lost.

The recurring pain of a pulled hamstring once forced Joyner-Kersee to withdraw from competing in the World Championships. Another time, her asthmatic condition got so bad she competed while wearing an allergen-filtering mask.

Neither condition stopped the athlete from pursuing her goal. By the time she retired from active competition in 1998, Joyner-Kersee had spent more than a decade winning championships, setting world records, and earning Olympic gold medals.

When God gives you a desire to achieve a specific goal, you can be sure He has provided you with the strength and ability to accomplish it—in the face of any obstacle. The road to success will have bumps, potholes, and dips; but obstacles do not mean defeat.

It is wonderful to know your goals are part of God's plan for your life. You can be confident that if He is backing you, you will not fail.

Talk to God about your situation. Let Him know you appreciate His involvement in your life, and how thankful you are that His strength is operating in you—pushing you even at times when you feel your weakest. Then, let His love, His mercy, and His grace help you hurdle, go around, or go through whatever desires to hinder you from reaching your goal.

GRACE FOR TODAY:

When God gives us a desire to achieve a specific goal, we can be sure He has provided us with the strength and ability to accomplish it.

LIVING THE TRUTH

The truth will set you free.

JOHN 8:52 NLT

In one of the longest running commercials of all times, a cute little kid named "Mikey" gobbles down a big bowl of cereal. In the late 1970s, a rumor got started that little Mikey had died. Supposedly, after eating six bags of carbonated pop rocks candy, Mikey swallowed six cans of soda—causing his stomach to explode.

Even though there was no truth to the rumor (the cereal company even redesigned their boxes to display a picture of the grown-up Mikey to prove he was alive and still in one piece), people were afraid to eat the once popular candy. It was even taken off the market for several years.

People act on what they believe. If they believe carbonated candy and soda can cause an internal explosion, they'll choose a different snack. No matter how sincere they are in their belief, they can still be wrong.

People believe things about God that are not true. Some believe He weighs good deeds against bad ones to determine whether people will enter heaven. Others believe His spirit lives within a statue or that He's really not there at all. Even if these people base their lives on these beliefs, the strength of their belief will never make what they believe true.

You can know what you believe and why. Look for the real truth by weighing what you hear against what the Bible has to say. Study up on why the Bible is a trustworthy source. Ask God to help you build your beliefs and corresponding actions on the whole truth and nothing but the truth.

GRACE FOR TODAY:

When looking for the truth, God is quick to shine His light on it for us.

NEW CREATURE

Maybe you lived a life filled with drugs, sexual immorality, stealing, lying, cursing, or other such sins before you found Jesus; and now you're having a hard time forgiving yourself. If so, you're not alone. Many people—young and old—struggle with this issue. They believe that God has forgiven their sins, yet they can't seem to forgive themselves. They still see themselves as dirty, rotten sinners.

If you are having trouble forgiving yourself for past sins, the Bible says you are a new creature in Christ Jesus. It's not just a new life, but you're a new creature. You're like the apostle Paul—the author

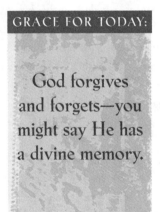

GRACE FOR TODAY:

God forgives and forgets—you might say He has a divine memory.

of most of the New Testament. Before he met Jesus, he killed Christians in the name of God.

That's a pretty dark past! But, once he had an encounter with Christ, he became a new creature. His name even changed from Saul to Paul. If Paul were able to forgive himself and become a shining vessel for the Lord, you can, too!

God removes our sins from us as far as the east is from the west. He doesn't remember your sin, and neither should you. Once you repent for your wrongdoing and turn toward God, the past is history. You are forgiven, so act like it!

In this new life one's nationality or race or education or social position is unimportant; such things mean nothing. Whether a person has Christ is what matters, and he is equally available to all.

COLOSSIANS 3:11 TLB

THE SPIRIT-FILLED LIFE

By John MacArthur Jr.

When Peter was filled with the Holy Spirit, he had the same power as when he was standing next to Jesus Christ! Now here's something exciting! Do you know what the Spirit-filled life is? It is living every moment as though you are standing in the presence of Jesus Christ! Not too complicated, is it?

Someone might think I am confusing the issue because the Holy Spirit and Christ are different. But by what name does Paul call the Holy Spirit? "The Spirit of Christ" (Romans 8:9). Jesus said that when He went away, He would send *allos* "another" Comforter (John 14:16). There are two words in the Greek for another: *heteros* and *allos*. *Heteros* means another of a different kind, and *allos* means another of exactly the same kind!

Here is my Bible. If I said to you, "Give me *allos* biblos," you would have to give another Bible exactly like mine, with all my markings and cuts and cracks. This is *allos*. When Jesus said, "I am going to send you another Comforter," He said *allos*, another exactly like Me. The Spirit-filled life is nothing more than living in the conscious presence of the indwelling Christ.'

—⁓—

HEAVENLY FATHER: I WANT TO LIVE FOR YOU, BUT SOMEHOW I ALWAYS MESS UP. THANK YOU FOR SHOWING ME THAT WHEN I AM CONSCIOUSLY THINKING ABOUT YOU, FEELING YOUR PRESENCE, YOUR GRACE KEEPS ME FROM WRONG CHOICES. AMEN.

Since we live by the Spirit, let us keep in step with the Spirit.

GALATIANS 5:25

DESTINED TO WIN

Do you not know that in a race all the runners run, but only one gets the
prize? Run in such a way as to get the prize.

1 CORINTHIANS 9:24

Every time the Olympics roll around, people all over the world swarm to their
television sets to watch the greatest athletes in the world go for the gold. It's an
amazing time.

Olympic athletes make it look so easy. Gymnasts stick their landings with ease.
Runners whip around the track at lightening speed. Ice skaters jump and spin—all with
smiles on their faces. What we don't see during the televised competitions are the grueling hours at the gym, the early morning workouts, the injuries along the way, and the
sacrifices they've made to become super athletes.

GRACE FOR TODAY:

God has great
plans for us, and
the best position
to prepare for
those plans is
on our knees
in prayer.

If you've ever been on a sports team, then you can
understand the importance of training. Juma Ikangaa,
the 1989 NYC Marathon winner, once said, "The will
to win means nothing if you haven't the will to prepare." Preparation is key—physically and mentally—for
athletes.

The same is true for Christians. We have to train
and prepare by reading the Word of God and spending
time in prayer. Becoming "buff" in the things of God
will help you succeed in His plans for your life. No
matter what hurdles lie ahead, you'll clear them all if
you're prepared.

Just like super athletes pull muscles and suffer set-
backs, you're sure to encounter trouble in this life; however, you'll come through a
winner if you keep your heart filled with God's Word and maintain a winning attitude.
You may never be a member of the Olympic team, but as a member of God's team,
you're destined to win!

Fear Factors

The LORD is with me; I will not be afraid.

PSALM 118:6

As the rain pounded steadily on the roof of the old house, Mary's attitude grew as dismal as the summer afternoon. Another dreary evening lay ahead. Nineteen-year-old Mary and her friends lit a fire in the hearth, preparing to entertain themselves with something befitting their "vacation" mood—reading ghost stories.

Inspired, the group decided to write their own stories, trying to "out-frighten" one another. Gray day after gray day passed without Mary coming up with a single idea. But, one evening Mary overheard her husband discussing the possibility of reviving a corpse with an electric current. The idea grew in Mary's mind—until she scared herself so badly she couldn't fall asleep.

That night "Frankenstein" was born. Today, people still enjoy reading Mary Wollstonecraft Shelley's classic horror story and others like it. That's because there's something exciting about being frightened—when you're in control. You can close the book, turn off the TV, or shut your eyes at the theatre if your fear gets too intense to handle. In real life, there's only one way to turn off your fear. That's by turning to God.

Although there are valid reasons to feel afraid, most of the fear you'll face in this life originates from the same place Mary's did—your mind. Fear of things like failure, embarrassment, powerlessness, or the future grow more ominous the more you focus on them. By focusing on your fears, you create your own monster.

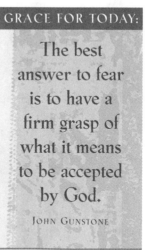

GRACE FOR TODAY:

The best answer to fear is to have a firm grasp of what it means to be accepted by God.

JOHN GUNSTONE

When life threatens to give you the creeps, change the channel. Focus on God, instead of your fears. Focus on His power, His promise to protect you, and His truth concerning what you're afraid of. Focus on who God says you are—a dearly loved child held securely in God's grace. Remember, God's in control, even when you're not.

GOD AND YOU MAKE TWO

I will ask the Father. And he will give you another Friend
to help you and to be with you forever.

JOHN 14:16 NIRV

Deserted!
That's how you feel every time you come home from school and there's no one there to greet you. But you're not alone.

According to statistics released in 2003, about one third of all school-age children, an estimated five million between ages five and thirteen, are latchkey children—kids who care for themselves while their parents are at work. In some schools in one midwestern city, fifty percent of the third and fourth graders were latchkey kids.

If they were to be honest with you, most parents would tell you they would much rather be at home with you rather than working hard at a job.

We live in a society where success seems to be determined by the amount of money we have, the kind of car we drive, and the size house we live in. To make ends meet, and "keep up with the Joneses," both parents must work.

But in many other cases, especially those that involve only one parent, working outside the home is not an option. Someone has to provide.

Thankfully, God has never left us alone, and He never will.

How do you find God when you are alone?

God's promise is that He will always be with us, His children, and that He will never leave us alone. God is always with you. Talk to Him. Pick up your Bible and read about Him. Pray and let Him know how you feel. Then thank Him for taking away that lonely feeling, and for being your friend.

You'll be surprised at just how safe and happy you can feel—right there in that seemingly empty place.

GRACE FOR TODAY:

God never leaves us alone. He is always with us.

WHAT'S YOUR BILLBOARD SAY?

We are Christ's ambassadors, and God is using us to speak to you.
We urge you, as though Christ himself were here pleading with you,
"Be reconciled to God!"

2 CORINTHIANS 5:20 NLT

There are some unique billboards popping up around the United States, especial-ly in large cities like Dallas and Philadelphia. They are written with white text against a basic black background with no sponsoring organization information includ-ed. They are simply called the "God Speaks" billboards. They say things like: "We need to talk. God," "Will the road you're on get you to my place? God," "Follow me. God," "Let's meet at my house Sunday before the game. God," "That 'Love Thy Neighbor' thing . . . I meant it. God," etc.

As billboards go, they are pretty effective. They aren't super-spiritual. They aren't judgmental. They aren't condemning. They are simple, yet they certainly stir your thinking as you cruise down the highway.

You may not be a billboard, but you communicate messages every day. What does your "billboard" say to your friends, enemies, or even strangers? We need to be con-scious of what we're communicating on a daily basis. If you act super-spiritual and judgmental, yet you claim to be a Christian, people will be turned off to you and Christianity. If you sport "Witness wear," yet you cheat in school, what message are you sending? You want your billboard to be effective, simple, and direct—just like the "God Speaks" billboards.

Ask God to help you become a good ambassador for Him. Ask the Holy Spirit to keep a guard on your mouth so you'll only speak what He wants you to say. Be con-scious of your every action, because chances are you're being watched and evaluated. Make sure your billboard points others to God.

GRACE FOR TODAY:

When we allow God to speak through us
—He has a lot to say.

KNEE TIME

The poster that reads: "Seven days without prayer makes one weak" packs a powerful message. We need to spend time in prayer every day—it's our life link to God.

In one of Evangelist Billy Graham's newspaper columns, he talks about the importance of prayer. He shares that when he first read in the Bible that we should pray without ceasing, he took it literally. Thus, he said he is in constant conversation with the Lord. That's a pretty good idea.

Jesus certainly understood the importance of prayer. Luke 5:16 tells us that Jesus often slipped away into the wilderness to pray. Now, if the Son of God felt it necessary to pray regularly, how much more should we pray on a daily basis?

It's not always possible to slip away into the wilderness for some alone time with God, but you can talk to God anytime, anywhere, about anything. You don't have to pray long, elaborate prayers to impress God. You don't even have to close your eyes. You don't even have to utter a single word. You can pray silently. Do whatever works best for you.

If you need some guidance in knowing how to pray, use the Lord's Prayer as an example. (You'll find it in Luke 11). If you still feel a bit uncomfortable when you pray, try journaling your prayers to God in a notebook you like. God looks forward to your next chat.

> **GRACE FOR TODAY:**
> No matter when we pray, no matter where we pray, God is there.

Devote yourselves to prayer with an alert mind and a thankful heart.

COLOSSIANS 4:2 NLT

OUR POWER SOURCE

John C. Maxwell

A friend of mine was discussing the implications of Micah 6:8 NASB with his seven-year-old grandson: "What does the LORD require of you but to do justice, to love kindness, and to walk humbly with your God?" The little boy, who was memorizing this verse, said, "Grandpa, it's hard to be humble if you're really walking with God." That's great theology coming from a seven-year-old. When we begin to get a glimpse of the unlimited resources at our disposal—the power of God Himself—then and only then will we sense the assurance that we are fully equipped to do whatever it is that God calls us to do.

We might feel like the little mouse who was crossing the bridge with an elephant. The bridge shook. When they got to the other side, the mouse looked at his huge companion and said, "Boy, we really shook that bridge, didn't we?"

When we walk with God, that's often how we feel—like a mouse with the strength of an elephant. After crossing life's troubled waters, we can say with the mouse, "God, we really shook that bridge, didn't we?"

Hudson Taylor, the great missionary to China, said, "Many Christians estimate difficulty in the light of their own resources, and thus they attempt very little; and they always fail. All giants have been weak men who did great things for God because they relied on His power and His presence to be with them."

Like David, who said, "The battle is the LORD's," we also need to understand that Jesus is our source, and we can be directly connected to Him (1 Samuel 17:47 NKJV).[2]

—◊◊◊—

HEAVENLY FATHER: YOUR GRACE HAS PROVIDED ALL THE RESOURCES I NEED TO LIVE A SUCCESSFUL, GODLY LIFE. WALK WITH ME THROUGH THIS DAY, I PRAY. TAKE MY WEAKNESSES AND MAKE THEM STRENGTHS FOR YOUR GLORY. AMEN.

I can do all things through Christ who strengthens me.

PHILIPPIANS 4:13 NKJV

GOT TIME?

Let the Word of Christ—the Message—have the run of the house.
Give it plenty of room in your lives.

COLOSSIANS 3:16 MSG

D id you know that there are 1,440 minutes in every day? That seems like a lot of time, so why is it that we have such a difficult time finding a few minutes for God each twenty-four hour period?

Life is busy. With school, extracurricular activities, homework, church obligations, chores, and downtime with friends—there's hardly enough time for sleeping and eating, let alone spending a few minutes with the Maker. So, you have to consciously make time.

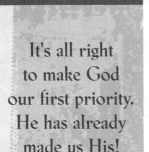

GRACE FOR TODAY:

It's all right to make God our first priority. He has already made us His!

Grab your calendar, planner, or your palm pilot and "pencil in" time with God (TWG) every day for the next week. Begin with five or ten minutes of prayer and Bible study. Once your TWG appointment is scheduled, you'll be more likely to keep it. Soon, you'll look forward to your TWG sessions and may even wish to increase that time.

Something else will happen, too. When you make time for God, He multiplies your time right back to you. It's as if He is rewarding you for your faithfulness.

A woman once shared that she committed to read Matthew, Mark, Luke, and John five times in one month. She felt impressed to do this, yet she had two small children at home, and they were still unpacking boxes from a recent move. Still, she pressed on and actually did what she set out to do—read the Gospels five times in one month. In addition, she was able to unpack all of the remaining boxes, care for her children, and refinish a piece of furniture. She still has no idea how she accomplished so much in thirty days!

God will help you make the most of your time if you give Him some time each day. Make Him #1 on your list of priorities today.

SOUL FOOD

Taste and see that the LORD is good.
Oh, the joys of those who trust in him!

PSALM 34:8 NLT

F rom sushi to salsa, burgers to bananas, God provides a grand buffet of nourishment to help you keep your body going and growing. Although God provides the source of your food, making good use of that source is up to you. Choosing a balanced diet is just the beginning. What matters most is actually eating it.

In the same way that your body needs food, so does your spirit. Without regular "soul food," your faith, hope, and love don't have the nourishment they need to grow. Your relationship with God begins to feel distant. Your efforts to do what's right and to help the world see God more clearly can become weak and ineffective. Before you know it, you're on your way to becoming spiritually anorexic.

Regularly feasting on the spiritual provisions God supplies prevents this from happening. There are four basic "food groups" for your soul: the Bible, prayer, worship, and spending time with others who want to grow closer to God. Read a chapter or two of the Bible every day. Talk to God about what you've read, asking Him to help you understand and apply what you read. Pray throughout the day about big things, little things, and everything in between. Worship God with your voice, your actions, and every aspect of your life. Get involved in a church where you can find out what real love is all about.

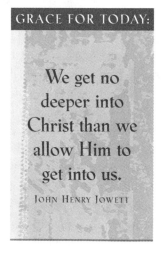

GRACE FOR TODAY:

We get no deeper into Christ than we allow Him to get into us.

JOHN HENRY JOWETT

Once you acquire a taste for real soul food, you'll never want to go hungry again. And there's no reason to. Simply choose to "eat" what God has graciously provided. It's guaranteed to be a meal that's joy–filled and fat–free.

BETTER FRIENDS

Let us come before him with thanksgiving
and extol him with music and song.

PSALM 95:2

For the second time this week you've stood by while others discussed their plans for the weekend. A beach party with lots of music and plenty of booze! All the things that go along with having a "good time."

Why are you never invited? you wonder.

You've done everything you know to show yourself friendly, yet for the most part you go ignored.

It sounds like you're already having a party. A pity party!

Why would you want to be invited to a party where you would not fit in, anyway?

When you became a Christian, you made a decision to come away from the things of the world. That included those wild parties where many of the things that happen are contrary to the new lifestyle you have adopted. The Bible says that you are not to be attracted to the world, or the things of the world. So, the fact that you are not invited to "hang out" with the in crowd and be subjected to ungodly situations is a good thing.

No doubt, your new way of living has become obvious to them. They recognize your respect for God.

Rest easy! You have nothing to feel sorry about. Your new way of living is speaking out as a witness to how God will keep you from doing wrong—even when you are tempted. If you want friends, tell God. He has plenty to send your way, and they will not try and get you to do wrong.

Remind yourself of the number of times you have felt left out, only to hear the sweet voice of God whisper a "welcome" in your heart. Then, thank Him that you have been accepted where it really counts—into the family of God!

GRACE FOR TODAY:

God values our friendship—another friendship is never worth sacrificing our relationship with God.

GOD—AT YOUR SIDE, AND ON YOUR SIDE

The LORD will guide you always; he will satisfy your needs.

ISAIAH 58:11

A re there certain people in your life who you're sure are against you? A class-mate, a sports rival, or even a teacher or family member?

If you suspect this is the case—even if you are sure this is the case—take heart because God is for you! He's on your side. All the time. And "all the time" includes right now. God is thinking about you, loving you, and supporting you, even as you read these words.

God is not a fair-weather friend. He offers His love and comfort to you even when you aren't doing everything right and your attitude toward Him is less than per-fect. You don't have to earn your heavenly Father's loyalty, and you won't lose it just because you make a mistake.

You have been created with a purpose in life—a purpose uniquely suited to your talents and temperament. And God is committed to seeing you fulfill that purpose. He isn't watching you from on high, hoping to see you fail. He's right beside you, cheer-ing you on, comforting you through failure, encouraging you through adversity.

Life can be tough sometimes, and if people in your life occasionally become your rivals, that can make things just that much tougher. But remember always that no mat-ter who your opponent is, you can't be defeated. That's because God is for you, and with Him in your corner, cheering you on and instructing you, you will ultimately have your hand raised in victory.

GRACE FOR TODAY:

Since God is for us, it doesn't really matter who might be against us!

NEVER ENOUGH

Langley Collyer was dead. At least that's what the anonymous caller told the NYPD. But when the police arrived at Collyer's three-story home, they found more than they were looking for. One hundred and twenty tons more. The house with filled from floor to ceiling with junk. Eleven pianos, two organs, the frame of an old Model T, a wine press, an old X ray machine, the folding top of a horse-drawn carriage, assorted tree branches, years worth of newspapers—the list went on and on.

Collyer had collected so much stuff over the years that it took the police two weeks to find his body amid the trash. Cause of death? Collyer had been crushed to death by a pile of junk he had set as a booby trap to discourage potential burglars.

Although hoarding to this extreme is often caused by a mental disorder, grabbing more than you want or need is a common occurrence. That's because every person longs for more than life can give. The problem with trying to fill this "empty spot" by eating another piece of cake or buying another pair of jeans is that the momentary joy they offer quickly fades. All you're left with is a couple of extra pounds or less money in your wallet—and a nagging feeling of discontentment.

God created that empty spot inside. It's a spot only He can fill. By allowing the things in this world to never really satisfy your heart, God openly invites you to fully turn to Him. The next time you're longing for something more, ask God to help you recognize and reach out for what you're really craving—a deeper experience of His own love and grace.

GRACE FOR TODAY:

God is the only one who can truly satisfy our hearts.

I have learned the secret of being content in any and every situation.
PHILIPPIANS 4:12

LEARNING GOD'S WORD

By John MacArthur Jr.

L et me share how I study the Bible, and how the Bible has come alive to me. I began in 1 John. One day I sat down and read all five chapters straight through. It took me twenty minutes. Reading one book straight through was terrific.

The next day, I sat down and read 1 John straight through again. The third day, I sat down and read 1 John straight through. The fourth day, straight through again. The fifth day, I sat down and read it again. I did this for thirty days. Do you know what happened at the end of thirty days? I knew what was in 1 John.

Next, I went to the Gospel of John. I divided the Gospel of John into three sections of seven chapters each. I read the first seven chapters for thirty days, the next seven for the next thirty days, and the last seven for thirty days. In ninety days, I had read the entire Gospel of John thirty times. Where does it talk about the Good Shepherd? Chapter 10,

right-hand column, starts in the middle, goes down, flip the page, go on down.

Where does it talk about the vine and the branches? Chapter 15. Where does it talk about Jesus' friends? Chapter 15, over in the next column and a little farther down. Where does it talk about Jesus' arrest in the garden? John 18. The restoration of Peter? John 21. The woman at the well? John 4. The Bread of Life? John 6. Nicodemus? John 3. The wedding at Cana? John 2.

You might say, "My, are you smart!" No, I am not smart. I read it thirty times. Even I can get it then![5]

—⁂—

HEAVENLY FATHER: YOUR WORD IS FILLED WITH GRACE AND TRUTH, AND I WANT TO KNOW ALL ABOUT IT. HELP ME TO KEEP MY COMMITMENT TO BE A GOOD STUDENT OF THE BIBLE. AMEN.

The unfolding of your words gives light; it imparts understanding to the simple.

PSALM 119:130 NRSV

THE REAL YOU

I say to you that you are Peter, and upon this rock I will build my church, and all the powers of hell will not conquer it.

MATTHEW 16:18 NLT

M ovie stars weren't always movie stars. In fact, some of the most glamorous starlets were just ordinary folks until they were "discovered." The late Lana Turner, who is best known for her Oscar-nominated performance in *Peyton Place*, was discovered while sipping a soda at Schwab's Drugstore on Sunset Boulevard. The late Marilyn Monroe, then nineteen-year-old Norma Jeane, was working on propellers when war photographer David Conover discovered her. Once that star quality in Lana and Marilyn was recognized, they became stars. The rest is Hollywood history.

You might say that Jesus "discovered" a lot of people, too. When He walked the earth, He saw people for who they could be—not who they presently were. Take Peter, for example. He was sort of a hothead. He often spoke before he thought. He was an up-and-down kind of guy. But, Jesus said to Peter in Matthew 16:18 MSG, "You are Peter, a rock. This is the rock on which I will put together my church."

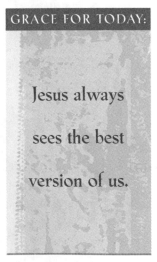

GRACE FOR TODAY:

Jesus always

sees the best

version of us.

Do you imagine the other disciples wondered if Jesus had really meant Peter? They were probably thinking, *Lord, are you sure? Remember, Peter is the guy You are always having to correct.* Still, Jesus saw Peter as the man of God he would eventually become.

Jesus continues to make discoveries today. He sees you for who you are destined to be in Him—not who you are right this moment. He always sees the best in you. So, even if you're a lot like Peter, Jesus sees the star quality in you. He sees your future, and it's a good one!

TAKE A FREE RIDE

Where the Spirit of the Lord is, there is freedom.

2 CORINTHIANS 3:17

Getting your driver's license can feel like a ticket to freedom. One minute you have to rely on your folks, your bike, or your own two feet to get you where you want to go. The next, you have the freedom to choose the back road, the short cut, or the scenic route. You can even choose to drive around just for fun—as long as you have money for gas.

But, this freedom comes at a price. You can't simply hop in the car and drive like you play a video racing game. You need to stop at a red light. Go on green. Stay in your lane. Drive the speed limit. When you follow simple rules like these, you and those around you are free to enjoy a safe and speedy journey. You enhance your freedom by choosing to restrict it in certain ways.

The same is true when you choose to follow God. Once you begin that relationship, you're given free license to drive through this world into the next, no roadblocks, toll roads, or traffic jams. But, God does provide a few rules for your journey. In the Old Testament, He gave the Israelites a list of ten basic commandments to follow. In the New Testament, Jesus provided the "cliff notes" of those rules. He encouraged others to love God with their heart, soul, mind, and strength, and to love other people in the same way they would love themselves. (See Mark 12:30.)

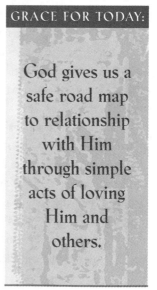

GRACE FOR TODAY:

God gives us a safe road map to relationship with Him through simple acts of loving Him and others.

Choosing to love God and love others gives you the freedom to move confidently down the road of life. If every action you take and decision you make is motivated by this simple rule, you can't make a wrong turn. That means you have more freedom to enjoy the ride.

SOUND ADVICE

Pride leads to arguments; those who take advice are wise.

PROVERBS 13:10 NLT

Y ou were excited about the possibility of directing this year's school play. Just the thought of being in charge of such an important project gave you a rush.

The drama coach had told you how impressed he was with your knowledge of theater, and then applauded your ability and skills as a leader. Even your classmates were encouraging when you told them about the offer.

The problem is, after praying about the position you did not feel it was what God wanted you to do. Your parents warned of some of the challenges you could expect by taking on such an important position. There would be stress and anxiety as the deadline approached. There was also the possibly that you could clash with fellow classmates when you made decisions that they did not agree with.

Despite the warnings, the sound of "director" played loudly in your head, and you accepted the offer. Now, reality has set in, and you're feeling the pressure. The workload is heavier than you imagined. The attitudes of the people you work with are even worse.

Do you give up and walk away? No. Go to God instead. Acknowledge your mistake in not listening to Him, or heeding the warnings from your parents. Ask His forgiveness, and then tell Him how much you need His help to bring order out of chaos and keep peace at the same time.

You can trust your heavenly Father to work in areas you were never capable of working. He always meets you where you are. His intervention can quickly bring things back together. Remember, He knows all about you. Just as He knew you were not able to handle the situation then, He knows you need His help now. Let Him help you.

GRACE FOR TODAY:

God's willingness to intervene at our invitation can quickly bring things back together.

YOU: A MASTERPIECE IN PROGRESS

Oh yes, you shaped me first inside, then out; you formed me in my
mother's womb. I thank you, High God—you're breathtaking!
Body and soul, I am marvelously made!

PSALM 139:13-14 MSG

King David had a way with words, as well as with a sling and stones. David
was unique—just as unique as you are. God crafted you. And there is no one
like you. One version of Psalm 139 says that God knitted you together. Consider the
implications of that image. Knitting is a careful, step-by-step method of creating something. This means that you aren't just another mass-produced clone, rolling off an
assembly line.

You are a carefully planned, meticulously created individual, placed with love on
this planet by a Master Artist. And the good news doesn't stop there. You aren't the
kind of work of art that just hangs in a gallery, waiting to be admired. The Bible promises that you are created to do "good works" that God has prepared for you to do. So
you don't just have artistic merit; you have a purpose. You have function as well as
form.

So the next time competition from peers at school—or messages from the media—
make you feel like you aren't attractive enough, intelligent enough, or physically gifted,
remember who made you. He made you carefully, He made you lovingly, and He made
you for a purpose. And you are precisely attractive enough, smart enough, and every-
thing-else-enough to accomplish all that your heavenly Father has planned for you in
your life.

GRACE FOR TODAY:

God lovingly made each one of us, and He
admires His handiwork.

THE WINNER'S CIRCLE

Competition equals drama. Whether it's a sporting event, a reality TV show, a video game, or even talk around the locker room about "who's going to ask out the new girl first," one thing is certain: Everyone wants to come out a winner. Unfortunately, what adds the drama to competition is for one person to win, another has to lose.

It's true that the spirit of competition has a positive side. It can push you to challenge yourself and teach you real life lessons about teamwork, sportsmanship, and grace. But it can also make you feel as though your self-worth is on the line. If you feel like you have to prove yourself to others, as though losing automatically makes you a "loser," chances are you'll also feel that way about your relationship with God.

Take another look at your heavenly Father. He doesn't play games with those He loves. Although your relationship with Him will lead you to do good things, you never have to prove your worth to Him. He knows what you're worth. He made you. All the good things you'll ever do will not make Him love you any more than He does right now. Blowing it won't make Him love you any less. God's love is perfect and unchangeable.

Not only can't you "win" God's love through good deeds, you're also never in competition with any of His other children. Just because someone you know spends two hours in prayer each day or gets to speak at your youth group's Christmas retreat doesn't mean you need to try and become more "spiritual" than they are. God has an individual race for each of His children to run. Though the finish line awaits you in heaven, the outcome has already been determined. God's declared you a winner.

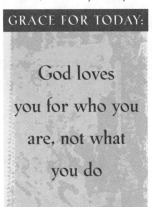

GRACE FOR TODAY:

God loves you for who you are, not what you do

Let us run with patience the particular race that God has set before us.

HEBREWS 12:1 TLB

WE CAN BELIEVE THE PROMISES OF GOD

By Luis Palau

Jesus' death and resurrection are our guarantee that God is faithful, that He hears our prayers, and that all His promises are true. Paul clearly explains this to the Corinthians because if they have any doubts about his integrity as God's messenger, they probably doubt God's message too.

I have a hunch that many Christians today, like the Corinthians, occasionally have trouble believing God's promises. Oh, the promises sound nice. Sometimes they even cheer us up. Yet I think many of us have, at least unconsciously, questioned whether God is faithful to keep His promises. We'll sometimes catch ourselves thinking, *Are the promises of God really true?*

None of God's promises ever has failed! The great evangelist D. L. Moody confidently stated, "God never made a promise that was too good to be true." Think about that! No wonder Jesus says not to worry about tomorrow. (See Matthew 6:34.) God did not create us to be self-sufficient. He created us to depend on Him. We don't have to rush around trying to solve all our problems and trials in thirty seconds. We don't have to exhaust all of our human problem-solving options before we turn to God as a last resort. Every trial we face is an opportunity for God to demonstrate His loving faithfulness to us.

God has been faithful to His people in the past and promises to be faithful in the future. Thus, we have no need to worry. We can rest assured that the God who is faithful will fulfill every promise we claim in the name of Jesus.[4]

—⁂—

HEAVENLY FATHER: THANK YOU FOR ALL YOUR PROMISES. WHEN I PUT MY TRUST IN YOU, I KNOW YOU WILL KEEP EVERY ONE OF THEM. I DON'T KNOW WHY YOU LOVE ME SO MUCH. IT MUST BE YOUR GRACE. AMEN.

God, who has called you into fellowship with
his Son Jesus Christ our Lord, is faithful.

1 CORINTHIANS 1:9

CHALLENGES EQUAL OPPORTUNITIES

Therefore I am well content with weaknesses, with insults,
with distresses, with persecutions, with difficulties, for Christ's sake;
for when I am weak, then I am strong.

2 CORINTHIANS 12:10 NASB

W hen a challenge arises in your life, do you retreat and pout, or do you see it as an opportunity for God to show Himself strong? Bernie Marcus fits into the latter category. You might not know the name "Bernie Marcus," but you probably have heard of his company—Home Depot. Sure, Bernie is hugely successful and very wealthy today, but it wasn't always that way. In fact, Bernie was fired in 1978 from a home-improvement chain called Handy Dan, leaving him jobless and frustrated.

GRACE FOR TODAY:

God wants to turn our tests into testimonies today!

You might say he was faced with a whopper of a challenge. Determined to succeed, Bernie Marcus did not run away from the home-improvement business defeated. Instead, he learned from that experience and decided he wasn't going to work for anyone else ever again. He began his own company. Today, Home Depot is the largest home-improvement retailer in the world.

God can use every challenge in your life to thrust you to a new level if you have a good attitude and keep your eyes on Him. Follow the example of Jesus. When He was asked to feed 5,000 men and thousands more women and children with only two fish and five loaves of bread, He didn't get mad and complain to His heavenly father. He saw the situation as the beginning of a mighty miracle. (See Luke 9:13–17.)

Whatever you are facing today—God is well able to handle it. Give it to Him and breathe a sigh of relief. Your challenge is simply an opportunity for God to show Himself strong on your behalf. Success is only moments away.

GET RICH QUICK

Where your treasure is, there your heart will be also.

MATTHEW 6:21 NKJV

The Phi Phi Archipelago in Thailand has long been home to treasure hunters. Its crystal blue coves and sheer pinnacled peaks were once a hiding place for pirates in search of gold and other riches. Today, people search the limestone cliffs for a different type of rare treasure—swallows' nests.

Fishermen risk their lives climbing unstable bamboo scaffolding to heights of over 1200 feet to retrieve this so-called "white gold." That's because they can make up to $750 per pound for what some believe holds the power to energize tired, aging bodies. It's hard to believe this treasure is nothing more than hardened swallow saliva.

What do you treasure? It doesn't have to be silver or gold. It may be your looks, your grades, your car, or your popularity. Your list will be as individual as you are. Caring deeply about something is not a bad thing. The key is making sure that God is always at the top of your list.

What you value most will determine how you live your life. If it's a swallow's nest, you'll learn all you can about where to find it. You'll climb perilous cliffs in search of it. You'll risk your life to acquire it. If it's God, follow Him with that same passion. But, the treasure you gain from going wholeheartedly after God enriches your life from the inside out—a treasure you can carry with you from this world into the next.

Be a treasure hunter, daily seeking after the riches only God can give. He promises that everyone who looks for Him, finds Him. No treasure map necessary.

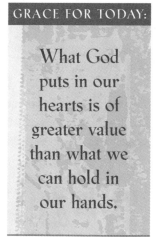

GRACE FOR TODAY:

What God puts in our hearts is of greater value than what we can hold in our hands.

BE THANKFUL

Don't be jealous of sinners, but always honor the LORD.

PROVERBS 23:17 CEV

Are there classmates who seem to have it all? They live in mansions, drive their own sports cars, wear stylish clothes, are never required to do chores or share their room with a brother or sister. Awesome! They live a glamorous, rich, carefree life. You admit that there are times you wish that you had what they have. Boy, you would like to trade places with them! Then, one day, you overhear them say that their family doesn't believe in God because they have everything that they need.

Suddenly, you think about how important God is to your family, and the Holy Spirit reminds you of your blessings. Your parents love you, and they work hard to provide the best they can afford. Your house is small and you share bedrooms, but laughter and peace in every room. Everyone helps with the chores because you love your parents and want them to rest after work. That is your small way of taking care of them. In the evening you might play games or watch television together. Then there is the family meal and prayer before bedtime.

All of you are healthy and well-groomed. The family car is almost ten years old, and your father still takes care of it like it was brand new. Weekend fun is usually simple, like a rented movie and microwave popcorn, a stroll through the zoo, or a picnic in the park. Every Sunday, you go to church to worship and praise God for His love and goodness.

You know that in God, your family has everything that you need. With a thankful heart, you realize that your lives are simple but rich in ways others might not understand.

GRACE FOR TODAY:

With God we are richer than we would be if we owned all the wealth of the world without Him.

God Has Your Life "Tivo-ed"

"I know the plans I have for you," declares the LORD, "plans to prosper you and not to harm you, plans to give you hope and a future."

JEREMIAH 29:11

Have you ever seen a movie before your friends—then gone to view it again with them? Or taped or "Tivo-ed" a sporting event and viewed it with your buds—after sneaking a peak at how the competition ended? If you have, you understand what it's like to watch those around you experience stress, doubt, and even sheer terror when the outcome is in doubt—while you can sit there, secure and confident because you know what will happen in the end. That's kind of the way the all-knowing God views your life.

For example, you might find yourself tangled in one of life's messes and hear yourself crying out, "I don't know how I can ever get out of this; I can't see any solution!" Or you might be engulfed by a cloud of depression that you think will never lift. *How can I ever smile, ever laugh again?* you ask yourself.

Take heart. God knows how your life will play out. He can see the happy ending right now. He views your life with confidence—because not only has He seen the "movie" of your life, He also wrote and directs it!

No element of danger, pain, confusion, or sadness will come into your life unless the heavenly Director allows it. That doesn't mean that you won't have to face the consequences of bad choices or disobedience. But it does mean that nothing can ruin the story of your life, as long as it's in the Author's loving hands.

GRACE FOR TODAY:

The story of our lives might take us to scary places, sad places. But no matter where we go, God will go with us.

THE REJECTS CLUB: EXCLUSIVE COMPANY

If you have recently experienced disappointment or discouragement, don't let it overcome you. You are in good company. Consider the following examples:

NBA superstar Michael Jordan was once cut from his high school basketball team.

After his first audition, screen legend Fred Astaire received the following assessment from an MGM executive: "Can't act. Slightly bald. Can dance a little."

Best-selling author Max Lucado had his first book rejected by fourteen publishers before finding one that was willing to give him a chance.

A so-called football expert once said of two-time Super Bowl-winning coach Vince Lombardi, "He possesses minimal football knowledge. Lacks motivation."

Walt Disney was fired from a newspaper because he lacked ideas. Later, he went bankrupt several times before he built Disneyland.

Upon his election as U.S. President, Abraham Lincoln was called "a baboon" by a newspaper in Illinois, his home state. The paper went on to say that the American people "would be better off if he were assassinated."

A young Burt Reynolds was once told he couldn't act. At the same time, his pal Clint Eastwood was told he would never make it in the movies because his Adam's apple was too big.

You can learn a truckload from rejection and disappointment. You might discover weaknesses that you need to bolster to reach your maximum potential. You might learn that people's judgments about you are highly subjective and that one key to success is simply finding someone who understands you and believes in you. All opinions about you are not created equal—or accurate.

Whatever the case, let rejection fuel your determination. And hang on to those negative letters, reports, and evaluations. You might want to frame them someday.

GRACE FOR TODAY:

We can always trust God to be the one who believes in us.

No matter how many times you trip them up, God-loyal people
don't stay down long; Soon they're up on their feet.

PROVERBS 24:16 MSG

EXPRESSIONS OF WORRY

By John MacArthur Jr.

The word *worry* comes from the Old English term *wyrgan*, which means "to choke" or "strangle." That's appropriate since worry strangles the mind, which is the seat of our emotions. The word even fits the notion of a panic attack.

We're not much different from the people to whom Jesus spoke. They worried about what they were going to eat, drink, and wear. And if you want to legitimize your worry, what better way than to say, "Well, after all, I'm not worrying about extravagant things; I'm just worrying about the basics." But that is forbidden for the Christian.

As you read through the Scriptures, one thing you learn is that God wants His children preoccupied with Him, not with the mundane, passing things of this world. He says, "Set your mind on the things above, not on the things that are on earth" (Colossians 3:2 NASB). To free us to do that He says, "Don't worry about the basics. I'll take care of that." A basic principle of spiritual life is that we are not earthbound people. Fully trusting our Heavenly Father dispels anxiety. And the more we know about Him, the more we will trust Him.

I believe in wise planning, but if after doing all you are able to, you still are fearful of the future, the Lord says, "Don't worry." He promised to provide all your needs, and He will.[5]

—⁓—

HEAVENLY FATHER: I THANK AND PRAISE YOU FOR THE MIRACLE OF YOUR GRACE—GRACE ENOUGH TO PROVIDE EVERYTHING I NEED. I EXCHANGE MY WORRIES FOR YOUR PROVISION, MY ANXIETY FOR YOUR PEACE. AMEN.

You can be sure that God will take care of everything you need,
his generosity exceeding even yours in the glory that pours from Jesus.
PHILIPPIANS 4:19 MSG

COUNT YOUR BLESSINGS INSTEAD OF SHEEP

Yes, you will lie down and your sleep will be sweet.

PROVERBS 3:24 NKJV

D o you ever have trouble falling asleep? It's a common problem. Millions of people get six or fewer hours of sleep each night—and that is not enough, according to Dr. James B. Maas, author of *Power Sleep.*⁶ Sleep is important. We need sleep to be able to function at our highest capacity. We need sleep to remain healthy. We need sleep to retain our strength. We need sleep to fight off depression. So, is it any wonder why the devil would try to steal our Zs? He will do anything to keep us from getting enough rest. His favorite way of stealing sleep is causing Christians to worry.

GRACE FOR TODAY:

God promises
His children
sweet slumber,
so we can
get some
worry-free Zs.

In fact, worry is one of the most common reasons for sleepless nights. Maybe you're worried about a number of things—getting good grades so you can get a scholarship; making enough money so you can do the whole prom thing in style; or dealing with your friends and their problems. If you're worried today, give all of your worries to God. He wants you to! First Peter 5:7 says, "Cast all of your cares on Him because He cares for you." He really, truly cares for you, and anything that bothers you, bothers Him. He is interested in every aspect of your life. As a child of God, you don't have to worry about anything.

The Bible also says that God never sleeps nor slumbers. He is watching over you at all times. Don't let worry keep you awake one more night. Quit counting sheep. Instead, give your worries to the Great Shepherd, and get some sleep.

BE A ROCK STAR

Let no one despise or think less of you because of your youth,
but be an example (pattern) for the believers in speech, in conduct,
in love, in faith, and in purity.

1 TIMOTHY 4:12 AMP

P icture yourself standing in front of a man the size of a giant. He's almost ten feet tall and wearing a coat of bronze armor that weighs over one hundred and twenty-five pounds. The iron point of his bronze spear, the point alone weighing fifteen pounds, is aimed directly at you—a teenager whose only weapon is a sling shot and five rocks. Doesn't seem like much of a fair fight, does it?

But, God is on your side. He's already chosen you to be the next king of Israel. So, you lean on God's strength and courage. Then, you do something you've done countless times before. You put a stone in your slingshot and let it fly. The giant falls dead at your feet.

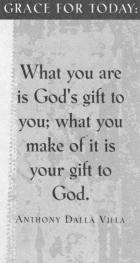

GRACE FOR TODAY:

You don't have to wait until you grow up to do "giant" things for God. David didn't. He risked what no other man in Israel's army would. He risked his life in a fight with the Philistine champion, Goliath. David wasn't skilled with a spear or a sword. He'd been trained as a shepherd, fighting off predators with his slingshot. When David sized up Goliath, he saw him for what he really was—just another predator.

Life is filled with giant-sized challenges. God offers you the same opportunity as He did David. The rocks in your hand are the skills you've acquired and the talents God has woven into your character. Simply use what you've been given right where you are, always remembering that God is by your side. You can make a positive impact for God, right here, right now.

What you are is God's gift to you; what you make of it is your gift to God.

ANTHONY DALLA VILLA

HONOR YOUR PARENTS

Honor your father and mother. Then you will live a long, full life.

EXODUS 20:12 NLT

I t will be so cool to have a driver's license and be able to go anywhere you want without waiting for someone to drive you there. You have the school permission form to take driver's education and training. All your mom and dad have to do is sign it and you are good to go.

Wait a minute! What is the problem? There is nothing to discuss! you think as they go to their bedroom to talk it over. They'll give you an answer tomorrow, they say.

The next day, the report is not good. You are not mature enough for such a great responsibility, they explain. Having a driver's license makes you responsible for your life and the lives of others. Maybe we can revisit it in a few months.

You plead your case, arguing that driving would help you grow up even more. Besides, most of your friends already have their licenses. But it gets you nowhere.

Disappointed, you decide to ask a friend with a driver's license to let you practice using his car. That way, when your parents finally give you the nod, you will already have driving skills. At first you practice in an empty parking lot, but soon you're on the back roads. One day you're driving when a drunk driver comes at you head-on. You swerve quickly and avoid what could have been a serious accident.

You thank God that no other car was close and ask His forgiveness for being disobedient. Later, at the police station, you look up to see your parents coming through the door. As you rush to their arms, all you can think about is how blessed you are to have a loving, wise God and parents looking out for you.

GRACE FOR TODAY:

God gave us parents to help Him look after us.

ZEST—IT'S MORE THAN A KIND OF SOAP

A glad heart makes a cheerful countenance.

PROVERBS 15:13 AMP

Have you ever had to baby-sit for a younger sibling, cousin, or neighbor? Then you probably understand the hassle involved in getting a toddler or grade-schooler to go to bed—and stay in bed. Kids just don't understand the point in retiring for the night while there is still energy in their bodies, snack food in the pantry, and a favorite show on Nickelodeon.

If you're a seasoned baby-sitter, you've probably heard all the excuses:

"But I'm not tired."

"Can't I watch just one more show?"

"Will you please read me just one more story?"

"My other baby-sitters all let me stay up late!"

"Okay, one more drink of water, then I promise I'll go to sleep."

Hearing a chain of excuses like these can be frustrating, but there is something to be admired in them as well. As a teen, your childhood years aren't that far behind you, and you should remember that childlike enthusiasm, that pure zest for living. Remember what it was like to enjoy life so much that you hated to go to sleep and risk missing something cool?

It's fine to leave behind some of the trappings of childhood—the nose-picking, the lisp, and the pajamas with feet on them. But it's okay, healthy even, to hang on to the childlike heart that allows you to play hard, laugh hard, and squeeze every drop of joy out of every day.

GRACE FOR TODAY:

God has blessed us with the joy of being child-like.

LOOKING INTO PEOPLE, NOT JUST AT THEM

A medical-school professor once posed this bio-ethics question to a group of students: "Here's a family history. The father has syphilis. The mother has TB. They already have four children. The first is blind. The second has died. The third is deaf. The fourth has TB. Now the mother is pregnant again. The parents come to you for advice. They are willing to abort their child if you decide they should. What do you say?"

After the students shared various opinions, the professor placed them into groups to make final decisions. After deliberating, every group reported that it would recommend an abortion to the parents.

"Congratulations," the professor told his class. "You just took the life of Beethoven!"

The lesson here? A person's inherent value and potential doesn't depend on their family background or social status or even the likelihood of success in life. God creates each person with worth and skill and promise. The way you treat those around you shouldn't be tainted by a prejudice based on race, economic status, physical appearance, or handicap. This advice might seem like a no-brainer, but many people are shocked when they honestly evaluate the way they perceive and treat others.

Like Beethoven, every person has potential to add music to the great symphony called life.

> **GRACE FOR TODAY:**
>
> God has given us much more potential than we have history or heritage.

So reach out and welcome one another to God's glory.
Jesus did it; now you do it!
ROMANS 15:7 MSG

WHAT WE WILL BECOME

By John C. Maxwell

Let's look at the Apostle Paul. I think one of the key ingredients in his life was his vision. Not only did he see what he was, but he also saw what the grace of God could enable him to become. It was that vision that kept him steady throughout his ministry. In Acts 26:19 NKJV, when he stood before King Agrippa, he said, "Therefore, King Agrippa, I was not disobedient to the heavenly vision." In spite of all the problems he had run into in his ministry, in spite of what was about to happen to him, he had been obedient to the dream God had given him.

What happened in Paul's life can happen in our lives. When we see ourselves properly, there are a couple of things that will happen. One, we'll see our position. We'll see where we are going. This can be discouraging because we may think, I'm not accomplishing what I want to accomplish; I'm not being what I want to become. But all people who have the potential for greatness first of all have to see themselves as they are, and usually that's discouraging.

When we have a vision from God and it stops us, we not only see our position, but thankfully, we also see our potential. We see our possibilities. The good news is that God believes in you, and He will not allow you to see yourself and your problems without allowing you to see your potential. He's not going to frustrate us; He's going to encourage us and help us see what we can become.[7]

—∾—

DEAR FATHER: I WANT TO SEE MYSELF AS I AM AND ALSO AS I CAN BECOME. I KNOW I DON'T HAVE IT IN ME TO GET THERE ON MY OWN, BUT I'LL RELY ON YOUR GRACE TO HELP ME REACH MY FULL POTENTIAL. THANK YOU FOR THE POSSIBILITIES YOU'VE PLACED IN MY LIFE.

Paul, called to be an apostle of Christ Jesus by the will of God.

1 CORINTHIANS 1:1 NRSV

A SELFLESS KIND OF LOVE

Love your neighbor as yourself.

LEVITICUS 19:18

E ver heard of Esther Kim and Kay Poe? If you're into Tae Kwon Do, their names are probably quite familiar to you. Esther, twenty, and Kay, eighteen, had been best friends and competitors in Tae Kwon Do since they were very young, when they discovered they would have to fight each other for the last remaining spot on the 2000 U.S. Olympic team.

GRACE FOR TODAY:

Selfless love makes us champions in God's eyes.

They both dreaded the match. Then the unexpected happened. Kay dislocated her kneecap in a fight prior to the finals and could hardly stand before the final match—the one that would determine her fate—the one against her best friend. Moments before the two competitors made their way to the mat, Esther forfeited the fight. She was simply not willing to fight her injured friend—even if it meant giving up her own dream. So in an act of complete selflessness, Esther gave her best friend the gift of a lifetime—a trip to the Olympics.

Esther's beautiful decision of friendship and love made headlines all over the world. People just couldn't get over her uncommon selflessness. Esther may not have earned a spot on the Olympic team that year, but she gained recognition as a true champion around the world.

The Bible tells us in First Corinthians 13 that love is not selfish, but that's one of those verses that is much easier to read than to live. Ask God to help you truly live the verses of First Corinthians 13. Ask Him to help you put others needs above your own. Look for ways to be a better friend. Live the love today!

SOMETHING'S GOTTA BLOW!

A fool gives full vent to his anger, but a wise man
keeps himself under control.

PROVERBS 29:11

O n the morning of August 24, the city of Pompeii was bustling with life. Thousands of people went about their usual daily routines, working, playing, planning for the future. By noon, nearby Mt. Vesuvius had erupted. The sky turned black, as a twelve-mile high cloud of cinder and ash blocked out the light of the sun. Rocky debris rained down on the city. Some people fled. Many others decided to wait out the eruption and see what the new day would bring. At midnight, lava, poisonous gases, and volcanic mud spewed from an open fissure on the mountain. But, it was a deadly surge of hot air the next morning that instantly killed the entire population.

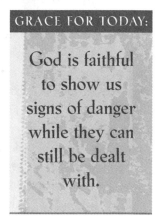

GRACE FOR TODAY:

God is faithful
to show us
signs of danger
while they can
still be dealt
with.

If only the people of 79 AD knew how to recognize the signs of potential volcanic activity like scientists can today. They would have been aware that pressure was building inside the volcano. They would have known it was inevitable that something was about to blow.

Can you recognize those same signs in yourself? After all, there's a potential volcano lurking inside each and every person. When anger, bitterness, and resentment get pushed down below the surface with no means of escape, the pressure starts to build. The inevitable explosion may be loud and showy, blasting dangerous hot air in the direction of others. Or, it may quietly release toxic fumes that poison your own heart, fueling depression and low self-esteem.

At the first sign of anger—even if it only feels like a minor annoyance—go to God. Talk to Him about how you're feeling. Ask Him to reveal any areas where you are wrong that need to be made right. Allow Him to help you replace anger with forgiveness, rendering the volcano within you fully dormant.

DON'T FOLLOW THE CROWD

[God] will direct and make straight and plain your paths.

PROVERBS 3:6 AMP

E ver tried to find your way through one of those mirror mazes at the fair? At first, you may have thought, *Oh snap! This will be easy. Just a few turns here and there, and I'll be out in no time.*

To your surprise and dismay, no time seemingly becomes hours as every turn you make leads nowhere. Suddenly, what started out as an innocent game has turned into a desperate attempt at escape. This maze is a real threat and not fun any more.

When we were born, we entered into a maze-like adventure filled with choices and options, detours and dead ends. Almost daily we're faced with opportunities to make right decisions or choose paths we know lead nowhere. How we respond to those choices determines how successful we become in life.

Choosing the wrong path is a lot like walking through a mirror maze. At every turn you see an image of yourself, but you are going nowhere. Making wise choices assures you will successfully reach your destination.

Whenever you are faced with a decision, always do what the Bible says is wise—trust in God and let Him direct you. Ask the Holy Spirit to lead you through the mazes of life, so that you don't stumble, fall, and get off track.

It may not be the natural thing to do, but it is certainly the right and honest thing. Making good moral choices is one of the clearest signs of the Holy Spirit at work in you. He will always help you to choose good and refuse evil.

GRACE FOR TODAY:

Life is a journey that, with God as our guide, will always end in success.

HEAR HERE

"My sheep recognize my voice, and I know them, and they follow me.
I give them eternal life and they shall never perish. No one shall snatch
them away from me."

JOHN 10:27–28 TLB

God wants you to hear his voice. He has words that will stir your heart and direct your mind. You want to be lifted up? God's words can make your soul soar above the stars. You want to be comforted? His healing message and soothing tones can heal your every heartache.

But first, you might have to put down the cell phone, turn off the TV, or give your eyes, ears, and fingers a rest from the video games. Because, as the music group Out of the Grey wisely points out, "He is not silent / He is not whispering / We are not quiet / We are not listening."

God yearns for you to hear Him, but it's been a long time since He spoke via a thundering voice in the sky. Thus, it's a good idea to occasionally silence all the noise pollution—all of the distractions—until the only voice you hear is His. (Sometimes God has to do the "silencing" for us, but He'd much prefer that we took the initiative.)

Yes, God is in heaven. Yes, He controls even the remotest corners of the universe. But He is also sitting right next to you. If you've accepted Him, His Spirit lives in your heart. He has much to say to you, words that will enrich your life in amazing ways. So take time to listen—He might have an important message for you—right now.

GRACE FOR TODAY:

God richly rewards those who discipline themselves
to regularly tune out competing voices and
hear only His.

LOOKING FOR LOVE

John Wesley did amazing things for God. Over the course of fifty years he preached over 40,000 sermons to crowds numbering up to 30,000 people. He founded the Methodist Church and was well known for his strong devotion to God. But on the dating scene, Wesley was not a shining example of loyalty. Back in the 1700s, he was considered a major flirt. He led several women to believe he wanted to marry them. Then he dropped them. When he finally did decide to get married, it was because he felt it would keep other women from pursuing him.

The woman he chose for the honor of being his wife was Grace Murray. After writing a forty-six page paper evaluating her spiritual qualifications and a list of thirty-two reasons why she would be a suitable wife, Grace chose to marry someone else. At almost fifty years of age, John eventually married Molly Vazeille. They separated twenty years later.

Loving God doesn't automatically make you—or help you find—the perfect date. But it should change the way you look at love and marriage. God says marriage was designed to give the world a picture of how He loves the people of His church. That kind of love isn't fickle. It doesn't use people or treat them with disrespect. It builds others up. It makes sacrifices. It always draws others closer to God, never further away from Him.

Loving like that isn't easy. As a matter of fact, apart from God, it's downright impossible. That's why it's important to put your love life in God's hands. Focus on loving others well—not just the opposite sex. Then, continue doing what you believe God wants you to do. God will lead you toward a deeper relationship at the right place and right time.

GRACE FOR TODAY:

When we draw close to God, He will lead us to deep and rewarding relationships.

Love is kind and patient, never jealous, boastful, proud, or rude.

1 CORINTHIANS 13:4-5 CEV

THROW AWAY THE MASK

By Luis Palau

When we live in godly sincerity, we don't wear masks. We don't try to act like fine Christians. We don't build up a "Christian" façade to impress other people. Godly sincerity simply means we are who we are in Jesus Christ. It means we walk in the light of the Lord, no longer putting on a show to deceive others.

Christians have no reason to live behind a mask. Christians are told to "walk in the light, as he is in the light" (1 John 1:7). This means we are to walk before God and others with the same transparency—or, as Paul says, sincerity—that Christ showed in His life. And by accepting the grace of God, we can do so.

When we place ourselves under the control of the indwelling Christ, we then are able to boast about our conscience and live in godly sincerity. When our hearts are transparent before God, we suffer no guilt from sin; we can boldly proclaim the message of Jesus Christ. We don't have to put on any kind of spiritual show because the power and authority of the Holy Spirit are at work within us.

Nothing is more humbling than the expectation of standing before the Lord Jesus in judgment. On that day, all façades will be exposed. Everyone who has hidden behind a mask will be revealed. But those who know the all-sufficient Father, and are controlled by His grace, can live with a clear conscience and godly sincerity until that day.[8]

—⁓—

DEAR LORD: I RECEIVE YOUR GRACE AS I LAY DOWN MY MASK AND RESOLVE TO WALK IN SINCERITY AND TRUTH. I KNOW THIS IS POSSIBLE ONLY BECAUSE OF JESUS AND THE WORK OF REDEMPTION. THANK YOU FOR RECEIVING ME JUST AS I AM. AMEN.

If we walk in the light as he himself is in the light, we have fellowship with one another, and the blood of Jesus his Son cleanses us from all sin.

1 JOHN 1:7 NRSV

DARE TO DREAM

I can do everything through him who gives me strength.

PHILIPPIANS 4:13

A sobbing little girl stood in front of a small church where she'd just been turned away due to space constraints. The pastor saw her crying and asked her why she was so sad. The little girl, dressed in shabby clothing, explained, "I can't go to Sunday school because there's no more room." The pastor took the little girl's hand and escorted her into the Sunday school class, finding a special spot just for her.

GRACE FOR TODAY:

God can accomplish much through us, even if we only have a mustard seed of faith.

About two years later, the girl died. Her parents called for the kind pastor who had found her a spot in Sunday school. They wanted him to do her funeral. While clearing out the little girl's belongings, they found an old, dingy red purse. Inside, there was fifty-seven cents and a note that said, "This is to help build the little church bigger so more children can go to Sunday school."

She'd been saving that offering for two years. The pastor shared this little girl's dream with his congregation, challenging his deacons to get busy and raise the rest of the money to expand the church. Soon, word of the little girl's fifty-seven cents hit the newspapers. A wealthy realtor read the story and offered the church a parcel of land worth thousands of dollars. Money came in from everywhere, and within five years, the little girl's fifty-seven cents had grown into $250,000—a lot of money for 1900. Today, that little girl's dream is evident to all in Philadelphia, Pennsylvania. Temple Baptist Church seats 3,300, and Temple University educates thousands every year.

Maybe you, too, have a dream that seems impossible. Just remember—God can do a lot with your little. Be willing to step out in faith and offer your best to God. That's all He needs to accomplish mighty miracles.

LIVING THE GOOD LIFE

We know that all that happens to us is working for our good if we love God and are fitting into his plans.

ROMANS 8:28 TLB

Fanny Crosby was an accomplished singer, songwriter, and musician. She was hired by a music company to write two to three songs a week, but often came up with the lyrics for six or seven. Out of the two dollars she earned from each song she wrote, she gave a large portion away to the poor. She was as generous with her time as she was with her money. She began teaching at the age of fifteen, and regularly volunteered to help those in need when she wasn't teaching English or History to her students. By the age of twenty-three, Fanny had become friends with President Grover Cleveland, and was speaking before Congress.

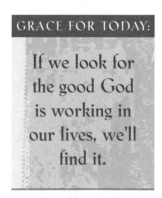

GRACE FOR TODAY:

If we look for the good God is working in our lives, we'll find it.

Even more remarkable than Fanny's accomplishments or her compassion for others was her attitude. The very first song she wrote, at the age of eight, tells her story: "Oh what a happy soul I am, although I cannot see! I am resolved that in this world, contented I will be. How many blessings I enjoy that other people don't. To weep and sigh because I'm blind, I cannot and I won't!"

When Fanny was six weeks old, a man pretending to be a certified doctor prescribed a medicine for Fanny that caused her to lose her sight. Instead of growing up bitter or resentful, Fanny freely told others how gracious God had been to her. She said that if she'd been able to see, she would have been distracted from writing the between 8,000 and 9,000 hymns she became known for.

God has the power, and the desire, to use everything that happens to you in a positive way. Your own attitude allows Him to help you live the good life, no matter what your circumstances may be.

A SECOND LOOK

Everyone should be quick to listen, slow to speak and
slow to become angry.

JAMES 1:19

C arly was proud of how well she had handled the situation with the stranger. The two had been sitting next to each other outside the doctor's office when Carly stepped away to go to the restroom. She had returned to find the girl casually thumbing through the teen magazine Carly had been reading—dog-earring page after page as she went.

What does she think she's doing? Carly thought as she watched the girl handling the magazine. She had to know that it was mine because she was looking right at me while I worked the crossword puzzle.

To make matters worse, the girl closed the magazine, shoved it into her shoulder bag, and stood as the receptionist called out her name. Carly started to demand her magazine, but not wanting to embarrass the girl or cause a scene, decided it wasn't worth it.

Thinking about the incident later that evening as she emptied out her shopping bag onto the bed, Carly was thankful she had not made a scene inside the doctor's office. Not only would she have embarrassed the girl, but if she had gotten angry and insistant, she could have damaged Carly's image as a Christian as well.

Carly looked down at the items she had purchased that day. To her shock—and embarrassment—there was her magazine!

How easy it is to assume things to be one way, only to find them to be just the opposite. That's one reason the Bible says be slow to speak. Acting on our assumptions can sometimes result in a world of trouble.

Thank God you have His wisdom, and that He always guides your actions. He sees a lot further than you, and He is always working on your behalf.

GRACE FOR TODAY:

God always looks for the good in us, even when what
He sees is not the prettiest picture.

SEE IT, THEN BE IT

Let wise people listen and add to what they have learned.
Let those who understand what is right get guidance.

PROVERBS 1:5 NIRV

A college student shot baskets on a side goal, as he watched his college's hoops team take to the court for their practice. Once a player himself, the student looked on with admiration as he watched. Occasionally, he would try to duplicate a shot or move he saw expertly executed on the court.

Midway through the practice session, one of the athletes sprained his ankle and hobbled out of the gym. Not wanting to continue the scrimmage with uneven teams, the coach approached the student on the sidelines and said flatly, "We need you to run with us. Put your ball down and get out on the court."

With a nervous gulp, the student stepped tentatively onto the court. The game was much faster than he was accustomed to, and he struggled to stay with a taller, quicker opponent.

However, as the scrimmage kicked into high gear, the student became more emboldened and less intimidated. He watched his teammates carefully, striving to emulate their moves.

Thus, as his teammates elevated their games, the student lifted his as well, carried along by the force of their momentum. Their power and skill brought out the best in him.

Could your life's "game" stand some improvement? Observing people whom you revere and respect is a great way to achieve this improvement, as is reading the Bible and studying the examples of Jesus and His faithful followers. However, don't just observe and make mental note of the examples you study. Apply what you see and read to your life. Ask to spend time with people whose lives you admire. It just might change the way you play the game of life. Forever.

GRACE FOR TODAY:

God created us to be more than observers, admirers of life. He wants us to get off the sidelines and experience the exhilaration of participation!

YOU ARE ROYALTY

Do you ever dream of being somebody else? Maybe a movie star? A famous singer? A millionaire? A professional athlete? While it's fun to daydream about being somebody else or having someone else's life, it is also quite dangerous. The Lord doesn't want you to waste your energies dreaming of being somebody else, because He already thinks you are awesome. Meditate on that a moment—the Creator of the universe thinks you are awesome!

Maybe you feel inferior today. Maybe you feel like you just don't measure up compared to those around you. Maybe someone has said something negative to you, and you continually hear that derogatory remark in your head. Well, I've got news for you. God creat-ed you just the way you are, and He doesn't care if your middle toe is longer than your big toe. He doesn't mind that your manicure is chipped. And, He's fine with the fact that you have trouble in math class. God loves you—flaws and all. So, quit dreaming about being somebody else and celebrate you! Your Heavenly Father created you, and He doesn't make mistakes.

Meditate on verses in the Bible such as Psalm 139:14. Look yourself in the mirror every day and say, "I am fearfully and wonderfully made." Say, "God made me, and He doesn't make any junk." Remember, when you became a Christian, you were adopted into the Royal Family. You now come from a royal bloodline. Bottom line—you are priceless.

GRACE FOR TODAY:

God loves us—flaws and all.

I will praise thee; for I am fearfully and wonderfully made:
marvelous are thy works; and that my soul knoweth right well.

PSALM 139:14 KJV

REPLACING WORRY WITH THE RIGHT FOCUS

By John MacArthur Jr.

G od wants to free His children from being preoccupied with the mundane. Colossians 3:2 says as directly as possible, "Set your mind on the things above, not on the things that are on earth." Therefore a materialistic Christian is a contradiction in terms.

The Greek word *prōtos* ("first") means "first in a line of more than one option." Of all the priorities of life, seeking God's kingdom is number one. It is doing what you can to promote God's rule over His creation. That includes seeking Christ's rule to be manifest in your life through "righteousness and peace and joy in the Holy Spirit" (Romans 14:17). When the world sees those virtues in your life instead of worry, it's evidence that the kingdom of God is there.

What is your heart's preoccupation? Are you more concerned with the kingdom or with the things of this world? Don't be anxious for the goods of this world—or anything else for that matter. As Sherlock Holmes would say, don't just see but observe. And remember what Jesus told you to observe: abundant evidence all around you of God's lavish care for the needs of His beloved.[9]

—⁂—

DEAR FATHER: HELP ME TO TAKE MY EYES OFF THE THINGS OF THE WORLD AND PLACE THEM ON YOU AND ALL THE THINGS YOU'VE GIVEN ME THROUGH YOUR GRACE. I BELIEVE THAT LIFE IN YOUR KINGDOM INCLUDES EVERYTHING I COULD POSSIBLY NEED IN THIS WORLD. I THANK YOU FOR GIVING ME MORE THAN ENOUGH. AMEN.

[Jesus said,] "Steep your life in God-reality, God-initiative, God-provisions. Don't worry about missing out. You'll find all your everyday human concerns will be met."

MATTHEW 6:33 MSG

RUN YOUR RACE

I'm off and running, and I'm not turning back.

PHILIPPIANS 3:14 MSG

W hen training for track, coaches often urge their runners to sprint the last leg of the predetermined distance—even during practice. You'll often hear veteran coaches call to their runners, "Finish strong!" Then, the weary runners—no matter how many miles they've already run—will kick it into gear and give it everything they've got until they cross the finish line. The drive to finish strong pushes them farther than they knew they could go and faster than they thought they could run.

> **GRACE FOR TODAY:**
>
> When we grow tired, we must remember—God is cheering us on to victory!

We have a heavenly coach giving us the same direction: "Finish strong!" No matter how hard it gets in life, God wants us to keep our eyes on the prize and finish strong. Maybe you're going through some tough times right now. Maybe you're feeling weary. Perhaps you're wondering if you'll ever finish the race that's been set before you. No matter how you're feeling, God wants you to know that He is in your corner. He is cheering you on to victory. He has already equipped you with everything you'll ever need to run your race. All you have to do is keep your eyes fixed on Him and stay on course.

Don't try to run anyone else's race. Refuse to compare yourself with others. God created you according to His own personal design for you. Just stay on your course and run the race that God has set before you. Push on, and you'll hear God saying something else to you—"Well done, good and faithful servant." Go ahead. Put on those track shoes and hit the pavement. You've got a race to run!

THE REAL THING

Popularity contests are not truth contests. . . .
Your task is to be true, not popular.

LUKE 6:26 MSG

From a distance, they look like the real thing—nonfat cream cheese, diet soda, imitation crab, veggie burgers. But, one taste exposes them for what they really are—imposters.

Imposters are not confined to the shelves of your grocery store. There may be an imposter sitting next to you in history class, competing against you in track, or even staring back at you when you look in the mirror. From a distance these people look like the real thing. They appear to have it all together, to be self-assured, the life of the party. It seems like they're living life from the heart of who they are.

In truth their heart is filled with fear. They're afraid that if people catch a glimpse of who they really are—with all of their faults, insecurities, and imperfections—they'll be rejected or ridiculed. The reality is, they may. Fear drives people to snub and make fun of others, as well as to put on a false front themselves.

God sees through it all. He created each person as an individual and wants each individual to follow His example of authenticity. God never puts on a false front, pretending to be more or less than who He is. When God introduced himself to Moses, He said, "I am who I am." Forever and always, God has been and will be authentically himself.

Risk being real. God asks for no more, and no less, from you. When you give up trying to impress others and simply be yourself, something wonderful happens. You can relax and enjoy life. Meanwhile, you'll discover that others are drawn to your God-centered joy and authenticity. Refuse to be an imposter. Be the one-of-a-kind miracle God designed you to be.

> GRACE FOR TODAY:
>
> If God had wanted me otherwise, He would have created me otherwise.
>
> JOHANN VON GOETHE

COME TOGETHER

From him the whole body, joined and held together by every supporting ligament, grows and builds itself up in love, as each part does its work.

EPHESIANS 4:16

"I've been thinking about this all weekend," Lisa said excitedly as she entered the room. "Just wait 'til you hear what I have planned."

I'm sure we can ALL wait, Gena thought to herself, glancing at the expressions on the faces of the others seated around the table.

Immediately, Gena felt remorseful over her thoughts. It was wrong for her and the others to feel that way about a fellow committee member and Christian. But with Lisa, it was hard to feel any other way.

Everyone knew how pushy Lisa could be—sometimes even to the point of tears when things did not go her way. She always had the perfect plan, regardless of what someone else might suggest.

Why does she always do that? Gena wondered, almost speaking out loud. *It's like she doesn't even realize how controlling she comes off looking. I spent just as much time as she did trying to come up with ideas. We are entitled to be heard too.*

Gena wanted to say just that to Lisa. And by the looks on their faces, she could tell the others were thinking the same. Unexpectedly, Gena thought about how patient Jesus was with people.

If He was patient with me while I got my act together, then surely we all can be patient with Lisa while God works all the kinks out of her, Gena reasoned.

"Great. Tell us about your ideas, Lisa," Gena said. "I'm sure they're good ones. And I'm sure the others have some ideas as well. It's so wonderful that God has called us all to work together."

GRACE FOR TODAY:

Despite a difference of opinion, God can help us to never miss an opportunity to walk in love.

Savoring Life's Flavors

He will yet fill your mouth with laughter
and your lips with shouts of joy.

JOB 8:21

Magic moments—you've had them. Chugging a cold soda after a hot day of athletic practice or outdoor work. Standing and cheering at the end of an inspiring song at a concert. Holding a child's hand on a walk to the park or ice cream shop. Seeing that familiar smile burst across your best friend's face when you unexpectedly bump into each other at the mall. Having a relative mention your name when thanking God for His blessings.

Every good and perfect moment like this is a gift to you from God—even the ones that seem like coincidence. He sends these gifts to remind us all that He is still in control, and that His supply of love and kindness will never run dry. And because of this, life is always worth living.

These gifts also remind us to keep our eyes, minds, and hearts open for the blessings, large and small, that await us in the future. Instead of dreading all that might go wrong tomorrow, next month, or next year, we should spend our energy being watchful for those magic moments, the ones that fill our mouths with laughter and make us want to shout with joy.

So the next time God drops one of these blessings on your tongue, take time to savor it, enjoy it. A seemingly momentary blessing can leave a sweet aftertaste that can last forever—so let it.

Grace for Today:

God had loaded us down with gifts, large and small.
We should take the time to open them all!

TRULY CONTENT

There's a beautiful song by the Christian group Avalon that goes: "You're everything to me. You're more than a story. More than words on a page of history. You're the air that I breathe. The water I thirst for. And the ground beneath my feet. You're everything to me."

If we truly feel that way about our Lord, we can be content no matter if we're the most popular student in school or the biggest nerd on the planet. Contentment—true contentment—comes only from the Lord. Sure, we can get "temporary contentment fixes"—things that make us feel fulfilled for a little while—but that lasting peace and sense of fulfillment comes only from Heaven.

Franklin Graham recently appeared on television and spoke of this emptiness. He said he once read an article in *Rolling Stone* about Kurt Cobane, the former lead singer of Nirvana who killed himself. The magazine actually printed portions of Cobane's suicide note that spoke of this empty hole that he couldn't fill. Graham relayed that only Jesus Christ can fill that hole. He further explores this concept in his book, *The Name*.

Truly, nothing can fill the hole in our hearts that yearns for Jesus. Only He can fill that void. Only He can cause contentment to be a way of life. That's why Paul and Silas could sing praises to God while locked up in a stinky prison. They were content—even joyful—in their circumstances. Why? Because Jesus was everything to them—period. Is Jesus everything to you today? If you've lost that passion you once had for Christ, spend some time with Him today. If He is your everything, you'll be content in everything.

GRACE FOR TODAY:

When Jesus is our everything, He'll help us be content in everything.

As the deer pants for streams of water, so I long for you, O God.

PSALM 42:1 NLT

HIS JOY

By Evelyn Christenson

I t was pouring rain as I started on an out-of-state trip. Three miles from home a truck, a compact car, and Evelyn stopped for a red light, but the car behind me didn't. Crunch. And all four vehicles accordioned into one. I recovered from the jolt to my nervous system, but as I drove during the following week I kept my eyes as much on the rearview mirror as I did on the road ahead of me!

The next weekend I was to drive to Minnesota, but I felt nothing but apprehension and fear at the possibility of being hit from behind. Just before I was planning to leave, God gave the answer as I was reading in the Psalms. A smile spread over my face as I read: "But let all those who put their trust in thee rejoice: let them ever shout for joy, because thou defendest them: let them also that love Thy name be joyful in thee" (Psalm. 5:11 KJV). Immediately I saw my problem— failing to trust Him! At that moment He

exchanged my fear for His—yes, literally—His joy. The apprehension disappeared, and I drove away, a changed woman.

My spiritual barometer for years has been 1 John 1:4: "And these things we write to you that your joy may be full" (NKJV). I can always measure the amount of time I'm not spending in the Scriptures by how much joy (not superficial happiness, but deep-down abiding joy) I have. When I find a lack of joy in my life, the first thing I check is how much time I'm spending in God's Word.[10]

—⁓—

DEAR FATHER: WHEN THINGS HAPPEN TO ME, I WANT TO EXPERIENCE YOUR JOY. OPEN YOUR WORD TO ME THAT MY HEART MIGHT BE TUNED TO SEE EVEN MY TRIALS THROUGH EYES OF GRACE. AMEN.

The precepts of the LORD are right, giving joy to the heart.

PSALM 19:8

WALKING IN THE F.O.G.

Surely, O LORD, you bless the righteous; you surround them
with your favor as with a shield.

PSALM 5:12

I f your father were the principal of your high school, would you expect special treatment? If your dad owned the local movie theater, wouldn't you expect to get in free and enjoy popcorn and sodas on the house? Of course you would, because you'd have favor with the guy in charge.

Well, guess what? You do have favor with the highest authority—God! The Bible says that He has crowned your head with glory, honor, and favor. He is wealthy beyond your wildest imagination. He can give you a whole lot more than free popcorn and sodas, and He wants to pour His goodness out on you! He delights in doing favors for you, because He adores you.

You can walk in the F.O.G.—the Favor of God— all the time. Thank God for His supernatural favor. Every morning before you head off to school, thank Him for favor with your teachers, your principal, your coaches, your peers, your parents, and anyone else you might encounter. It's amazing, really. Once you start giving God credit for His supernatural favor, you'll notice more of it in your life.

God appreciates that you notice all of the nice things He does for you. When you get the last corn dog in the lunch line at school, thank God for His favor. When you get the best parking spot in the entire school lot, acknowledge His goodness. When you forget to do your math homework, and your teacher allows you to turn it in late without penalty; realize He had a hand in their decision. Enjoy living in the F.O.G. today!

GOD CAN HEAR YOU NOW

Don't worry about anything; instead, pray about everything; tell God
your needs and don't forget to thank him for his answers.

PHILIPPIANS 4:6 TLB

W hat do you talk about with your best friend? Chances are, everything from great news to big problems, along with all the minor details in between. Sometimes you may simply need reassurance that you're loved and not alone in this world. Whatever the reason, it's always great to spend time with someone you care about who loves you in return. But there will be times when you're unable to chat face-to-face. That's where a cell phone comes in handy. Then, you can have instant access into your friend's presence anytime, anywhere—depending on your carrier.

God's long distance plan beats anything you can find here on earth. You have unlimited minutes, no roaming charges, and equipment that never needs recharging. With God's Spirit as your long distance carrier you never have to worry about a lousy connection. You always get through loud and clear. And God doesn't subscribe to call waiting. Every individual gets His undivided attention.

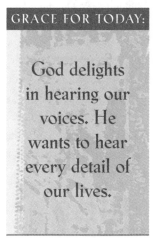

GRACE FOR TODAY:

God delights in hearing our voices. He wants to hear every detail of our lives.

Until you have the opportunity of meeting God face-to-face in heaven, prayer is the cell phone that can bring you straight into God's presence. Like your best friend, God's interested in every detail of your day. He delights in hearing your voice and wants to know what you're thinking and feeling. There isn't any secret password or fancy language necessary to get His attention. Just be honest and open. Share your heart. Then, take time to listen. Sit quietly and wait for God's whisper. The more time you spend with Him, the more you'll be able to recognize His voice—the same way you do with any new friend.

Make a habit of calling God as often as you do your best friend. He always answers on the very first ring.

WHY ME?

Blessed are you when people insult you and persecute you, and
falsely say all kinds of evil against you because of Me.

MATTHEW 5:11 NASB

A nger rushes through your mind as you rehearse the words you just heard from
your principal.

"Cheating is dishonest, and absolutely will not be tolerated," he had admonished.

Why would someone lie that way and get you in such trouble? You wonder. You
want to defend yourself. But more than that, you want to get even with whoever lied
about you.

This is a perfect place to stop and ask: What would Jesus do?

The Bible is very clear on how Jesus would respond in such a situation. On a
number of occasions people lied about Him and tried to destroy His credibility. Each
time, He chose to endure the abuse and mistreatment, and forgive those who had come
against Him. That's what God expects of you.

It is difficult to overlook an offense, especially when you don't understand why you
are being attacked. As a Christian, you should expect persecution to come in some
form. But don't let it get you down. You may not understand why certain things happen, but He does. And because you are His child, He will protect you.

When someone falsely accuses you, don't try and fix it. Let God step in and defend
you. Your job is to continue to walk in love. The life you live before people speaks
more about your character than anything else. People who know you will recognize
when you are falsely accused.

Thank God that the accusation against you is not true. Trust Him to reveal the
truth; and then, as an act of your faith in Him and His Word, forgive the ones who have
come against you.

GRACE FOR TODAY:

God is our defense in every situation.

LOVE CHANGES EVERYTHING

I'll call nobodies and make them somebodies; I'll call the unloved and
make them beloved.

ROMANS 9:25 MSG

Jesus' love changed a lot of people. Paul turned from a heartless persecutor of
Christians to a heart-on-his-sleeve encourager and self-sacrificing missionary.
Zaccheus was transformed from a shrewd, greedy tax collector to a repentant, open-
hearted giver.

One of the most dramatic transformations occurs early in the Gospel of John.
Jesus, who is Jewish, meets a woman who is Samaritan, a people hated by Jews.
Further, she has had five husbands and is currently living with a man she is not mar-
ried to—that's scandalous, even by today's standards.

But Jesus talks with her, which amazes her. In fact, it shocks even His disciples.
The Lord doesn't judge her. Instead, He offers her (again, a sworn enemy of the Jewish
people) the "fresh, living water" of salvation.

Finally, Jesus inspires her (some theologians say He actually assigned her) to go
into her village and tell everyone about Him.

It's significant that the villagers responded to her words and went to see the
Messiah for themselves. Why did they trust the words of a woman of dubious reputation—a woman who admitted to conversing with "the enemy"? They must have been
able to sense that her loving encounter with Jesus had changed her forever.

Jesus' love can do the same for you—no matter what you have done. His love can
soothe the pain and shame of your past—and give you energy, hope, and purpose for
your future. Jesus has been using love to transform lives for thousands of years; He's
quite good at it. Let Him show you, personally.

GRACE FOR TODAY:

Just as a little seed can grow a beautiful tree, even a
little of God's love can grow a beautiful life.

SUPERNATURAL FAVOR

There are bullies lurking in every school in the world. They love to abuse and humiliate others. In fact, they thrive on it. Maybe you've been the victim of a bully. Maybe you haven't been bullied, but there is a group of teens who don't particularly like you. Well, that can be subject to change.

Did you know that God can cause people who don't like you to suddenly change their minds about you? He can even cause them to do nice things for you. When the Israelites left Egypt and headed for the Promised Land, they left in a hurry as Moses had instructed. On the way out of town, however, they asked the Egyptians for gold and silver and for clothing and shoes. Now the Israelites and Egyptians hadn't exactly been friendly with each other, yet the Israelites were given all they asked for and more. Can't you just see the Egyptians loading up sacks of these precious items to give to the Israelites and saying, "I don't know why I am giving this stuff to you, but enjoy it! Have a great trip!"

God can even use your enemies to treat you favorably. He can cause the bully who has been giving you grief to like you. He can cause that group of kids who hate you to suddenly want to bless you. God can do it! Just honor Him and His Word, and thank Him for His supernatural favor. Praise Him for causing your enemies to bless you. It works!

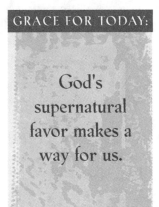

GRACE FOR TODAY:

God's supernatural favor makes a way for us.

The LORD had made the Egyptians favorably disposed
toward the people, and they gave them what they asked for;
so they plundered the Egyptians.

EXODUS 12:36

KEEPING TRACK

By Evelyn Christenson

A re you aware that each of us have an internal "bookkeeping" system? We have one column in the ledger where we record the good things that happen to us, and another where we keep track of the wrongs leveled against us. Year after year these accumulated statistics tip the balance one way or the other. The side outweighing the other has a strong effect on our whole being. If it is the "bad" side, it can affect us adversely.

I heard of a woman who actually has a little book with a page for each acquaintance. She makes an entry each time someone says or does something against her. Then when she comes to a predetermined number, she draws a dark diagonal line across that page—slashing her off her list of friends!

But forgiving does a strange thing to the forgiver's column of hurts. It wipes clean the statistics that have been hoarded in the internal ledgers. In 1 Corinthians 13:5, that great love chapter, we read, that love "keeps no record of when it has been wronged" (NLT). In other words, as in the Phillips translation, "It does not keep account of evil."

We may feel there is a personal gain in the satisfaction we derive from exercising our "right" to refuse to give up our angry, negative, accusing, wounded spirit. But in reality just the opposite is true. We are the losers. The emotional and physical gains come when we take our spiritual eraser and wipe the ledger clean—by forgiving."

—∽∾—

DEAR GOD, HELP ME TO REMEMBER THAT WHEN I WAS A "LOSER" YOU REACHED DOWN, POURED OUT YOUR GRACE ON ME AND SAVED ME. GIVE ME A HEART THAT FORGIVES LIKE YOURS DOES—FULLY. AMEN.

Love covers over all wrongs.

PROVERBS 10:12

POWER PRAYERS

That's why I urge you to pray for absolutely everything, ranging from
small to large. Include everything as you embrace this God-life,
and you'll get God's everything.

MARK 11:24 MSG

"**W**heel . . . of . . . Fortune!" Can't you just hear that famous game-show
music now? "Wheel of Fortune" is a fun game show to watch. Who
wouldn't want to spin a gigantic wheel full of money, free spins, and special prizes? Of
course, sometimes the hopeful contestant is yelling, "C'mon! Big money! Big money!"
and the wheel stops on the bankruptcy spot, and that contestant loses everything accumulated up to that point in the round. That's what hap-
pens when you play a game of luck.

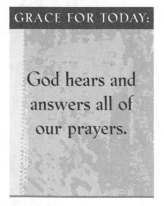

GRACE FOR TODAY:

God hears and
answers all of
our prayers.

God doesn't have a big "Wheel of Fortune" that
determines whether or not your prayers get answered.
Imagine if every time you prayed, God spun that big
wheel in the sky, determining your outcome.
Sometimes you'd get prizes, but other times you'd get
"lose a spin," and then the angel, Gabriel, (standing in
for Vanna White) would tell you about your lovely
parting gifts.

Some people actually believe their prayers are
answered in a "Wheel of Fortune" kind of way. They
pray any old prayer and simply hope for the best. As Christians, we don't have to leave
the outcome to chance. Unlike the wheel on the "Wheel of Fortune," God is the same
yesterday, today and forever. What God has done for others, He will do for you.

He loves you and wants to bless you. So don't approach prayer like a game of
chance. Instead, believe that God will hear and answer your prayers at the appointed
time. That kind of communication is powerful. In fact, when you pray with that attitude, you always win.

SIGNED, SEALED, AND DELIVERED

Love never gives up, never loses faith, is always hopeful,
and endures through every circumstance.

1 CORINTHIANS 13:7 NLT

I magine receiving an incredible love letter. In it, the author elaborates on how important you are and how much he cherishes you, going so far as to say he would sacrifice his life for yours. Page after page talks about how your true love longs to be with you, and how you will be together forever, soon. What would you do with that letter?

You'd probably put it in a safe place, reread it often, share what was written with your closest friends, and perhaps even memorize a line or two. It would undoubtedly be a source of joy and encouragement, something you'd plan your future around.

Every time you read the Bible, you hold that letter in your hands. It's God's heartfelt love letter to you. In it, He describes what a masterpiece you are and how much you mean to Him. He also tells how your True Love sacrificed His life on a cross so you could spend eternity with Him. Along with God's promises and love poems, He also shares stories about people just like you—people who faced tough circumstances and wanted to do what was right, people who tried and

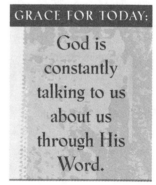

GRACE FOR TODAY:

God is constantly talking to us about us through His Word.

succeeded, others who tried and failed, and some who didn't seem to try at all. He gives you the opportunity to learn from their lives.

The overall message of the entire letter is one of love. The more you read God's love letter, the more you'll understand how much He cares about you, and the more excited you'll be about the fantastic plans He has for your future.

Pick up God's letter today. Read 1 Corinthians 13. Consider what it means to be the focus of God's perfect love—and how that love changes your view of today, tomorrow, and forever.

READY TO GIVE

As we have opportunity, let us do good to all people, especially to those who belong to the family of believers.

GALATIANS 6:10

You had looked longingly for this day for some time.
Finally, a Saturday with no obligations! No soccer practice. No tutoring sessions. No exams to study for. Your parents have even excused you from mowing the lawn and told you to enjoy the day. Now, a friend is on the phone asking your help in preparing for the math session of the PSAT.

Why me? You wonder. *I need this time to myself.*

There will be times when it seems like people are drawing on you from every side. You should always be willing to do whatever you can to help others, when you feel that God is leading you to do that. There will be times when you feel God telling you to enjoy time in fellowship with Him or just relaxing by yourself.

Be sensitive to the prompting of the Holy Spirit. He will instruct you what to answer when others need your help or want your company. The important thing is to be in tune with Him. It always pleases God when we put the needs of others above our own. But if you are so busy that you never have time for yourself, then you are too busy.

Ask God to help you keep your life organized so that you can be available when others need your help. If people are calling on you for help, it's because they trust you to help them. They have confidence in you. Be thankful that you are known as a person of compassion, and not one who is selfish. Thank God that your desire is to help those in need, then ask Him to let you always be willing to help in the time of need.

GRACE FOR TODAY:

God will give us more time for ourselves
as we find time for others.

LOVED "JUST BECAUSE"

God is love, and anyone who doesn't love others has never known him.

1 JOHN 4:8 CEV

D o you ever wonder what makes the people in your life—your family and friends—like you, even love you? What is it about you that inspires affection in those around you.

People might adore you for your charming sense of humor, your musical talent, your generosity, your intelligence, your "cool factor," your loyalty, even your physical attractiveness. But that's not the way it works with God. He loves you because He is love. He's not merely loving, or love-prone. Love isn't merely one of God's tendencies or traits. More than any other aspect of His character, love defines who God is.

This means that He loves you because it's in His nature to do so. He doesn't have to read poetry to get in the mood to love you. He doesn't have to practice being loving or make a love "to-do" list for each of His people. His love is unprompted, unearned, and unrelenting.

The difference between God's love and imperfect human love is that God loves you when you don't feel lovely—or are, in fact, unlovely. He loves you even when no one else feels like it. He loves you when others are distracted or too focused on themselves to even think about you.

Friends may abandon you. It might seem that your parents neglect you. Adults you admire might ignore you, or even turn against you. But God isn't swayed by how anyone else feels, and His love doesn't ride the bumpy waves of popular opinion. He will love you. Forever. No matter what.

GRACE FOR TODAY:

God doesn't love us because of our goodness, but, rather, because of His.

FRIDAY

A GIFT THAT FITS JUST RIGHT

Think of your most valuable possession. It could be a guitar, your first car, even a collection of baseball cards. Chances are, the more you care about this "treasure," the more you'll take care of it. You're not going to leave your baseball cards on the front porch during a snowstorm or use your guitar to hammer a nail into your bedroom wall. You don't want what you care about to get ruined. You want to keep it in mint condition, so it will hold its value and so that you can enjoy it for as long as you can.

The most valuable "possession" God's given you is your physical body. However, it's easy to take it for granted. One reason for that may be because it's so well made. Even with little sleep, a diet of fast food, and an exercise routine that consists solely of pushing buttons on your video controller, your body keeps on going—for awhile. But even your body has limits.

God designed your body with a built in alarm system to remind you to take care of yourself physically. You get tired. You get hungry. You feel run down, stressed, or headachy. Regularly choosing to do things that hurt your body, instead of keeping it healthy, shows that you're not only ignoring what God's trying to tell you, but that you don't really value the priceless gift God's given you.

Take a fresh look at the way you were made. Thank God for how intricately He's designed your body. Thank Him for the things that work well and pray to Him about those that don't. Then, continue to show God your gratitude by making healthy choices throughout this day—and your lifetime.

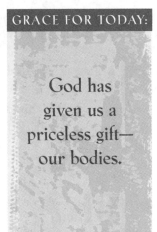

GRACE FOR TODAY:

God has given us a priceless gift— our bodies.

Use every part of your body to give glory back to God.

1 CORINTHIANS 6:20 TLB

HOW CAN YOU BECOME CONFIDENT?

By John C. Maxwell

When you want to establish your worth, you should do it by using God's value system. God demonstrated your importance to Him in two great acts. First He created you in His own image, and second He—through Jesus Christ—died for your sins. God thought so much of you, believed in you, and saw you as a person of such worth, that he allowed His Son to die so that you could live. When we begin to see ourselves in light of God's actions on our behalf, then we immediately begin to have more confidence. There is nothing more humbling than the realization that if you were the only person on this earth, Jesus would have died for you. That makes you priceless.

Confidence is not the result of an absence of problems. It is very clear in Psalm 27 that the psalmist encountered many problems and difficulties. He mentions his enemies, evildoers who want to devour his flesh, adversaries, and a host encamping around him.

Confidence is a result of trusting God in our problems. In the midst of his difficulties, the psalmist kept focusing on God and not on his difficult situation.[12]

—*m*—

HEAVENLY FATHER: I DON'T KNOW WHY YOU LOVE ME SO MUCH OR CARE SO MUCH ABOUT ME, BUT YOU DO. HELP ME TO SEE MYSELF THE WAY YOU SEE ME—A PERSON OF GREAT WORTH. I THANK YOU FOR YOUR GRACE THAT GIVES ME THE CONFIDENCE I NEED TO ASK FOR YOUR HELP. AMEN.

The LORD is my light and my salvation—whom shall I fear? . . .
When evil men advance against me . . . they will stumble and fall.
Though an army besiege me. . . . even then will I be confident. . . .
I am still confident of this: I will see the goodness of the LORD in the land
of the living. Wait for the LORD ; be strong and take heart
and wait for the LORD .

PSALM 27:1–3, 13–14

NO REGRETS

"Come on!" Jesus said. Peter then got out of the boat and started walking
on the water toward him.

MATTHEW 14:29 CEV

When you think of the Apostle Peter, what first comes to mind? If you're like most, you remember him for denying Jesus three times before the rooster crowed. Peter is also remembered for trying to walk on the water and sinking because he took his eyes off of Jesus. And, he is remembered for being a hotheaded, reactionary apostle—the one who often spoke before he fully processed his thoughts. Peter was much more than that. He was a risk taker.

GRACE FOR TODAY:

**If we step
outside the boat
for God,
He will never
let us sink.**

When all of the other disciples saw Jesus walking on the waves toward their boat, they never volunteered to step outside the safety of their vessel to meet Jesus on the stormy sea. Peter was the only one who had faith to take that first step outside the boat. He didn't consider his own welfare, even though the wind was swift and the water quite turbulent. He only knew that Jesus was out there, bidding him to come.

As Christians, we need to be willing to do what God asks us to do—no matter what. So if He says, "Give money to the poor kid in your English class," you should be willing to do just that—no matter how awkward or uncomfortable it feels. If God impresses on your heart to ask the meanest girl in your whole school to youth group, you should be willing to "step outside the boat" and ask her.

Just as Jesus was there for Peter when he began to sink, He will be there for you should you run into trouble. Trust in God and listen for His quiet urgings. Get out of the boat and make a difference today!

CALLING ALL SPIRITUAL GIANTS

The church is Christ's body, in which he speaks and acts, by which he fills everything with his presence.

EPHESIANS 1:23 MSG

R eal giants inhabit this earth. Some of them have been alive since before Jesus was born. Some are taller than the Statue of Liberty and wider around than a school bus.

They live along the California coast, in the Sierra Nevada mountain range, and in one remote spot in China. They are the largest living thing on earth, larger than elephants and blue whales. These real-life giants are redwood trees.

But despite the immensity of these natural wonders, a redwood's roots only grow six to ten feet deep. That means that storms and high winds could bring them down relatively easily. So, how can they remain standing for over 2,000 years? Community. Redwood grow together in groves, their roots intermingling to provide strength

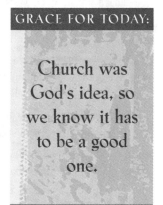

GRACE FOR TODAY:

Church was God's idea, so we know it has to be a good one.

To become a giant in the spiritual world, you need to take a lesson from the redwoods. Place yourself in a grove, instead of trying to go solo. Then, when emotional storms build or the winds of doubt start to blow, you'll have the support you need to stand strong and tall.

Allow a local church to be your God-given grove. Find a place where you can plant yourself, where relevant, Bible-based teaching provides water for your thirsty soul. Get involved in a small group, where you can intermingle your spiritual roots with others, growing closer together as you strengthen each other through prayer, study, and holding one another accountable. Use the gifts and talents God's given you to serve others, providing the support others need as they in turn support you.

Allow God to show you the joy and strength that can be found by getting involved with others who long to know Him like you do.

GET PAST THE WORDS

Above all things have intense and unfailing love for one another, for love covers a multitude of sins [forgives and disregards the offenses of others].

1 PETER 4:8 AMP

Y ou hide your face, ashamed for anyone to see that you have been crying. But it is hard to hold back the tears after the way she just talked to you.

How could she call herself a Christian and act that way? you whisper to yourself. *I will never forgive her.*

Wait a minute! Listen to what you just said. You are surprised, perhaps even angry, that a fellow Christian has used harsh words to hurt you. And now you are prepared to strike back by holding it against her forever.

That's not how God responded to you all those times you turned your back on Him and chose to disobey His Word. Instead, He loved you and forgave you for doing wrong, and welcomed you back into fellowship with Him with opened arms.

Being a Christian does not protect you from life's ups and downs. Your teacher may give you a bad grade unjustly. Or a classmate may say or do something to embarrass you in front of others. Everyone gets his or her feelings hurt at one time or another, but nothing gives us permission to retaliate or try and get even.

When this happens to you, do what Jesus did. Forgive. Instead of thinking of ways to get revenge, pray for those who have wronged you. That's what God would expect from a child of His. If you have problems forgiving others, be honest and tell God. Ask Him to help you overcome anger so that you are always ready to repay evil with good.

GRACE FOR TODAY:

God's love can help us correct any wrong.

You Can't Shock God

Such love has no fear because perfect love expels all fear.
If we are afraid, it is for fear of judgment, and this shows that his love has
not been perfected in us.

1 John 4:18 NLT

In a large corporation, a middle manager welcomed an employee to his depart-
ment—an employee who was transferring from another division of the same company. In the weeks and months that followed, many of the new employee's co-work-
ers were surprised—both pleasantly and unpleasantly—by some of their colleague's
work habits, attitudes, words, and actions. A few of them mumbled, "I'm not sure the
boss knew what he was getting himself into when he hired her!"

The boss, however, knew exactly what he was getting himself into. Before agree-
ing to the transfer, he carefully examined his prospective employee's personnel file—
including performance reviews, college transcripts, and complaints from previous coworkers. He spent hours with the person's current and former managers and coworkers. And he conducted several lengthy interviews with the prospective employee
herself.

So, while others around him sometimes dropped their jaws in amazement, the
manager remained unsurprised and unruffled.

It's kind of like that with God and you. There will never be a day when He grabs
a nearby angel and blurts, "Did you see what _____ just did? I can't believe it!"

God knows your personality quirks, your habits, your thoughts, and your heart.
He knows your faults and every wrong thing you've done. He even knows about the
good things you should have done, but didn't do. During your life, you will disappoint
and, yes, shock, the people closest to you, but not God. He has perfect knowledge of
and perfect love toward imperfect people just like you.

Grace for Today:

If we say to God, "You want me? Do you know what
you're getting yourself into?" He will reply, "I love
you. That's what I'm getting myself into."

RICH IN GENEROSITY

A s Jesus was speaking to a group of religious leaders, He noticed people giving their offerings at the temple. Lots of rich people walked by, placing large sums of money into the offering box. Then a teenage girl walked over and took a single dollar bill out of her wallet. She placed her offering in with the others'.

Jesus commented that the girl's offering was worth more than all the rest, because Jesus knew how much it really cost her. The girl didn't give out of what she had left over. She gave all she had, not knowing when more money would be coming her way. She gave because she believed that's what God wanted her to do.

Okay, so the girl was a little older than you are. In fact, she was an elderly widow. But this widow had the heart of a teen. She gave all she had to do what she believed was right.

You don't have to wait until you grow up to live a life of generosity. That's because generosity isn't measured by the size of a gift. It's measured by the size of the heart of the person who gives it. You may not have a job. You may not even have a steady allowance. But that doesn't mean you have nothing to share with someone in need.

Ask God to help you see the needs around you that He'd like you to help fill. Be generous with your time, your possessions, your talents, and your money. God can use any heartfelt gift, no matter how small, to accomplish great things.

GRACE FOR TODAY:

God's compassion is stirred when we give with our hearts.

Whoever shares with others should do it generously.

ROMANS 12:8 GNB

FINDING SOLUTIONS

By John C. Maxwell

Everyone faces problems. The ability to creatively find solutions will determine the success or failure of each difficulty.

The Chinese symbol for crisis means danger. It also means opportunity. The key is to use a crisis as an opportunity for change. You'll never succeed if you throw up your hands and surrender. The Greek poet Homer understood the value of a crisis. He wrote, "Adversity has the effect of eliciting talents which in prosperous circumstances would have lain dormant."

Remember the story of the chicken farmer whose land was flooded virtually every spring? Even though the floods caused him horrendous problems, he refused to move. When the waters would back up onto his land and flood his chicken coops, he would race to move his chickens to higher ground. Some years, hundreds of them drowned because he couldn't move them out in time.

One year after suffering heavy losses from a particularly bad flood, he came into the farmhouse and in a voice filled with despair, told his wife, "I've had it, I can't afford to buy another place. I can't sell this one. I don't know what to do!"

His wife calmly replied, "Buy ducks."

Creativity is a trait not always admired by those who don't have it. They interpret creativity and inventiveness as stupidity and impracticality. If they see the creative person as salvageable, they will try to pull him back into the mainstream of thought. He will be told to stay busy, follow the rules, be practical, and not make a fool of himself. Traditional thinkers don't realize that creative thinkers are the geniuses of the world. Had it not been for someone's inventiveness, they might not have jobs![15]

⁓⁓⁓

FATHER GOD: HELP ME NOT TO SQUANDER THE CREATIVITY YOU'VE PLACED IN MY LIFE. I WANT TO STEP OUT BY FAITH READY TO APPLY YOUR GIFT OF GRACE TO THE PROBLEMS AROUND ME. THANK YOU FOR SOLUTIONS THAT ARE PLEASING IN YOUR SIGHT. AMEN.

Do not be conformed to this world, but be transformed by the renewing of your mind, that you may prove what is that good and acceptable and perfect will of God.

ROMANS 12:2 NKJV

FEELING GROUCHY

You will always give thanks for everything to God the Father
in the name of our Lord Jesus Christ.

EPHESIANS 5:20 NLT

T-shirts bearing funny sayings are quite popular today. One that is making its rounds, says: "Warning: Feeling Kind of Grouchy Today." Be honest. Does this motto fit your usual mood? If so, you need to know that grouchiness and godliness do not go hand in hand. (Hey, that might make a cute T-shirt saying!)

If you're grouchy more days than you're happy, you need to ask God to keep a watch over your mouth. Ask Him to help you quit complaining and start praising.

GRACE FOR TODAY:

God looks forward to our praise. It's music to His ears!

Complaining and grouching your way through life is no way to live. It sabotages your future, and it angers God. The Israelites found that out the hard way. Consequently, their journey to the Promised Land took them forty years—instead of the forty days it should've taken. God had just rescued them from slavery, caused the Red Sea to part so that they could walk across on dry land, provided manna from heaven for them to eat, yet they still complained.

In fact, they got tired of the manna and even grouched about that. They were basically saying, "Hey God, we're really sick of this manna. Could you send down a few pancakes?" And their habitual complaining led to a lack of faith and unbelief in God's plans. When they found out the Promised Land was inhabited by giants as well as delicious food, they gave up on God, instead of trusting Him to provide again. This unbelief forced them to wander around in the wilderness for many years.

If you've been wandering around in your own wilderness lately, you probably need an attitude check. God can't work in your life to the extent He would like if you're grouching around all the time. So, change today. Ask God to fill you up with His joy. Start each day praising God instead of murmuring your way through breakfast. Put that "Feeling Kind of Grouchy" T-shirt in the trash and put on the garment of praise! Just like you put on a coat for winter—make it a point to deliberately praise God today.

JUST SAY "YES"

Teach me to do your will, for you are my God.

PSALM 143:10

M iriam wasn't sure whether to scream or fall to her knees. She'd heard of angels, but never imagined she'd come face-to-face with one right there in her room. But, there he was, just as real as she was. He said he'd come with a message from God. But surely, this was some kind of a mistake. After all, Miriam was just a typical teenager.

But, the message Miriam received was even more fantastic than the messenger. The angel said Miriam was going to become pregnant before she got married, and give birth to God's Son.

Miriam, or Mary as she's referred to in English, became the earthly mother of a heavenly Savior. She suffered the embarrassment of an unwed mother, the tension of sharing this news with her fiancé, and the agony of watching her Son suffer and die before her eyes. Mary had a choice in the direction her future would take. Mary's choice was to say yes to God's plan.

GRACE FOR TODAY:

The center of God's will is our only safety.

BETSIE TEN BOOM

It isn't always easy to do what God asks of you. He asks you to forgive those who've hurt you, even when they aren't sorry in the least for what they've done. He asks you to study for tests, instead of cheating on them. He asks that you wait until you're married to be physically intimate with your spouse. The more you get to know God, the more you'll discover that finding His will isn't hard.

God is a loving Father who only wants your best. The better you get to know Him, the easier you'll find it is to trust in His love and plans for you. Say yes to God and you'll find you've said yes to an adventure even bigger than your dreams.

GIVE FREELY

Each one must do just as he has purposed in his heart; not grudgingly or under compulsion, for God loves a cheerful giver.

2 CORINTHIANS 9:7 NASB

I t was almost quitting time when your boss asked you to do one last thing before leaving. Smiling obligingly, you agreed to do whatever he asked. On the inside, however, you screamed to be free from that dead-end job, flipping burgers and cleaning up after people.

Everyone wants to take, and nobody ever gives, you think as you head to the stockroom to stack the boxes of supplies that had come in earlier in the day. *Why does it always have to be me who gives?*

It's funny how easily we see ourselves as victims rather than servants when it comes to giving our time to help others. It's good for us that Jesus did not have that attitude when it came to doing "one last thing" before leaving this earth. In fact, He voluntarily came to the Earth to sacrifice His life so that we could have a renewed relationship with God—His Heavenly Father and ours.

Not even the most vivid of imaginations can realize the pain and agony Jesus suffered during that sacrificial moment. Yet, He chose to endure that awful form of death because of His love for us.

As a born-again child of God, you have the same giving spirit as Jesus—who told His disciples to "give as freely as you have received" (Matthew 10:8 NLT). Giving of your time, your energy, and yourself pleases God just as much as Jesus sacrificing His life. Sometimes it may be inconvenient, but if it helps someone else then it is worth it.

Ask God to help you to see that you are a living image of Him. When you sacrifice your time to help others, you represent Him and show others His love.

GRACE FOR TODAY:

Jesus' giving was painful; ours should be a pleasure.

Consider the Ants

"Be imitators of God, as beloved children; and walk in love, just as Christ also loved you and gave Himself up for us.

Ephesians 5:1-2 NASB

Have you ever devoted time to observing an ant colony? The constant flurry of activity, carrying food and building materials to the ant hill? The danger from other insects—or from the giant shoes of careless or malicious humans? Have you ever thought, *I'd really like to trade place with those ants. I think it would be a lot of fun to be closer to the bottom of the food chain?*

What human would want to swap lives with ants—have their tiny, ant-sized brains and giant, people-sized problems? What appeal is there in a life in which a really good day is one in which you manage to avoid being stomped on? Who would give up their current life—friends, a variety of food, laughter, entertainment, and love—for a mound of dirt and a brief life of taxing manual labor?

But that's what Jesus did. He left heaven for earth, where even the grandest mansion available would be the equivalent of a hole in the ground in heaven.

Think about this sacrifice the next time you see a trail of ants scurrying about their business. The God of the entire universe gave up heavenly comforts and privileges and powers to become a born-in-a-barn mortal. Just to be with us.

And there's something else to consider about the lengths Jesus went to. Once He got to earth and experienced first-hand things like pain, disease, hunger, hatred, and persecution; He could have changed His mind at any point. He could have returned to the comforts of heaven, saying, "I just can't live like this."

The New Testament says that love endures all things, and it's hard to imagine one thing Jesus didn't endure because of His huge love for us. He traded places with us because He wouldn't trade His love for us—not for anything in the world.

Grace for Today:

Jesus loves us with a love that goes the distance—in every sense of the word.

PRAY FOR WHO?

Think of the person in your life who most aggravates you. It may be a sibling. It may be a person in your high school. It may even be someone in your church youth group. Okay, got the visual? Now, pray for that person. "What?" you say, "Pray for that person!" No matter how odd that seems, it's exactly what you must do if you want to experience true freedom in your life.

Don't pray from your mind. If you do, you'll probably want to call down fire upon them. Instead, pray out of your spirit. Pray blessings upon your enemy. Pray for God's favor in their life. Pray mercy and grace for them. It may not change the way that they treat you, but your prayers will definitely change your attitude toward them. Suddenly, when you see them, you won't have that twinge in your heart that makes you feel irritated. You'll begin to have compassion for this person that used to be your enemy. You'll begin to see them through the Father's eyes. You'll even begin to love them with a pure heart. It's possible!

Make a list today. Write down all of your enemies, listing the people who have hurt you. Then spend some time praying over each one. This may be a gradual process. It may seem uncomfortable at first, but stay with it. It's not just a good suggestion; it's a command from God. You'll find that praying for your enemies will heal your heart and set you free. Go ahead, hit your knees today.

> **GRACE FOR TODAY:**
>
> God loves our enemies just as much as He loves us.

Love your enemies, bless them that curse you, do good to them that hate you, and pray for them which despitefully use you, and persecute you.

MATTHEW 5:44 KJV

SEIZED BY A DREAM

By John C. Maxwell

W hen you receive a vision that could change your life or you're grabbed by a dream that could really help you become what you want to be, there's a natural sequence that happens. First there's the "I thought it" stage. That's when a dream just flashes by. Could it be? Maybe this is for me. What would happen if I did that? Every person goes through this stage. We go from the "I thought it" stage to the "I sought it" stage. After we think about some of the dreams that we have and the visions that God gives us, we get excited, and we begin to talk about that dream and see ourselves in it.

I think everyone goes through these first two stages. But stage three makes the difference for the person who will be successful. It's what I call the "I bought it" stage. After we catch that dream, there's a time when we have to put a deposit down on it. There comes a time when we have to make an investment in it to make it happen. No dream comes true automatically. We have to buy that dream.

The fourth stage is the "I caught it" stage. This is where desire comes in: we begin to want it so much that it possesses every part of us. Finally comes the "I got it" stage: I can touch it with my hands. This is where I say, "It's mine; I'm glad I paid the price; I'm glad I dreamed the dream." [14]

—⁓—

HEAVENLY FATHER: I KNOW YOU'VE PLANTED A DREAM IN MY HEART. I ASK FOR YOUR GRACE AS I REACH OUT TO TAKE HOLD OF IT. THANK YOU FOR TRUSTING ME WITH YOUR DIVINE PURPOSE. AMEN.

The plans of the righteous are just.

PROVERBS 12:5

SAY WHAT GOD SAYS

Death and life are in the power of the tongue:
and they that love it shall eat the fruit thereof.

PROVERBS 18:21 KJV

While many Christians would never say anything negative about other people, they use their own mouths to say ugly things about themselves. That's equally destructive. According to this verse in Proverbs, life and death are in the power of the tongue. That being the case, wouldn't it be better to use our mouths to speak words of victory instead of defeat?

Successful athletes have been using their mouths in this way for many years. The Golf Channel recently did a feature story about golf legend Gary Player. In this interview, Player shared something very interesting. He said that from the time he took up golf at age fourteen, he would wake up, look himself in the mirror, and say, "I'm going to be the best golfer in the whole world." It's no wonder that in 1965 at age twenty-nine, he won golf's Grand Slam—the Masters, the U.S. Open, the British Open, and the PGA. At that time, he was the youngest competitor to ever reach that pinnacle. How did he do it? He saw himself as a winner and a champion long before his talents merited such talk. He understood the power of words. He didn't speak poorly of himself; rather, he spoke words of victory about himself. You can do the same!

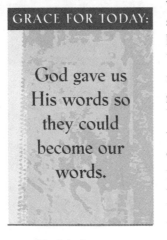

GRACE FOR TODAY:

God gave us His words so they could become our words.

Think before you spew words everywhere. Say only what God says about you in His Word. He says you are more than a conqueror. He says you can do all things through Him. He says you are highly favored. Get into the habit of saying good things about yourself, and if you can't say anything positive, then just zip it up! Ask the Holy Spirit to help you be more aware of the words you say about yourself. Change your words, and you'll change your world.

FLOATING ON FAITH

We live by faith, not by sight.

2 CORINTHIANS 5:7

T he final bell has just rung to begin gym class. You wish you were dressed in your usual shorts and tee shirt, getting ready to play flag football or even run the track two or three times. Instead, you're wearing a swimsuit. Your toes are curled tightly over the edge of the pool as you prepare to jump in the water. The teacher promised that before the semester is over, you'll be able to swim. When the whistle blows, you tentatively step off the edge of the pool, hoping the water's warmer than it looks.

Sinking below the surface, unable to swim, you tightly hold onto this truth: I know I can float. As your body rises again to the surface, you relax and roll over onto your back. You trust the water will support your weight, even though you may not totally understand the physics behind why it does.

Faith is a lot like floating. It's resting on what you know is true. Consider just a few of the truths you know about God: He loves you. He's all wise and all-powerful. He wants your best. He hears your prayers. He has a purpose for you in this world. Resting on these truths can give you the courage to move forward in tough situations, especially when you feel you're in over your head.

What you see with your eyes doesn't tell the whole story. Faith gives you a glimpse of what's going on below the surface. It helps you see your situation from God's point of view. Let what you believe open your eyes to the big picture of life. Let it support you throughout the day. Rest on God's promises. Relax in the faithfulness of His character. Then, dive on in to whatever the day ahead may hold.

> **GRACE FOR TODAY:**
>
> When we rest on God's promises, we are floating on the sea of faith.

CHILL OUT!

Behold, I will do something new. . . . I will even make a roadway in the
wilderness, rivers in the desert.

ISAIAH 43:19 NASB

T he news that the family would be moving was a big surprise, but to discover
you would be leaving North Carolina and going all the way to Texas—1,200
miles away from all your friends to a place you knew nothing about—even more dev-
astating.

Suddenly, fear sets in as all kinds of questions bombard your mind.

Why so far away, and why Texas of all places? What about all my friends? What
kind of school will I attend? Will the kids there like me? Will I get a spot on the football team? Why would Dad pick my senior year in high school to make such a move?

Imagine how shocked Abram must have been when God told him to pack up, take
his wife, and move to a distant land. At about seventy–five years old, surely he had no
plans for relocation. But he obeyed God.

Not many people today would take such a step without some guarantee of security. Abram had faith in God, who had said to him, "I will cause you to become the
father of a great nation. I will bless you and make you famous, and I will make you a
blessing to others (Genesis 12:2 NLT)."

Someone once said that growth without change is impossible. God makes changes
in your life as part of His plan to develop and mature you into the person He wants
you to become. How you handle those changes determines how far you succeed in life.

Change may not be convenient or comfortable, but don't be afraid or stress out
because of it. Pray and ask God to strengthen you and help you do whatever is necessary to make the adjustment comfortably. Even when you are confused, you can rely on
Him to make things clear and give you peace.

GRACE FOR TODAY:

With God, change is not the end but the beginning of
something new and exciting.

CUSTOMIZED LIVES

Love does not delight in evil but rejoices with the truth. It always
protects, always trusts, always hopes, always perseveres. Love never fails.

1 CORINTHIANS 13: 6-8

H ave you ever burned a custom CD for yourself? It's a rush to consider the array of options when you're in control of the song-selection process. You can say yes to the current top-40 hit, but no to the long instrumental cut that you don't care for. Yes to the time-tested classic, but no to the over-produced knock-off. Yes to the band of real musicians; no to the posers who can't play a note and get by on looks and image.

What would life be like if personal relationships were like that? What if, for example, you could custom-design your parents? Yes to the generous allowances, but no to the curfews and lectures? Or how about younger siblings—yes to the cute smiles and goodnight hugs, but no to the annoying questions and uninvited entrances into your room?

Life and love might be less complicated and easier if we could pick and choose all of its elements, but that kind of life wouldn't be authentic. That's because true love isn't finicky. It doesn't accept just the attractive things, the easy-to-deal-with things. It accepts all things.

That's how God looks at us—as a package deal. Even if the package is damaged or missing some of its contents. And this is how He wants us to treat the people in our lives. He wants us to accept the good along with the bad—and to be patient and hopeful toward all that "bad."

So follow the ideal set by the Lord when it comes to people. (And save the picking and choosing for CD burning and MP3 downloading.)

GRACE FOR TODAY:

When it comes to loving His people,
God chooses not to be choosy.

87

GOD'S BEST IS
ON ITS WAY

Barely visible through the falling snow, the neon sign looks like an answer to prayer: "Fresh Hot Pizza." After spending all day snowboarding with your friends, then hours stuck in traffic on an icy freeway, you anxiously pull into the parking lot. You're seated right away, despite the crowd. Visions of piping hot pepperoni dance through your head as you glance at the menu. When the waiter arrives, you and your friends order an extra large with everything, commenting on how hungry you are to the waiter.

The waiter takes pity on you. You're tired. You're hungry. You need to eat fast. Within minutes the waiter's back at the table holding a pizza pan. On it is freshly made dough piled high with every topping imaginable—uncooked. "I knew you wanted it as soon as possible. Bon appetite!" You quickly call him back to

explain that "fast" isn't as important as "done."

The same is true of God's timing. People want fast. When they pray, they want relationships to be healed, needs to be filled, and bad habits to be broken in the blink of an eye. But God is not a clueless waiter filling orders. He's a loving Father who wants to help His children grow. He wants the answer to their prayers to be "cooked to perfection" before they're delivered.

Sometimes that can take quite awhile. He may even change the order altogether, bringing what you really need into your life, instead of what you think you want.

The next time you're waiting for God to act and you're feeling impatient, remember how much He cares about you. Part of His perfect answer for you lies in His perfect timing.

> **GRACE FOR TODAY:**
> God's timing is always perfect— even when it means we have to wait!

I wait eagerly for the LORD's help, and in his word I trust.

PSALM 130:5 GNB

THE TROUBLE WITH PLAYING IT SAFE

By John C. Maxwell

I love the story about the old farmer, ragged and barefooted, who sat on the steps of his tumbledown shack, chewing on a stem of grass. A passerby stopped and asked if he might have a drink of water. Wishing to be sociable, the stranger engaged the farmer in some conversation.

"How is your cotton crop this year?"

"Ain't got none," replied the farmer.

"Didn't you plant any cotton?" asked the passerby.

"Nope," said the farmer, "'fraid of boll weevils."

"Well," asked the newcomer, "how's your corn doing?"

"Didn't plant none," replied the farmer, "'fraid there wasn't going to be enough rain."

"Well," asked the inquisitive stranger, "what did you plant?"

"Nothing," said the farmer, "I just played it safe."

A lot of well-intentioned people live by the philosophy of this farmer, and never risk upsetting the apple cart. They would prefer to play it safe." These people will never know the thrill of victory, because to win a victory one must risk a failure.

C. T. Studd made a great statement about risk-taking: "Are gamblers for gold so many and gamblers for God so few?" This is the same missionary who, when cautioned against returning to Africa because of the possibility of his martyrdom, replied, "Praise God, I've just been looking for a chance to die for Jesus." How can a guy like that fail? He has everything to win and nothing to lose.[15]

—⁓—

DEAR LORD: YOUR GRACE HAS GIVEN ME EVERYTHING I NEED TO WIN. HELP ME TO STEP OUT BY FAITH AND TAKE HOLD OF YOUR PLAN AND PURPOSE IN MY LIFE. I DON'T WANT TO PLAY IT SAFE. I WANT TO COURAGEOUSLY PURSUE ALL YOU HAVE FOR ME. AMEN.

By You I can run against a troop, By my God I can leap over a wall.

PSALM 18:29 NKJV

TURNING YOUR TEST INTO A TESTIMONY

Consider it pure joy, my brothers, whenever you face trials
of many kinds, because you know that the testing of your faith
develops perseverance.

JAMES 1:2-3

P roblems happen. Until we get to heaven, we're guaranteed to have our fair share of trouble. But that's okay. Whether we're walking on sunshine or dodging storm clouds, we're destined to win. In the Bible God tells us that we are more than con-
querors. That's why we can rejoice—no matter what problem comes our way.

The Apostle Paul certainly knew this principle. Whether he was shipwrecked, beaten, thrown in prison, or ridiculed by those he loved, he learned to press through with joy. He sang praises to the Lord while imprisoned. Some Bible scholars believe he wrote much of the New Testament while in a dirty, smelly, dark jail cell. Paul was able keep such a positive attitude because he knew that at the end of the day, God was still in his corner. He also knew that when he felt his weakest, God could do His very best work and always did.

God will do the same for you. No matter what test you're going through right now—family challenges, loneliness, trouble in school, lack of finances, health problems—God can turn your test into a testimony if you keep a right attitude and press through.

Knowing this truth will help you face trials with joy in your heart. Your friends may even wonder how you can be so happy when they are so stressed out and upset all the time. If they ask, tell them: "These problems are nothing for my God. I can remain joyful because I know He will come through for me." When you're a Christian, God's got you covered!

A JOB WELL DONE

Not that I have already obtained all this, or have already
been made perfect, but I press on to take hold of that for which
Christ Jesus took hold of me.

PHILIPPIANS 3:12

G etting a job in Hawaii sounds like a wonderful opportunity. But, the job Father
Damien went to do was far from a vacation. He volunteered to work at a leper
colony. One hundred years ago, a diagnosis of leprosy, which is a disfiguring and often
fatal disease, meant immediate exile to the island of Molokai. People of all ages were
sentenced to live out their lives without the help of hospitals, doctors, or teachers.
Other lepers were their only companions—until Father
Damien arrived.

Surprisingly, the people on the island didn't welcome Father Damien's arrival. Instead, they questioned
his motives. They couldn't believe he was there just
because he cared. For the first ten years, Father
Damien lived virtually as an outcast among outcasts.
He was lonely and discouraged, but God's grace gave
him the strength to go on. He continued to work,
devoting much of his time to building caskets and dig-
ging graves for those who died.

GRACE FOR TODAY:

God's hands
are the perfect
place to grow
something
beautiful.

It was only after Father Damien contracted leprosy that the island residents accepted him. For the next
six years, he continued to work with them, building
water systems and homes. He also organized schools, a band, and even a choir.

Father Damien persevered doing a job that was difficult, and often unappreciated.
He never gave up because he believed he was doing what God wanted him to do.
When he died from leprosy at the age of forty-nine, Father Damien was proud of what
had been accomplished. He felt he'd spent his life on something worthwhile.

It isn't easy to persevere. The things that are most worthwhile often don't come
easily. Take one day at a time, giving your heart fully to what God wants you to do.
His grace will turn your faithful efforts into something of eternal value.

THE RIGHT THING

I will instruct you and teach you in the way you should go;
I will counsel you and watch over you.

PSALM 32:8

For years, it was your dream to play on the same tennis team as your younger brother. As a senior, you've enjoyed quite a ride playing in the number–one spot for the past three years. Now that your kid brother is entering high school, he can carry on the family name by following in your footsteps.

It is the day before team tryouts, and you're excited at the showing the two of you will make. Only, your brother does not seem quite as enthusiastic. You ask if there is something wrong, only to hear him say he has no plans to play tennis.

"I know we grew up playing tennis together, and I really do enjoy it," he confides. "But I've never been as good a player as you. I've prayed about it, and I'm sure God wants me to focus on my studies so I can be ready for college. You know, I've always wanted to go to medical school."

A sibling following in your footsteps, or even those of your parents', is commendable, but only if it is part of God's plan for his or her life. Just as God had a plan for you when you entered high school, He has one for your brother.

Be thankful he is using godly wisdom in trusting God to take care of him just as He has you. Instead of trying to talk him into doing what you want, support his decision to follow what he knows God wants him to do. Encourage him to pray for God's direction and wisdom in his decision-making.

God has the right plan for his life, and He will take care that he fulfills it.

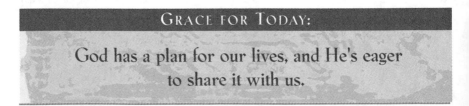

GRACE FOR TODAY:

God has a plan for our lives, and He's eager
to share it with us.

TRAVELING IN THE LIGHT

Let us run with endurance the race that is set before us, looking unto
Jesus, the author and finisher of our faith.

HEBREWS 12:1-2 NKJV

E ven though you are young, you might feel that you have already been on a long
and painful life journey. You might be carrying a heavy emotional or physical
load right now. You might have already experienced the death of people you love. You
might have felt the sting of friends who have turned against you or abandoned you.

It might seem that your life's goals are unattainable. You can't discern a way to get
from where you are to where you hope to be someday. Your home might be filled with
boiling hostility or cold indifference.

In short, life might be making you tired and discouraged. Take heart. God never
said that life's journey would be easy or free of problems. But He did say that there is
joy to be found in that journey—and that its ultimate destination will make everything
worthwhile.

As you travel, God will not provide you with everything you desire. But He will
give you everything you need. He won't do everything you want—but He will, always,
always, do what is right and what is best.

No matter what your journey brings, God will forever be with you, walking
beside you, filling you with His Spirit. And even if you sometimes collapse from fatigue
and discouragement, He will help you up and make sure you get home.

GRACE FOR TODAY:

No matter how hard life's journey may be,
our voyage will be a success as long as we have God
as our traveling companion.

SURRENDER ALL

Have you ever heard the expression, "Let go and let God?" It's easier said than done. We sing songs in church about giving our all to God, such as "All to Jesus, I surrender," when the whole time we're holding something back. Many times Christians run to God and ask Him to take over every part of their lives, and then later discover still another part of their hearts they'd somehow held back from God.

It's silly, isn't it? Why would we ever want to hold out on God? He doesn't want us to give Him our all so that He can make us miserable. He wants us to give our all so that He can bless us beyond our wildest dreams. God isn't some big ogre in the sky, just waiting for us to give our all to Him so that He can control us like puppets.

He simply wants us to give our all so that we can walk in the plan that He has for us. So, if you're struggling with giving your all today, ask God to help you. Go ahead—let go and let God. He will give you much more in return. You give Him sickness. He gives you health. You give Him anger. He gives you peace. You give Him hate. He gives you love. It's a pretty great deal when you think about it that way.

Jesus gave His life for us. It's only right for us to give our lives back to Him. He has so many good things in store for you, if you'll do as the song says, "Surrender all."

> **GRACE FOR TODAY:**
>
> When we give our all to God, He gives so much more in return.

I'll give him and his descendants the land he walked on because he was all for following GOD, heart and soul.

DEUTERONOMY 1:36 MSG

WHAT GOD DESIRES

By John MacArthur Jr.

Talking about sin and salvation is offensive to some people. Who wants to hear about sin? Most people mask it. Sin is not sin. Oh, no. Sin is "a prenatal predilection," psychologists tell us. Sin is an "idiosyncrasy of individuality." Sin is "poor secretion of the endocrine glands"!

But God's will is that people be saved! And basic to salvation is the recognition of sin. This lays it right at your feet. Either you are not saved from your sin, and you need to come to Christ because that is God's will; or you are saved and need to reach others with the message of salvation. There is a world out there that needs Jesus Christ. God wants them to be saved, and you and I are the vehicles for the transportation of the Gospel. That is God's will.

You say you do not know what God's will is, but I'll tell you what it is. First, that you know Christ and then that your neighbors hear about Christ. That is His will. So often we sit around twiddling our thumbs, dreaming about God's will in some far distant future when we are not even willing to stand up on our own two feet, walk down the street, and do God's will right now.

God so desired that men be saved that He gave the One whom He loved most, His Son, and sent Him to die on a cross. That is the measure of His love, and that indicates how much He wills that men be saved![16]

—⁓—

DEAR LORD: YOUR GRACE LEAVES NO ONE OUT—YOUR WILL IS FOR ANYONE AND EVERYONE TO COME AND EXPERIENCE IT. I WANT TO WALK IN IT EVERY MOMENT FOR THE REST OF MY LIFE, AND I WANT TO SHARE IT WITH OTHERS. THANK YOU FOR THE GREATEST GIFT EVER GIVEN. AMEN.

Now is the right time to listen, the day to be helped. Don't put it off.

2 CORINTHIANS 6:2–3 MSG

GOD REALLY CARES

The very hairs on your head are all numbered. So don't be afraid;
you are more valuable to him than a whole flock of sparrows.

LUKE 12:7 NLT

D id you know that an average head has approximately 100,000 hairs on it? Red
heads have about 90,000 hairs. Brunettes have about 110,000 hairs, and
blondes have about 140,000 hairs. So isn't it amazing to think that God actually knows
the exact number of hairs on your head? He cares so much for you that it's important
to Him to know how many strands of hair you have.

GRACE FOR TODAY:

God loves us—
from the top of
our heads to
the bottom of
our feet.

You wouldn't think that the Creator of the universe
would have time to consider such trivial information,
but He does. He knows everything about you. Psalm
139:15–16 MSG says: "You know me inside and out, you
know every bone in my body; You know exactly how
I was made, bit by bit, how I was sculpted from nothing into something. Like an open book, you watched me
grow from conception to birth; all the stages of my life
were spread out before you, the days of my life all prepared before I'd even lived one day."

That's how much God adores you. When you feel
like no one cares, remember God does. He cares about
the smallest details of your life. He wants to be
involved in every aspect of your day. He wants to be the first one you turn to when
you need to talk. He wants to be your very best friend. Let God be involved in your
day-to-day life. Don't believe the lie that no one cares about you. Almighty God—the
Alpha and the Omega—the Beginning and the End—cares about you.

MAKE A WISE MOVE

If any of you need wisdom, you should ask God,
and it will be given to you.

JAMES 1:5 CEV

P icture yourself in an anatomy class. You're learning about your muscles, lungs, and the cortex of the brain. You pay attention to the lecture. You diligently study the textbook. You get an A on your dissection lab—and ultimately on the final. To cel-ebrate the end of the semester, you head downtown with your friends, and light up a cigarette along the way. Your report card may show that you're knowledgeable about the human body, but your actions reveal you cer-tainly aren't putting what you know to good use.

While it's important to work hard and get the most you can out of school, knowledge and intelligence are only able to take you so far. They may help you land a great job, but only God can help you live a great life. One way He helps you do that is by helping you become wise, instead of just smart.

God knows everything. He would get an auto-matic "A" in anatomy because He literally wrote the book. He is also wise. He applies what He knows in ways that make a positive difference in this world. When you act wisely in your life, your choices should reflect God's desires for your life.

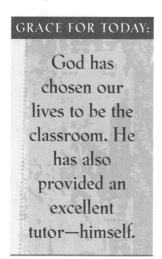

GRACE FOR TODAY:

God has chosen our lives to be the classroom. He has also provided an excellent tutor—himself.

You can't take a quick class in wisdom. God has chosen your entire life to be the classroom. He has also provided an excellent tutor—himself. He promises that if you ask for wisdom, you'll receive it. When you're struggling to determine the right thing to do, ask God for the wisdom to know what's best and the courage to go ahead and do it.

WHEN LITTLE IS BIG

Whatever may be your task, work at it heartily (from the soul),
as [something done] for the Lord and not for men.

COLOSSIANS 3:23-24 AMP

I t feels like years since you started work at the pizza shop, and despite consistent pay raises, you're still doing the same job.

How nice it would be to not have to get dirty every day mixing pizza dough, you think. *Besides, anyone can make pizza. Working the register is a whole lot cleaner, and it probably pays better.*

Before being so quick to downplay what you have in favor of something else, pray about it. Ask God why He has you making pizzas instead of counting out money.

The Bible says that God gives everyone certain talents, skills, and abilities based on what He knows each is capable of doing. If you are good at counting money, it is good to work where finances are involved. But if you lack math skills, handling money could be disastrous for you.

It is not wrong to want more, or better. But it is best to let God decide what that more or better should be. He has a reason for everything He does. He also knows what you are best suited for because He made you.

The Bible said not to discount small things as though they count for nothing. Your job may not seem as important as someone else's, but if you are doing what God has assigned you to then it is important. Be thankful that He sees you as trustworthy, and that He has entrusted you with responsibility. Then, commit to do the best job you can.

When you see your job as an assignment from God—a special opportunity to serve Him—and you are faithful to perform it, you can trust Him for promotion when He knows the time is right.

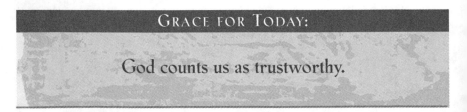

GRACE FOR TODAY:

God counts us as trustworthy.

Take a Load Off

Don't worry about anything; instead, pray about everything. . . . His peace will guard your hearts and minds as you live in Christ Jesus.

Philippians 4:6-7 NLT

D o you ever feel you're on information overload? Cell phone going off all the time? E-mails building up faster than you can answer them? Answering machine blinking incessantly? Pop-up ads invading your Web searches? Teachers assigning more and more homework? Parents asking if your chores are done yet?

Believe it or not, Jesus knows how you feel. True, the only Net that He dealt with was the kind used to catch fish. But He did know the stress of having so many people crowd around Him that sometimes He and the disciples didn't even get a chance to eat. On at least one occasion, He had to preach from a boat, just to keep from being suffocated by an eager audience.

Indeed, your Lord understands the fatigue of information overload. And He provides a great example of how to deal with it. In the book of Mark, the writer tells us, "The next morning Jesus awoke long before daybreak and went out alone into the wilderness to pray." (Mark 1:35 NLT). Now, you might not be crazy about the "early morning" thing, but if even God's Son himself needed some private, quiet time, that should speak volumes to you.

Your Lord understands the pressure you feel, the barrage of information that bombards you every day. So find a quiet place, a quiet time, through which you can bring your stresses to Him. The next time you feel you're on overload, remember that there is someone who can share that load with you.

Grace for Today:
God will sometimes put us in situations where His voice is the only one we can hear.

READY. OK.

Have you ever watched a college cheerleading squad? Their motions are perfectly timed, in sync, on beat, and very sharp. If one member is behind a half of a count, you'll be able to tell. Even minor flaws and mistakes are greatly magnified when the rest of the team is so good.

Maybe you hang out with the popular crowd at school and church. Maybe your best friend is the Prom Queen. Perhaps you're among beautiful, smart people all day long.

Do you ever feel like that cheer-leader who is a half step behind the entire routine? Do you feel inferior compared to your friends? The devil loves to point out our shortcomings and whisper things like: "Hey, you're a loser. If you were a better person, you would have more friends. If you were smarter, you'd do better in school. If you were thinner,

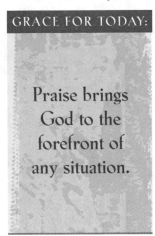

GRACE FOR TODAY:

Praise brings God to the forefront of any situation.

you'd have more attention from the opposite sex."

See, the devil knows what buttons to push in order to make you feel the very worst, but don't let him have access to your buttons. When you start to compare yourself with another person, stop that destructive behavior right then. Immediately, begin to thank God for giving you the wisdom and strength to be the best person you can be.

When you respond to the devil's button-pushing with praise for the Father, you will send the devil packing. He doesn't want to hear about the goodness of God. The next time you start feeling badly about yourself, start praising. It will change your attitude and the entire atmosphere surrounding you.

I will praise you as long as I live.

PSALM 63:4

JUST GO!

By John MacArthur Jr.

A Fizzie is a small tablet used to make a soft drink; it's sort of a flavored Alka-Seltzer. Put it is a glass of water, and its flavor is released throughout the water. This concentrated, compact power pill is no good as long as it sits on the bottom of the glass. It has to release its energy to fill the glass, and then it turns the water into something new.

If it is a grape Fizzie, you get a glass of grape drink. The flavor of the tablet determines the flavor of the water.

This is a good picture of how the Spirit of God operates in a human life. He is in the Christian all the time as a compact, concentrated, powerful force of divine energy. The question is—has He ever been able to release that power, to fill your life so that you can become what He is? A Christian not yielded to the Spirit does not manifest the Christ-life. The Spirit of God has to permeate a life if that life is to radiate Him.

I have a glove. If I say to the glove, "Play the piano," what does the glove do? Nothing. The glove cannot play the piano. But if I put my hands in the glove and play the piano, what happens? Music! If I put my hand in a glove, the glove moves. The glove does not get pious and say, "Oh, hand, show me the way to go." It does not say anything; it just goes. Spirit-filled people do not stumble and mumble around trying to find out what God wants. They just go![17]

—∞—

HEAVENLY FATHER: ONLY BY YOUR GRACE CAN I LIVE A LIFE THAT IS PLEASING TO YOU. FILL ME WITH YOUR HOLY SPIRIT SO THAT I CAN BE A LIVING, BREATHING EXAMPLE OF YOUR LOVE TO OTHERS. AMEN.

Live in order to please God, as in fact you are living. Now we ask you and urge you in the Lord Jesus to do this more and more.

1 THESSALONIANS 4:1

GO FOR IT!

I know what I'm doing. I have it all planned out—plans to take care of
you, not abandon you, plans to give you the future you hope for.

JEREMIAH 29:11 MSG

N ovelist Sinclair Lewis was scheduled to deliver an hour-long lecture to a
group of college students who planned to be writers. Lewis opened his lecture with one question, "How many of you really intend to be writers?" All hands
went into the air. "In that case," said Lewis, "my advice
to you is to go home and write." With that, he left.[18]

GRACE FOR TODAY:

Aim high,
for nothing
is impossible
with God!

Sometimes, whether you feel qualified or not,
you've just got to go for it. You've got to go after your
goals with everything in you. No matter the odds. No
matter what your critics say. No matter how you're
feeling. Just go for it!

The good news is this—as a Christian, you don't
have to go after those goals alone. God promises that
He will never leave you nor forsake you. He's got your
back! He promises to help you achieve your dreams.

Many people dream big dreams, but they never
take action to make those dreams a reality. Some say, "But, what if I miss God? What
if I get out of His will?" Don't let fear of failure or worry of missing God keep you
immobilized when it comes to pursing your dreams. Go after them!

The Word of God says that the steps of a righteous man are ordered of God. So
go ahead. Walk with God, and walk in your dreams. Aim high, for nothing is impossible with God.

BUILT TO LAST

God so loved the world that he gave his only Son, so that everyone who believes in him will not perish but have eternal life.

JOHN 3:16 NLT

S arah Winchester was an heiress who believed she lived under a curse. When her husband died, Sarah received a lump sum of twenty million dollars, along with an additional thousand dollars a day. If this sounds like a lot of money to you, imagine how much more incredible it sounded back in 1881.

Sarah spent this incredible fortune on only one thing—building a house. That's because Sarah believed that as long as carpenters and craftsmen continued building, she wouldn't die. For thirty-eight years, night and day, workmen built bedrooms that would never be slept in, staircases that led nowhere, and doors that opened onto blank walls. One hundred and sixty rooms later, Sarah died in her sleep at the age of eighty-three. All of that hammering did nothing but make a fortune disappear.

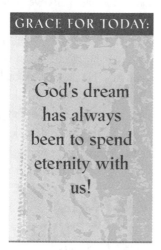

GRACE FOR TODAY:

God's dream has always been to spend eternity with us!

People do crazy things to find eternal life. Today, some people are putting their faith in cryogenics. When they die, they have their head frozen in the hope that technology sometime in the future will be able to bring them back to life. There is no science, technology, or carpenter's blueprint that holds the key to life without end. Only a Jewish carpenter, Jesus, holds that key. And He is holding it out to you.

That's been God's plan from the beginning. You were meant to spend eternity with Him, to live a life that doesn't end with death. To accept the key to life all you need to do is accept who God really is—your Creator, your Lord, your Savior, your eternal Friend.

A BRIGHT FUTURE

As far the as sunrise is from sunset, he has separated us from our sins.

PSALM 103:12 MSG

E ver looked at the world around you and wondered, *Why am I here?*
Or, maybe you've wished you could take a peek into the future just long enough to see what it holds for you.

You're not alone.

At some point we all have wondered what it would be like to glimpse into the future, hoping to discover it held something good.

But what if the picture you see is not so good? What if your future was based on your past? Would there be anything to look forward to?

Your Heavenly Father, who wants to direct your life, does not base your future on your past. He planned a wonderful future for you before you were born.

When you invited Him into your heart, anything you did in the past that would hinder your future has been forgiven—and forgotten. God, who keeps record of all that you do, wiped your slate clean and removed any recollection of wrongdoing by taking all your sins and throwing them into the sea of forgetfulness.

He will not use them against you, because He has chosen never to remember them.

You don't need the assistance of a psychic or the horoscope to show you what the future looks like. You have God's Word and His promise. Look at your past long enough to be sure you have acknowledged your wrong, turn away from it, and ask Jesus to be Lord over your life. That's the best way to know that your future is secure in Him.

GRACE FOR TODAY:

God provided a way for us to escape a checkered past
and enjoy a bright and prosperous future.

THE PATIENCE PRINCIPLE

Patience is better than pride.

ECCLESIASTES 7:8

"I speak without exaggeration," Thomas Edison once said, "when I say that I have constructed three thousand different theories in connection with electric light, each one of them reasonable and apparently likely to be true. Yet in two cases only did my experiments prove the truth of my theory."

Think about it, then do the math: Thomas Edison, a renowned scientific genius, developed 2,998 failed theories in order to produce two successful experiments. In fact, the entire story of the light bulb is a tedious tale of repeated trial and failure. Yet, through it all, Edison was watching attentively and learning from each mistake, each false start.

Another lesson can be learned from Edison's adventures with electricity. As his various attempts to carbonize a cotton thread and use it as a lightbulb filament failed, Edison realized that he had to combine extraordinary determination with extraordinary care and patience. Indeed, the more intent a person becomes on a task, the more patience that must be exercised to avoid ruining the results of those earnest efforts.

So, follow Edison's lead. When failures mount up, step back. Re-examine what you are doing. Ask God for His precious gift of patience. And remember, patience is more of a decision than an emotion. And it's a foundational part of good character.

As you develop and test your own bright ideas, remember and emulate the patience exemplified by people like Thomas Edison. If you are patient and prayerful about problems, solutions will come to light.

GRACE FOR TODAY:

God grants His people the ability to bear defeat without losing heart.

A POSITIVE PERSPECTIVE

In Second Kings 6, King Aram was very angry with the prophet Elisha. Every time King Aram and his troops would plan an attack against the Israelites, Elisha would let the King of Israel know ahead of time. Finally, King Aram could stand it no more—he sent his army to kill Elisha.

That night, King Aram's army surrounded the city where Elisha and his servant slept. When they awoke the next morning, the situation appeared grim. Elisha's servant panicked, saying, "Oh, my lord, what shall we do?" (2 Kings 6:15). Elisha didn't panic. Instead, he prayed, "O LORD, open his eyes so he may see" (v. 17). At that moment, the Lord opened the servant's eyes, and he saw the hills full of horses and chariots of fire, totally surrounding and protecting them. Suddenly, King Aram's army didn't seem quite so threatening.

The servant certainly gained a new perspective. He went from a total panic mode to "bring it on!" Once he saw that God had "their back," he was no longer fearful. You might say, he got a positive point of view.

That's what we all need—a healthy, positive perspective. Ask God to help you see every situation through His eyes. You can see your world differently and face every challenge in faith, not fear. Put on your eyes of faith today!

> **GRACE FOR TODAY:**
>
> **When we place our hope in God, He charges our batteries with a positive perspective.**

Now faith is being sure of what we hope for and
certain of what we do not see.

HEBREWS 11:1

GOD'S GIFT OF HOLINESS

By Luis Palau

I n our own power and wisdom, it's impossible for us to understand and live out the concept of holiness. Yet God is holy and demands that His people be holy too.

In the midst of the world's degenerate moral condition, it's tough for Christians to live in holiness. Those who live in holiness are truly set apart from the world. But if we are to have a conscience about which we can boast, we must live in holiness.

God, however, does not forget. He will not tolerate sin. When we commit immorality or other unholy actions, we dishonor God and will reap the penalty of our sin. When we stubbornly continue in our sin, we devastate our own lives and that of others. But when we walk in holiness, transparent before the Lord, our lives will reflect His power and authority.

Living in holiness is not impossible, Jesus' death and resurrection paid the penalty for our sins, making holy living possible. The Holy Spirit, living within us, gives us the power to follow Christ's example of holy living so that we can have fellowship with a holy God. . . .

The wonderful news is that we can begin holy living at any moment. The blood of Jesus Christ truly cleanses us from all sin and restores our relationship with God.

—*m*—

PRECIOUS SAVIOR: THANK YOU FOR THE GIFT OF HOLINESS. TEACH ME TO LEAD A LIFE THAT IS PLEASING TO YOU AS I CALL UPON THE POWER OF YOUR GRACE. AMEN.

Make every effort to live in peace with all men and to be holy; without holiness no one will see the Lord.

HEBREWS 12:14

INTEGRITY

Remember this—a farmer who plants only a few seeds will get a small crop. But the one who plants generously will get a generous crop.

2 CORINTHIANS 9:6 NLT

Have you ever heard the expression, "You reap what you sow"? Everyone says it, but it actually comes from the Bible. (You can read more about it in Mark 4.) If you are playing around in school instead of working; cheating on tests; lying to your parents; and talking behind your friends' backs; you're sowing some bad seed. And, you're giving God very little to work with.

God desires to bless His children, but if we show a lack of integrity, we tie His hands. He can't bless us, because He can't work in violation to His Word. But, you say, "You don't understand. Everybody plays around at school, and everyone cheats. My parents don't respect me, so why should I respect them? I only talk about the people who talk about me." Well, maybe that's true, but you don't want to sow bad seed just because everybody else is doing it. You know why? Because you don't want to reap that kind of negative harvest.

GRACE FOR TODAY:

God always rewards integrity, even if no one else notices.

No matter how badly it seems that your parents treat you, give them respect every day. Do it unto the Lord. No matter how many people cheat at school, you determine to abstain from that dishonest activity. Give God something to work with. Take the high road in every situation. Ask God to help you. Pretty soon, you'll enjoy a harvest of favor at school, good grades, a good relationship with your parents, loyal friends, etc. Your blessing crop can't be far off!

A QUIET PLACE

Be still, and know that I am God.

PSALM 46:10 NKJV

You're sitting in front of your computer, listening to music as you're writing a research paper and instant messaging a dozen or so of your closest friends. A new instant message pops on the screen: "Can we talk?" It's signed, "God."

It's true that IM isn't God's usual method of communication, but who knows? If He can use a burning bush He certainly can handle the Internet. The real question isn't "could He do that?" but "what's your response?" Do you turn off your music, sign off with your friends, stop writing, and give Him your full attention? Or, do you continue on as you were—chatting, working, listening, and talking to God all at once?

Trying to fit God into a busy life and a noisy world doesn't work. He's way too big. So are His plans for your life. That's why it's good to get alone with Him now and then. It's good to focus just on Him. And doing that takes practice.

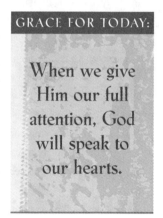

GRACE FOR TODAY:

When we give Him our full attention, God will speak to our hearts.

You're a natural born multi-tasker. God designed you that way. That's why it's so hard to just sit quietly and listen for God's voice or to simply enjoy His presence. There are so many distractions that try to grab your attention.

Purposefully give God your full attention today. The best time may be as you read a Psalm or two out of the Bible. It may be as you walk to school, just you and God, enjoying the things He's made along the way. It may be via e-mail. Who knows?

The key is to keep your eyes and ears open. Turn down the volume of life every now and then. Take time to be still, inside and out, so you can hear God speak.

THE WRONG REASON

If someone falls into sin, forgivingly restore him,
saving your critical comments for yourself. You might be needing
forgiveness before the day's out.

GALATIANS 6:1 MSG

You didn't mean to eavesdrop. But now that you've heard the conversation, you are not sure how to handle the information. If others knew what he did, it could certainly hurt his reputation. In fact, it could practically ruin any chance he has of making captain of the football team—a position you both have been eyeing since freshman year.

Stop right there!

It's a perfect setup, and you're about to fall for it.

How would it make you feel to learn that someone knew something about you and planned to use that information to destroy your reputation? The devil does it all the time. In fact, the Bible says he watches your every move, waiting for you to mess up or do something wrong so that he can accuse you and embarrass you before others.

Everyone has faults, and everyone makes mistakes. God sees them all. But He is not interested in exposing wrong and making you a living spectacle. Instead, He is more interested in helping you overcome the wrong and finding a right relationship with Him.

That should be your motivation as well.

It is not your place to expose people and try to ruin their reputation. And it is certainly not right to rejoice because someone else's downfall could mean something good for you.

God says when you see someone doing wrong, help them. Sometimes, you may not be able to go to them directly, because even that would embarrass them. But you can pray and ask God to restore them.

GRACE FOR TODAY:

God is interested in helping us overcome wrong and find a right relationship with Him.

A ROLE PLAY

Never tire of doing what is right.

2 THESSALONIANS 3:13

L ong ago there were two jars. Each was carried by a king's water bearer on opposite ends of a long pole. One jar was perfectly made, with no cracks or chips. The other was unglazed earthenware—with a long, jagged crack at its base.

Daily, the water bearer would walk to a river and fill both containers, then carry them to the king's palace. Once inside, the first jar offered its full contents into the king's cistern. The other had less to offer since most of its contents had leaked through the crack during the journey.

Despondent, the cracked jar pleaded with the water bearer, "Please, sir, replace me. I am a failure. I spill so much that my offering cannot compare to what the perfect jar brings. I'm ashamed!"

The water bearer smiled in response. "Take a look at the hill we climb each day," he said one day. The jar obeyed. All along the path bloomed beautiful wildflowers. "I've been planting seeds as I walk up this hill," noted the water bearer. "And those flowers you see now have grown from your water, little jar. Flowers that please the king and all his people."

Like the jar in this tale, if you do your job diligently, you will be able to survey the landscape of your life and see the flowers of faithfulness that you have grown. Not because you are perfect, but because you were faithful to your task.

GRACE FOR TODAY:

God's joy in our lives is the best reward for
our diligence.

FULL STRENGTH PAIN RELIEVER

W hen you choose to follow God, your life changes. It has true purpose and power. But it also still has problems. Even Jesus said so. He told His disciples, "In this world you will have trouble." (John 16:33). He didn't say "maybe." He didn't say "probably." His words are more like a guarantee: Trouble will come your way.

Jesus didn't want those who followed Him (which includes you!) to be surprised when life didn't go smoothly. But He also didn't want them to worry. Right after He talked about trouble, Jesus assured those He loved they'd have what they needed to win over any trouble they faced.

But while you're on that road to victory, you may experience what feels like defeat. At times, disappointment, discouragement, or depression can take hold. That's what happened to Elijah. After God used him to raise a widow's son from the dead and miraculously end a drought, Elijah was so pumped he even outran a chariot. Then, Elijah received a death threat. What did God's great prophet do? He hid out in a cave and moaned to God about wanting to die.

What God did next for Elijah is what He'll do for you. He'll comfort you. God's comfort may come wrapped in the face of a friend that He brings your way just to listen. It may show up in the encouraging words of a Bible verse. It may appear as a feeling of peace that dissolves your worries. It may even arrive through the counsel of a youth group leader or professional counselor— if your feelings of depression linger longer than they should.

However God's comfort arrives, watch for it. Don't be hesitant in asking for it. Then, anticipate it with a hopeful heart.

GRACE FOR TODAY:

It will greatly comfort you if you can see God's hand in both your losses and your crosses.

C. H. SPURGEON

As a mother comforts her child, so I will comfort you.

ISAIAH 66:13 NRSV

RUNNING THE RACE

By Warren W. Wiersbe

In the races, each runner was to stay in his assigned lane, but some runners would cut in on their competitors to try to get them off course. This is what the Judaizers had done to the Galatian believers: they cut in on them and forced them to change direction and go on a "spiritual detour." It was not God who did this, because He had called them to run faithfully in the lane marked "Grace."

The believer who lives in the sphere of God's grace is free, rich, and running in the lane that leads to reward and fulfillment. The believer who abandons grace for law is a slave, a pauper, and a runner on a detour. In short, he is a loser. And the only way to become a winner is to "purge out the leaven," the false doctrine that mixes law and grace, and yield to the Spirit of God.

God's grace is sufficient for every demand of life. We are saved by grace. (See Ephesians 2:5.) Grace enables us to endure suffering. (See 2 Corinthians 12:9.) It is grace that strengthens us, so that we can be victorious soldiers. (See 2 Timothy 2:1.) Our God is the God of all grace. (See 1 Peter 5:10.) We can come to the throne of grace and find grace to help in every need. (See Hebrews 4:16.) As we read the Bible, which is "the word of his grace," the Spirit of Grace reveals to us how rich we are in Christ (Acts 20:32 and Hebrews 10:29).

"And of His fullness have all we received, and grace for grace" (John 1:16).

How rich we are![20]

—⁂—

FATHER GOD: KEEP ME RUNNING IN THE LANE MARKED "GRACE." AND IF I SHOULD EVER LOOK TO MY OWN GOODNESS TO GAIN SALVATION, PULL ME QUICKLY BACK FROM MY DETOUR. I WANT TO LIVE EACH DAY FULLY DEPENDING ON YOU. AMEN.

I strain to reach the end of the race and receive the prize for which God, through Christ Jesus, is calling us up to heaven.

PHILIPPIANS 3:14 NLT

THE GREEN-EYED MONSTER

Seek first the kingdom of God and His righteousness, and all these things shall be added to you.

MATTHEW 6:33 NKJV

Jealousy. It's one of those sneaky little emotions that lurks on the inside of every person. It's that raging green-eyed monster that rears its ugly head when your best friend gets the car of your dreams. It's that sick feeling in your stomach that overtakes you when you hear your cousin made student council and you didn't. It's that force inside of you that erupts when you learn that your crush now likes your best friend.

Maybe you're struggling with jealousy right now. You can probably think of a million reasons why you deserve something more than someone else. No matter how you're feeling, refuse to allow jealousy to overtake you.

GRACE FOR TODAY:

When we seek God first, His blessings flow freely.

Here's your assignment. It's pretty simple, really. You are to follow God's ways first, and then He will make sure you receive every blessing with your name on it. Now, there may be some blessings you wanted God to give you that don't come your way. If that's the case, it just means that God has something better in store—something more suited for you. God's ways are higher than our ways. You have to trust Him to give you the things He knows are best for you.

Nothing can stop the blessings that flow from God to you—except you! Don't let jealousy clog that blessing waterway. When you feel jealous, purposefully think of God's love. Then, you'll be able to celebrate victories with your friends—even if their blessings arrive before yours do.

THE POWER OF YOUR STORY

Always be prepared to give an answer to everyone who asks you
to give the reason for the hope that you have.

1 PETER 3:15

S ome people see the courage of a teenage girl surviving a shark attack as the heart
of Bethany Hamilton's story. But Bethany knows the heart of the story is really
all about God. "I look at everything that's happened as part of God's plan for my life,"
Bethany has frequently said to friends, strangers, magazine reporters, and TV talk
show hosts.

The story that's brought so much attention
Bethany's way began the morning of October 31, 2003.
Thirteen-year-old Bethany was surfing near her home
in Kauai when a fourteen-foot tiger shark bit off her left
arm at the shoulder. As Bethany remained amazingly
calm, the quick efforts of a friend's father helped get her
to shore before she bled to death.

Just a few months after the accident, Bethany was
back on her surfboard, placing in several national competitions and earning a spot on the USA's national
surfing team. But, Bethany's influence has moved far
beyond the world of surfing. Her recent book, *Soul
Surfer,* and her many interviews and inspirational talks
have given her the chance to tell others about God.

"I know I have something to say. Something that
people need to hear—but sometimes they get so caught
up in the story part, that they miss the meaning," she explains on her Web site.

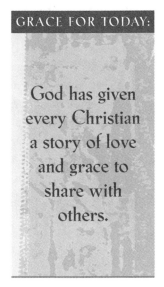

GRACE FOR TODAY:

God has given
every Christian
a story of love
and grace to
share with
others.

Just like Bethany, you have a story to tell. It may not seem as exciting or dramatic as surviving a shark attack. But, that doesn't make it any less important—or less
powerful. Tell your story to those around you. Share how God is at work, rewriting
the story of your life. The message you share may be just what someone needs to hear
to be able to see God and His love more clearly.

DON'T DELAY!

Go to the ant, you sluggard; consider its ways and be wise!

PROVERBS 6:6

Since ninth grade, it had become a regular thing that you and "the guys" meet after school each day to shoot a few hoops. But suddenly, your interest in after-school basketball starts to wane.

Now in your junior year, college is not too far away. The smart thing to do is buckle down and use your time to do something more productive—like studying. With the first semester almost over, finals are just around the corner, and you certainly can't afford to fail any of the exams.

The Bible relates an interesting illustration of the ant and how it lives out its life.

It has no commander, chief, or ruler, the Bible says. Yet, the ant is wise enough to know that winter is coming. So, she uses the summer months to carefully gather in her food so she and her family will not go hungry.

That's called planning and preparation.

It took God six days to create heaven and earth. He could have made it all at once, but He planned it out and took the time to do it right. In the end, God had produced something He was so proud of that He called it "good."

God gives you just the right amount of time to do everything you need to do, including the fun stuff. Most people would rather spend their time doing fun things than planning for the future. But putting things off to the last minute usually means they don't turn out right.

Don't let that be the case where your future is concerned. Learn to use your time wisely. Develop a plan and strategy for how you do things. In the long run, it can mean the difference between success and failure.

GRACE FOR TODAY:

God set the example—careful planning provides a future.

A SWEET 16

Let wise people listen and add to what they have learned.

PROVERBS 1:5 NIRV

Here are sixteen ideas for adding life to your every day:

1. Appreciate the value of time. Grab it, use it wisely, and savor every moment of it.
2. Remember that it's easier to prevent bad habits from forming than it is to break them once they have formed.
3. As you drive the road to success, consider letting others travel with you. The trip will be much more fun.
4. You should always have a good reason for speaking out; you don't necessarily need a good reason to remain silent.
5. Of all the items you can wear to school, church, or work, your facial expression is the most important.
6. Avoid being paranoid or overly sensitive.
7. Receive both praise and constructive criticism with grace.
8. Be bold in what you stand for. Be careful of what you fall for.
9. Never give up on miracles. They do happen—for people with eyes to see them.
10. Don't rain on other people's parades. Only a drip would do that.
11. Don't postpone joy. Laugh and celebrate now.
12. Find ways to sincerely compliment friends, classmates, and teammates on a job well done.
13. Get real. If you're already there, keep it real.
14. Choose to give others the benefit of the doubt.
15. Be public with praise for others, private with criticism.
16. Always remember to say "Thank you"—especially to God.

GRACE FOR TODAY:

When we count our blessings, we find that God
is the source of every one of them.

GOD'S AS GOOD AS HIS WORD

The sun comes up in the east and goes down in the west. Ocean tides rise and fall. Spring follows winter, year after year after year. . . . Some things seem dependable because they've been predictable for so long. But God says all of these things, the sun and the moon and even life on this earth, will end. There's only one thing that will never change. That's God. He is exactly the same as He's always been and always will be—loving, forgiving, merciful, just, and abundant in grace. That's what makes Him the only thing in this life—and the next—you can totally depend on.

God's faithfulness means every promise He makes, He keeps. That's one reason why your relationship with Him looks so different from any other you've experienced. People who love you, even your closest friends and family, can make promises with a sincere heart yet fail to keep them. They're human. They're fallible. They're just like you. But nothing will ever keep God from doing what He says.

God's faithfulness is something worth meditating on. That doesn't mean you have to sit in a lotus position or repeat a meaningless syllable over and over again like in some Eastern religions. You aren't clearing your mind when you meditate on God. You're filling it up with Him.

Spend a few quiet moments just thinking about how God's faithfulness makes a difference in your life. Focus on how God's promises to love you, guide you, forgive you, and prepare a home in heaven for you change the way you look at the world, other people, and yourself. Allow God to strengthen and encourage you with His faithfulness. He is one solid Rock that will never move.

The LORD is faithful to all his promises and
loving toward all he has made.

PSALM 145:13

WE OWED A DEBT

By Warren W. Wiersbe

God's Word teaches that when we were unsaved, we owed God a debt we could not pay. Jesus makes this clear in His parable of the two debtors. (See Luke 7:36–50.) Two men owed money to a creditor, the one owing ten times as much as the other. But neither was able to pay, so the creditor "graciously forgave them both" (literal translation). No matter how much morality a man may have, he still comes short of the glory of God. Even if his sin debt is one–tenth that of others, he stands unable to pay, bankrupt at the judgment bar of God. God in His grace, because of the work of Christ on the cross, is able to forgive sinners, no matter how large their debt may be.

Thus when we trust Christ, we become spiritually rich. We now share in the riches of God's grace (Ephesians 1:7), the riches of His glory (Ephesians 1:18; Philippians 4:19), the riches of His wisdom (Romans 11:33), and the "unsearchable riches of Christ" (Ephesians 3:8). In Christ we have "all the treasures of wisdom and knowledge," and we are "complete in Him" (Colossians 2:3 and 2:10 NKJV). Once a person is "in Christ," they have all that they need to live the kind of Christian life God wants them to live.[21]

—∞—

PRECIOUS FATHER: THANK YOU FOR MAKING ME SPIRITUALLY RICH, FOR TAKING MY DEBT AND REPLACING IT WITH THE RICHES OF YOUR GRACE. TEACH ME TO WALK IN THOSE RICHES DAY BY DAY. AMEN.

The grace of God that brings salvation has appeared to all men.
It teaches us to say "No" to ungodliness and worldly passions, and to live self–controlled, upright and godly lives in this present age.

TITUS 2:11–12

GRAY-HEADED WISDOM

Wisdom belongs to the aged, and understanding to those who
have lived many years.

JOB 12:12 NLT

R especting elders is a common practice in many cultures. Take the Chinese culture, for example. It is said in their culture, "When there is an elder, there is a
treasure."

Maybe your parents aren't exactly white-headed right now, but you've probably
given them a few gray hairs, right? They know a few more things than you do. You
have to admit they've been around a lot longer, and
they've probably walked down many of the same roads
you're encountering today. While it might seem somewhat "uncool" to ask the counsel of your parents or
grandparents, it's a wise move. Some of their life lessons will save you some trouble down the road. Why
not ask for their advice today? If you're struggling with
something, try asking your parents or grandparents or
other respected elders for their input.

GRACE FOR TODAY:

God has all
the wisdom
we will ever
need.

This practice is even gaining popularity in the
United States. In fact, Elder Wisdom Circle, a
California based non-profit association comprised of
elders who offer advice and seekers who want it, is
putting wisdom-givers and wisdom-seekers together on a daily basis by way of the
Internet. The organization's Web site says, "The mission of our association is to promote and share elder know-how and accumulated wisdom."

Interesting, isn't it? Young people are so hungry for wisdom; they are even turning to elderly strangers for advice. Well, you don't have to do that. Even if you don't
know any elderly Christians, God is available to you. He has all of the answers, and
He is more than willing to share His wisdom with you. Go ahead—get some wisdom
today!

A PLACE OF PEACE

God's peace, which is far beyond human understanding, will keep your
hearts and minds safe in union with Christ Jesus.

PHILIPPIANS 4:7 GNB

There is a house in Amsterdam where people wait in line for hours just so they
can walk into its small, barren rooms and remember the life of a teenage girl
they've never met. Some people say she was just an ordinary girl living in extraordinary circumstances. But, in God's world nothing, and
no one, is "ordinary." Everything He has made is
extraordinary, including Anne Frank.

Anne's life was different from yours, but her heart
was much the same. For two years she and her Jewish
family hid from the Nazis in a small apartment, concealed behind a bookcase. In her diary, Anne wrote
about boys, the difficulty of being a teenager, and her
hopes and dreams for the future. She covered the walls
of her room with pictures of current film stars and
postcards from around the world. Anne died in a concentration camp at the age of fifteen, just a few weeks
before the prisoners there were set free.

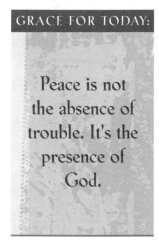

GRACE FOR TODAY:

Peace is not
the absence of
trouble. It's the
presence of
God.

War and hate are a reality of life in a world that often turns its back on God. But,
God has given you a path to peace, no matter what your circumstances. Whether you
are watching a scary movie with a friend, struggling through the divorce of your parents, or caught up in the chaos of a real war, Jesus promises you peace.

The peace Jesus offers is the quiet assurance of God's presence and protection
wherever you are, no matter what's going on around you. The next time you find your
emotions on a roller coaster ride of panic or worry, stop. Ask God to help you feel the
comfort of His love and see the situation through His eyes. Allow His peace to change
your life from the inside out.

NEVER ALONE

There is a friend who sticks closer than a brother.

PROVERBS 18:24 AMP

The expression on her face is a familiar one.

It wasn't too long ago that you found yourself right where she is: sitting alone and feeling like the "new kid on the block" at a new school after moving here from halfway across the country.

You wonder if she feels as lonely and homesick as you did—like you were on the outside looking in.

Feeling lonely is no fun.

Jesus, who was abandoned by all His followers just before he was crucified, knew what it felt like to be lonely. He may have been thinking about that when He told the disciples that He would be leaving them soon.

He knew they would miss His presence. Because of His love and compassion, Jesus wanted to make sure they would not be lonely while He was away.

"I will not leave you comfortless," Jesus told them. "I will come to you" (John 14:18 KJV).

God loves you with the same compassion. That's why He has sent His Holy Spirit to live inside you—so that you are never alone. He has also given you His Word as an encouragement and assurance of His presence when you feel alone.

When you see someone who needs to be comforted, pray and ask God if you should approach that person. If He says yes, then trust Him to show you how to take time to help that person to feel loved. As a Christian, you can be His Word to someone who is in need or feeling lonely.

GRACE FOR TODAY:

We are never on the outside when God is inside us.

GETTING OUT OF DEEP TROUBLE

By doing good you will put a stop to the talk of foolish people.
They don't know what they are saying. God wants you to stop them.

1 PETER 2:15 NIRV

A group of frogs was hopping through the woods. Suddenly, two of them plunged into a deep pit, which had been covered by loose grass and weeds. As the other frogs circled the pit, they quickly concluded that their amphibious cohorts were doomed. Frantically, the two misfortunate frogs began leaping with all their strength.

"Give it up," their cohorts scolded them. "You are as good as dead."

But still the two frogs kept jumping.

After a half-hour, one of the trapped frogs became discouraged, curled up in a dark corner of the pit, and waited to die. But the other frog kept leaping, even though his companions above the pit continued to jeer.

Finally, with one mighty lunge, the frog propelled himself to the top of the pit, barely grasping its rim, then pulled his way to safety.

"Wow! You sure have hops!" one of the surprised frogs shouted. "I guess it was a good thing you ignored our taunts."

The now-safe frog looked at his companions, a puzzled expression on his green face. Then, through a series of frog sign-language gestures, the once-trapped creature explained to the others that he was deaf and couldn't hear anything. In fact, the frog signed, when he saw their frantic gestures and flapping frog jaws, he assumed they were encouraging him!

You can accomplish amazing feats when you turn a deaf ear—or two—to the discouraging words of negative-thinking naysayers. When you're faced with adversity, remember that, because of the courage and strength God provides, hope expressed can become hope realized.

GRACE FOR TODAY:

Because of the courage and strength God provides, hope expressed can become hope realized.

OPEN DOOR POLICY

Ninepence is an odd name for a five-year-old Chinese girl. But then, Ninepence had led a rather odd life. She'd been kidnapped by a beggar who thought having a young child would make others more willing to give her a handout. But a British missionary saw the young girl, sick and covered with sores, and offered to buy her outright—for nine cents. That's how "Ninepence" came to live with Gladys Aylward.

Soon after, Ninepence brought home a young orphan boy. She promised Gladys she'd eat less food if the boy could also make his home with them. Gladys warmly invited the boy in, promising to supply enough food for both. But in honor of Ninepence's heartfelt offer, Gladys nicknamed the boy "Less." Around two hundred other orphans eventually became part of Gladys' family. When China went to war, around half of the children escaped the country with the help of a friend. Gladys led the other 100 children twelve days on foot through the war-torn wilderness of the Chinese countryside. That is hospitality in action.

The word "hospitality" usually brings to mind images of elaborate dinner parties held in perfectly decorated houses. But when God asks His children to be hospitable to others, He is more concerned with the condition of their hearts than their homes.

Even if you aren't old enough to own a home, like Ninepence, you can still practice hospitality. The key is making others feel at home. Invite a new student to eat at your table in the cafeteria. Share your lunch with someone who's forgotten his. Serve any guests in your home with kindness and compassion—whether they're your parents' friends or yours. Treat strangers with loving respect. Welcome others the way God has welcomed you.

GRACE FOR TODAY:

With God at home in our hearts, we have all we need to make others feel at home anywhere.

Be hospitable to one another without grumbling.

1 PETER 4:9 NKJV

PONDERING OR PRAYING?

By Evelyn Christenson

Much of what we think is prayer actually is only pondering. Even when we are on our knees in our prayer closets, it is easy just to roll our own thoughts and our own answers around in our minds, not really including God at all. This is not a prayer; it is only pondering.

My dictionary defines ponder like this: "to consider something deeply and thoroughly; to meditate over or upon, to weigh carefully in mind; to consider thoughtfully; to reflect, cogitate, deliberate, ruminate." This is a healthy process as it helps us sort out whys, unravel perplexing puzzles, come to conclusions, and even put to rest hurtful events. But people frequently think they have prayed when they have spent time pondering. Pondering is not prayer. Only when we involve God in this process does it turn into prayer.

In the supernatural battle for our families, pondering is inadequate. It is powerless to change the family problem that we are deliberating.

But when we include God, our pondering suddenly involves the omniscient, all-wise God of the universe. The God who never makes a mistake. The God who knows all the whys, all the outcomes, all the perfect He intends through everything that happens to our families. When God becomes personally involved in our pondering, there are accurate conclusions and correct attitudes in and for our families—supplied by a loving, caring, all-knowing God.[22]

—⁂—

DEAR FATHER IN HEAVEN: THANK YOU FOR PROMISING TO HEAR ME EVERY TIME I PRAY. I CALL ON YOUR GRACE CONCERNING THE ADVERSE CIRCUMSTANCES IN MY LIFE AND ASK YOU TO TAKE CHARGE, DOING FOR ME WHAT YOU THINK BEST. IN JESUS' NAME. AMEN.

Draw near to God, and He will draw near to you.

JAMES 4:8 NRSV

ALL ABOUT ME

If you want to be first, you must be the slave of the rest.

MATTHEW 20:27 CEV

Happy Bunny has become quite popular in all of his cute pinkness and his in-your-face sayings on notebooks, posters, magnets, t-shirts, and more. One example says: "It's all about me. Deal with it!" While that sounds kind of funny coming from Happy Bunny, it's not so cute when it comes out of your mouth, is it? Many people feel just like Happy Bunny, they just aren't as honest.

GRACE FOR TODAY:

We don't have to look out for Number One, because God is already looking out for us.

The world says, "If you don't look out for number one, nobody else will." But, the Bible says whoever wants to be first among you must be your slave. Those two statements are in direct contradiction, aren't they? It's hard to survive in this world without developing a "Me, Me, Me," mentality, but your mission is to become a reflection of the image of God.

God gave some additional reasons why we should choose to go His way. Proverbs 16:18 MSG says, "First pride, then the crash—the bigger the ego, the harder the fall." The Bible says a lot about humility. It says that God gives grace to the lowly and that He promises to save the humble. Sounds like God looks out for those who aren't so concerned with looking out for themselves, doesn't it?

You don't have to look out for Number One because the Creator of the universe is already looking out for you. Put down your "It's all about me. Deal with it!" sign, and begin focusing your attention on God. Trust in the Lord. He is your protector and defender. He will see to it that you're not overlooked or neglected. Forget Happy Bunny. Your new sign should read, "It's not about me. It's all about Him."

ABOVE US ALL

As high as the heavens are above the earth,
so high are my ways and thoughts above yours.

ISAIAH 55:9 GNB

K nowing God and understanding Him are two different things. It's like the difference between knowing planes can fly and then being able to explain how they do it. Even the pilot who flies the plane may not fully understand the physics of flight, just like the mechanic who fixes the plane may not understand how to land a 747 in heavy fog. They both know what they need to know to do their job. In the same way, God allows you to know what you need to know to live your life in a relationship with Him.

You can understand more about God by spending time with Him. And just like the pilot and mechanic can choose to learn more about flight and flying, you can study the Bible to learn more about God's way of living and loving. But, there's a limit to what your human brain can hold.

That means you'll have to live with some unanswered questions. Doubts may creep into your mind now and then. Your friends may ask you things about God that you won't be able to fully explain. That's okay. God and His grace are much bigger and more powerful than words or thoughts. He'll provide you with what you need to know—when you need to know it.

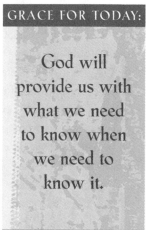

GRACE FOR TODAY:

God will provide us with what we need to know when we need to know it.

It may not be clear in your mind how a heavy metal plane weighing a couple of tons actually soars through the air. But that doesn't mean you don't climb aboard, especially when there's a fantastic destination waiting for you at the end of the ride. Give your doubts, as well as your faith, to God. Then, take your reserved seat and relax. You're in for the ride of your life.

DON'T BE DISTRACTED

But the LORD's plans stand firm forever;
his intentions can never be shaken.

PSALM 33:11 NLT

You were so sure the lead role in the school play would go to you. Considering all the time you put into rehearsal for the part—memorizing the lines and studying the character's demeanor—there's no way the role could go to someone else.

But it did. Not only that, but you ended up with one of the smallest parts in the entire production. A walk-on without a single speaking line!

Sometimes, even our best efforts are not enough when it comes to getting what we want. We put our best foot forward, doing everything we know to assure we'll get where we want to go, and still things don't go our way.

And we are disappointed.

Maybe what we want is not exactly what God had in mind.

When He made us, God put into us certain abilities based on the plan He had for our life. Just because we see something we like or want does not mean we are suited for that particular thing. It just may be that God has reserved whatever it is for someone else, and that He has something different and better in store for you.

The best way to know we are going after the right thing is to pray and ask God. Then, life for us will not be a hodgepodge of trial and error. God made us, and He for sure has our best interest at heart. He will not sit idly by while we fail.

GRACE FOR TODAY:

When God is steering us down life's highway
we will never veer off course.

"1" CAN BE A LONELY NUMBER

Two are better than one, because they have a good return for their work:
If one falls down, his friend can help him up. But pity the man who
falls and has no one to help him up!

ECCLESIASTES 4:9-10

The famous Lone Ranger, old-school star of TV and movies, was misnamed. In reality, he wasn't "Lone" at all. He didn't defeat bandits or escape danger by himself. He had the help of his faithful friend, Tonto, as well as that of his fast and trusty horse, Silver.

Even the most heroic of humans aren't designed to conquer life by themselves. Whether it's studying for a challenging final exam, pushing your stalled car out of an intersection, or just coping with the stress of teen life in general, some situations require a call for help from a trusty sidekick—or a few of them!

You might be one of those people who have trouble asking for help. If so, just remember that the help you need is available. God has a way of putting people in our lives to act as His hands and feet.

Sure, it might take some effort and a move out of your comfort zone to connect with a counselor, youth pastor, friend, teammate, or family member to help you in your time of need; but asking for help is definitely worth it. Sending up an SOS when you need it is a sign of maturity, not weakness. Ignoring or refusing the help of those God has place around you is, at best, an ungrateful decision. (And, at worst, it's downright foolish!)

Finding the support or guidance you need can make a huge difference in your attitude toward life. So don't hesitate to reach out when you need a lifeline. And remember, the person you seek help from today might be the one who needs your expertise, guidance, or moral support somewhere down the road.

GRACE FOR TODAY:

In our time of need, the human resources God has
provided for us are only a cry of "Help!" away.

THE REAL YOU

What are you worth? Ask Jesus. You are priceless in His eyes. He gave His life to save yours, because you are so deeply loved. But at the same time, the Bible says people are really no more than dust. That's because without God's touch, without His gift of life, people are literally nothing.

Finding a balance between these two truths is what true humility is all about. It's recognizing your value to God and in His plan for this world, as well as your total dependence on Him to accomplish even the smallest task—like breathing, for instance.

Pride, which is the opposite of humility, tempts people to take credit for what they do without acknowledging the part God plays in the whole picture. Pride always has its eyes on others, instead of God. It likes to brag and boast, demand center stage, and is secretly pleased when others wind up in second

GRACE FOR TODAY:

God is even more pleased about our success than we are.

place. Pride pretends a person's worth depends on things like talent, beauty, income, popularity, or position in society. In the end, it deceives people into believing they don't need God. It whispers, "You control your own destiny."

Pride is a liar. Humility lives out the truth. Being humble doesn't mean you shouldn't feel pleased over an accomplishment or proud of how hard you worked or how far you've come. God is just as pleased about your success as you are. He's been there helping you every step of the way. The more you remember that fact, and thank God for it, the more humble your heart will become. Humility isn't something you can work harder to achieve. It's something that gradually grows in your life—the more you recognize how big God is, how small you are, and what wonderful things you can accomplish together.

Humble yourselves before the Lord, and he will lift you up.

JAMES 4:10 GNB

WHO DO YOU SAY I AM?

By John MacArthur Jr.

Jesus was talking to His disciples and asked, "Who do men say that I am?"

They answered, "Oh, some people think You are Jeremiah; some people think You are Elijah; some people think You are one of the prophets."

He said, "Who do you think I am?"

Peter responded, "Thou art the Christ, the Son of the living God" (Matthew 16:16 KJV). Then, I feel sure, he wondered, *Where did that come from?*

Jesus said, "Blessed are you, Simon son of Jonah, for this was not revealed to you by man, but by my Father in heaven." (Matthew 16:13–17).

Peter probably said, "I thought so. I surely didn't know that." You see, when Peter was near Jesus, he not only did the miraculous, he said the miraculous. Is it any wonder he wanted to be near Him?

When he was near Christ, Peter had miraculous courage. He was in the Garden of Gethsemane when a whole band of soldiers—as many as 500—came to arrest Jesus. They came marching in with all their regalia. In front of them came the chief priests, and before the chief priests came the servants of the priests. Peter was standing with the Lord. Maybe his thoughts went something like this: "They think they are going to take Jesus away. No, they won't."

Since Peter did not ever want to be removed from the presence of Jesus, he took out a sword. He started with the first guy in line, who happened to be Malchus, the servant of the high priest. The Bible says Peter cut off Malchus' ear, but if I know Peter, he was going for his head. Peter was ready to take on the whole Roman army. You see, when he was with Jesus, he had miraculous courage.[23]

—⟋⟍⟋—

PRECIOUS FATHER: I WANT TO KNOW YOU THE WAY PETER DID—INTIMATELY, MIRACULOUSLY, COURAGEOUSLY, WALKING DAILY IN THE FLOW OF GRACE THAT COMES FROM YOUR PRESENCE. AMEN.

It is God who arms me with strength and makes my way perfect.

PSALM 18:32

LOOKING GOOD

God sees not as man sees, for man looks at the outward appearance,
but the LORD looks at the heart."

1 SAMUEL 16:7 NASB

The Duchess of Windsor has been credited with coining the phrase, "You can never be too rich or too thin," and women around the world have bought into that mentality. One look at today's stars such as Lara Flynn Boyle and Calista Flockhart reveals that our role models are no longer the voluptuous Marilyn Monroe types. They are thin—super-thin! For guys, there's the whole "I must look like I drink steroids for breakfast," with muscles exploding into more muscles. In fact, so many guys are overdosing on exercise, there's a new phenomena called "bigorexia."

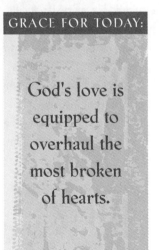

GRACE FOR TODAY:

God's love is equipped to overhaul the most broken of hearts.

Feeling good about yourself is tough for everyone. Let's face it, it's important to look good, but it's more important to work on your inner appearance. Eating right, exercising regularly, dressing in the right clothes, driving a hip car—those are all part of fitting into the all-important social scene at school. But, there's so much more to you than your outward image.

In order to become the whole package, you need to work on your inner man. Feed your spirit the Word of God. Develop your faith by praying and spending time meditating on the promises of God. Allow the Lord to overhaul your heart, filling you with more of His love. He will help you grow in Him and become the total package.

God can even cause you to outshine the most popular group in your school. Ask Him for the right friends and favor with your peers. It's available to you. Forget the magic pills that promise "Lose thirty pounds in thirty days" and the protein shakes that guarantee biceps the size of boulders. Instead, put your trust in God. The Master wants to give you an inner makeover.

MOVING BEYOND SUCCESS TO VICTORY

Overwhelming victory is ours through Christ, who loved us.

ROMANS 8:37 NLT

Time for a little sports trivia: What famous baseball player struck out 1,330 times? What professional basketball player was cut from his high school freshman team? These two "losers" are Babe Ruth and Michael Jordan. Although they're known as two of the greatest athletes of all time, they didn't achieve their success by never losing a game. Both Babe Ruth and Michael Jordan blew it now and then, looking exactly like the "not-so-greats" whose names never made it into the record books. What set them apart is they understood that failure was part of success—and so they risked trying again.

Is there any area in your life where you've labeled yourself "a failure?" God wants to talk to you about it. He'll be happy to show you what you can learn from the experience. Then, put what you've learned into practice. Try again. Success may be closer at hand than you first thought.

Success is only part of the picture. You can succeed without being wholly successful, particularly in God's eyes. That's because your own effort and hard work will never tell the whole story of who you are. God wants you to be more than successful. He wants you to be victorious. That means on the inside, where others cannot see, God longs for you to win over your toughest competition.

GRACE FOR TODAY:

God is ready to help us win over our toughest competition.

Everyone's inner "World Series" will look a little different. Yours may be a battle with depression, anger, or pride. Whatever it is, God has given you the ability to beat it, as moment-by-moment you rely on Him.

You may strike out every so often along the way. But, don't let that throw you. Learn what you can from what happened. Then, try again. God's on your team, making your victory as certain as His deep love for you.

SHAPING YOUR FUTURE

But it takes only one wrong person among you to infect
all the others—a little yeast spreads quickly through the
whole batch of dough!

GALATIANS 5:9 NLT

A t first it seemed innocent enough.
"Sampling the goods" is how your friends described it as they urged you to
take a few pieces of candy from the open bin in the grocery store.

"It's the only way you're gonna know which ones to buy," they say laughingly.

In a way, what they say makes sense, but something on the inside tells you this is
not right. You realize that in the three weeks that you've been part of this "taste–testing" adventure, you have yet to see your friends buy any candy.

Thankfully, you never agreed to be part of their little game. And now that you
realize what they were doing was stealing, you're glad.

God has given you His Holy Spirit to help you to see when something is not quite
right. When you are good, you have a strong sense of peace that confirms God's presence inside you. On the other hand, doing wrong always brings about a feeling of guilt.

Your friends may not see the danger in what they are doing. Because you do, it
becomes your responsibility to tell them how wrong they are.

Whether they realize it or not, they are establishing a pattern of sin that could follow them for life, and cause a lot of trouble. Ask God to help you show them how such
a small thing can lead to something much more serious. Then, pray about your choice
of friends. It may be God wants you to reevaluate the kind of company you keep.

GRACE FOR TODAY:

When we're headed in the wrong direction,
God will always wave a caution flag.

THE CONTENTS OF CONTENTMENT

Make sure that your character is free from the love of money,
being content with what you have.

HEBREWS 13:5 NASB

On a cool spring afternoon, an expert wood carver sat on his front porch, sipping lemonade and enjoying the view. Around him on the porch sat his various creations. A friend of the carver's stopped by for a quick visit and was surprised to see the artisan relaxing. "It's only one-thirty in the afternoon," the friend observed, "a little early in the day for a break, isn't it?"

The artisan swallowed a mouthful of lemonade and yawned. "This isn't a break," he answered, "I'm done for the day."

The friend, a young marketing executive, was puzzled: "What do you mean? It's too early in the day for you to stop carving. You need to produce more. If you carve more figures, you can make more money. You could even hire an assistant to help you with the business end of things. You could buy new tools. You could buy a shop, so you wouldn't have to carve here at your house."

"Why would I want to do all of that?" the carver asked.

"So you can make more money—are you dense?" his friend sputtered.

"And what would I do with all that extra money?"

"Why—enjoy life, of course!"

The carver sipped from his lemonade again, then leaned back in his chair, and closed his eyes. Before he drifted off into an afternoon nap, he mumbled contentedly, "Enjoy life? What do you think I'm doing right now?"

GRACE FOR TODAY:

God provides an abundance of blessings every day—
we must make sure we're not too busy to enjoy them.

SPENDING DOWN TIME LOOKING UP

The very first week of recorded history was a productive one. God created the heavens, the earth, and every little detail of life right down to the tiniest dust mite. After working hard for six days, God took time off. He didn't need a vacation. He hadn't run out of energy or ideas. He'd simply completed what He'd set out to do. So He took a break. He didn't play video games, reward himself with a hot fudge sundae, or take a trip to the mall. God simply spent the day taking a good look at everything He'd accomplished. And He declared it good.

On the seventh day, God didn't stop maintaining what He'd made the week before. The planets kept on spinning, and plants kept right on growing. God just stopped creating so He could spend time contemplating. God encourages you to do the same.

The Sabbath, which is celebrated

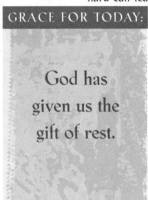

GRACE FOR TODAY:

God has given us the gift of rest.

every Saturday by Jews and on Sundays by most Christians, is God's gift to you. Unlike God, you do get tired. Working hard can leave you stressed out, burned out, and out of sync with God and others. Pausing from your regular week-day can help renew your energy so you're ready to tackle the new week ahead.

But there's more to Sabbath rest than just vegging out. Look back over the past week, just like God did. Thank Him for all He's done. Get involved at a church where you can worship God and serve others. Go ahead and eat, laugh, spend time with your friends, make your bed, help your mom—do whatever needs to be done to maintain the life God's entrusted to you. Just make sure God's at the center of it all, helping you regain your focus on Him before another week of work arrives.

For six days, work is to be done, but the seventh day is a Sabbath of rest, holy to the LORD.

EXODUS 31:15

LIVING AND ACTIVE

By Evelyn Christenson

The beach at Lake Michigan is my favorite place to read God's Word and let Him speak to me. Every day while we are on vacation I rise early, and, weather permitting, take my Bible down to the edge of the lake and read until He speaks. One morning I read such a great psalm about our God that I found myself skipping down the beach instead of doing my usual hiking. God had changed an ordinary, run-of-the-mill vacation day into one of exhilaration and exploding joy, joy that could not be contained in ordinary steps. The thrill that sent my body soaring like the eagle's blurt out in impromptu songs of praise as I adored Him for who He is and praised Him for what He is. Changed by a Psalm? Yes, changed!

Fifty-nine years of underlining answers for actual situations have proven to me that the Bible truly is a liv-ing Book. "For the word of God is living and active," Hebrews 4:12 NASB tells us. Yes, it is alive. It has answers in the midst of our knowledge explosion today—or tomorrow—on this planet and in outer space. And precept upon precept as I let it renew my mind, my attitudes, and wisdom to live by, I am changed. Changed into what is His perfect will for me to be.[24]

—∽—

WONDERFUL FATHER: AS I STUDY YOUR WORD, I LEARN MORE AND MORE ABOUT THE PROMISES YOU'VE GIVEN ME—EACH ONE FILLED WITH GRACE AND TRUTH. THANK YOU FOR YOUR LIVING WORD THAT HELPS ME TO LIVE IN THAT GRACE. AMEN.

God means what he says. What he says goes. His powerful Word is sharp as a surgeon's scalpel, cutting through everything, whether doubt or defense, laying us open to listen and obey. Nothing and no one is impervious to God's Word.

HEBREWS 4:12–13 MSG

A NEW BEGINNING

Count yourself lucky, how happy you must be—you get a fresh start, your
slate's wiped clean.

PSALM 32:1 MSG

Video games are addictive. Hours pass, and it seems like only minutes. Your
calloused fingers manipulate the joystick with great precision and then—boom!
The enemy strikes and you explode. If you're not too far into the game, and nobody is
watching, do you ever just restart the game, declaring the first round as simply a "practice round?" (C'mon, be honest!)

In real life, we don't get many "do-overs." When you stick your foot in your
mouth in front of your best friend, you can't rewind and
start again. When you forget to study and your math
teacher gives you a quiz, you can't go back in time and
prepare. When you let anger get the best of you and yell
at your parents, you can't take back those words. When
you miss the basket at the end of the game, you can't
push back the time clock and take the shot again. There
are very few "do-overs" in real life.

GRACE FOR TODAY:

With God, we always get a second chance.

Aren't you glad that with God, we always get to
start over? No matter what we've done. No matter
how awful we've acted. No matter how disappointed
we are in ourselves, God still loves us and will forgive us if we'll only ask Him. God
promised that He would remember our sins no more. It's like He hits the ultimate
delete button and we get to start again! All we have to do is repent, and then we get to
move forward with our Heavenly Father—no penalties, no guilt, no shame. With God,
we always get a fresh start!

FAMILY TIES

Children, obey your parents because you belong to the Lord.

EPHESIANS 6:1 NLT

H is parents were frantic. They'd traveled all day long assuming their twelve-year-old son was with the other relatives who'd also gone to Jerusalem. But, when nightfall came, Jesus was nowhere to be found. Mary and Joseph took the long walk back to Jerusalem, undoubtedly worried the whole way. The next day they found their son in the temple, listening and asking questions of the religious leaders.

Like any mom, Mary quickly reprimanded her son for making them worry. Jesus explained why He felt it was important for him to remain in Jerusalem, to be in His "Father's house." The book of Luke says that Jesus' parents didn't understand what He was saying. But, it also says that Jesus went back to Nazareth along with His parents and was obedient to them.

Jesus was not your typical teenager. At this point in His life, Jesus was God wrapped up in an adolescent body. But He still chose to obey His parents. That's because Jesus knew that one way of honoring His heavenly Father was through honoring His earthly mom and dad. The same is true for you.

GRACE FOR TODAY:

God gave us parents to help us learn His ways.

There will be times when your parents won't understand you. Jesus knows how you feel. But, He's also shown you the right thing to do, to respect your parents by listening to them and doing what they ask. Not only will this help you grow in patience, self-control, and wisdom, it can help your parents do the same. You're there to help each other grow—finding out firsthand what unconditional love really means.

JUST SAY IT!

My power works best in your weakness.

2 CORINTHIANS 12:9 NLT

S hawn panted heavily as he wiped the sweat from his face. It was obvious he was disappointed and embarrassed at the poor showing he had made while running the 4/40 relay in the high school competition.

"Man, that was lousy," you could hear him complain beneath his breath as he plopped down beside you after coming in fifth place. "I should have done a lot better than that."

Yeah, but you ran pretty hard out there, you think of your teammate's performance. *You gave it your best.*

That's a very good response to someone's obvious failure. But don't just think it. Say it to him. The one thing he can really use right now is to be encouraged. And you're just the person for the job.

Sometimes, things that seem to be obstacles to us are simply opportunities for God to show us His love and faithfulness. God never requires that we be perfect. Doing our best is all He ever expects.

He knows there will be times when, after we've done our best, we will run out of steam—our strength weakens. It's in those times that God steps in to provide that extra nudge we need to make it through. His strength, He says, is never failing. It's enough to get us through when our strength is seemingly all used up.

When you feel you've given all you've got, and it was still not enough; pray and ask God to help you. He has all the strength you need.

GRACE FOR TODAY:

When we feel our weakest, God gives us
His strength to build on.

TURNING THE TIDE

Diligent hands bring wealth.

PROVERBS 10:4

I f you asked teens across the country to name one famous newspaper—besides their hometown paper—the most popular answer would no doubt be *The New York Times*, which is bigger than many huge corporations today.

However, the now–famous *Times* was just a struggling little paper (with a paltry 9,000 subscribers) in a battle for survival with a dozen other New York dailies, when it hired a man named Adolph Ochs as publisher back in 1896.

Assuming the helm of this sinking ship, Ochs promptly lowered the paper's retail price from three cents to a single penny and vowed to publish the news "impartially, without fear or favor." Then he cut out the paper's fiction section, as well as columns he deemed stale. His slogan for the publication became "All the news that's fit to print."

Ochs also launched a Sunday magazine section, with photographs to provide variety and visual appeal.

The results of his efforts? By increasing value while decreasing price, Ochs quickly boosted the paper's circulation to 350,000—an astounding 39-fold growth! Today, that little paper that once sold for a penny is a multi–billion–dollar enterprise that is closing in on 100 Pulitzer Prizes won.

The lesson for you? Don't be discouraged if you're part of a small and/or unsuccessful team, club, or band—or if your scholastic career isn't going the way you would like it to. By focusing on quality work and being willing to make changes, you can turn things around. God promises that diligent effort will make a difference. Maybe not an instant difference, but one that can be realized over time. And that's good news that's fit to print anywhere.

GRACE FOR TODAY:

God promises our sincere efforts are never for
nothing, always for something.

STANDING BY!

Y ou had heard that your friend's parents were having problems and were going through a divorce, but not wanting to pry you decided to keep quiet. Now, your friend is calling. She wants to talk to you because she trusts you.

It is good to have someone to go to when you are faced with a problem—someone who will understand what you are facing and will take the time to help you get through it.

Jesus, who always made himself available to those in need, understood that there would be times when we would need that kind of support. That's why He promised to always be with us and to never leave us alone. In fact, He gave us His Holy Spirit as a permanent comforter—one who would be by our side at all times.

As a Christian, you have the same

love and compassion as Jesus, who went everywhere looking to be a blessing to others. You also have the ability to comfort those around you because you have the Holy Spirit inside of you.

God's love becomes the tool you operate with when others come to you for help. His compassion becomes your motivator when others need you to spend time praying with them and offering them encouragement.

Tell them how God has changed your life. Share His Word with them, and help them to see for themselves how He graciously provides, and that He is always present. He promises to never leave them alone. That's how true, godly friendship operates.

GRACE FOR TODAY:

God will never walk away, but will stay by our side.

He will be with you; he will neither fail you nor forsake you.

DEUTERONOMY 31:8 NLT

STAYING PURE

By John MacArthur Jr.

I think sex is a glorious thing. God invented it. If He invented it, it is good. But He designed it for the beauty of the marriage relationship and nowhere else. For a person to think that they can cheat God and get kicks out of sex apart from marriage is to believe the devil's lie.

It is absurd for a young person (or anyone else) who is living in sexual impurity to say, "God, show me your will." Such a person is not even doing what this text of Scripture says is His will. Why should God disclose some further will?

Stay away from immoral sex. That is a simple principle. Someone inevitably says, "How far away?" Far away enough to be pure. Sanctified. Set apart wholly unto God.

Am I saying that you can't hold hands with the one you love? That is not the issue. Do I mean that you can't kiss? I don't mean that, either. The Bible says, "All things are lawful unto me, but all things are not expedient; all things are lawful for me, but I will not be brought under the power of any" (1 Corinthians 6:12 KJV). You can be blessed by God only so long as you are controlling what you do for His honor. When lust controls you, you have crossed the line. It's a simple principle.[25]

—⁂—

DEAR GOD: I WANT TO KEEP MYSELF PURE, DESPITE ALL THE TEMPTATIONS THAT FLY AROUND ME. I DON'T WANT TO BE A SLAVE TO ANYTHING BUT YOUR MARVELOUS GRACE. HELP ME AS I STRIVE TO LIVE A LIFE THAT IS PLEASING TO YOU—A LIFE THAT HONORS THE BODY YOU'VE GIVEN ME. AMEN.

You know the guidelines we laid out for you from the Master Jesus. God wants you to live a pure life.

1 THESSALONIANS 4:2–3 MSG

ENCOURAGE YOURSELF

David encouraged himself in the LORD his God.

1 SAMUEL 30:6 KJV

I t's difficult to be happy every single day. Stuff happens—large amounts of home-work, fights with friends, endless chores, conflicts with parents, and zits. Until we get to heaven, we're going to have difficult days. It's simply a fact of life. On those days, it's so important to encourage yourself in the Lord. Don't let depression rob you of joy, because the joy of the Lord is your strength. Even David—a man after God's own heart—had to encourage himself in the Lord.

Once, he and his 600 men were returning from an exhausting battle, when they discovered their hometown burned, belongings gone, wives and children taken captive, and their lives turned upside down. The men were hurt, disappointed, and angry. Heartbroken, they turned their anger toward David.

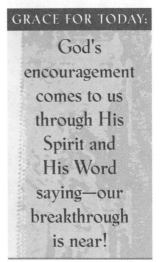

GRACE FOR TODAY: God's encouragement comes to us through His Spirit and His Word saying—our breakthrough is near!

This was a very difficult day for David. Not only had he lost everything and everyone he'd ever loved, but his men talked about killing him! If ever there was a time to get down in a hole and hide, this was it. But, David didn't do that. Instead, he encouraged himself in the Lord. He reminded himself of all the times God had come through for him. Seventy-two hours later, he was crowned King of Israel.

We're all going to face battles in this life with great opportunities to become depressed, but instead of wal-lowing in self-pity or giving up, we can learn from David's life. Encourage yourself in the Lord. Keep your joy intact. Let God's grace envelop you and make a way for you. After all, your breakthrough may be just seventy-two hours away!

DIRTY LAUNDRY

Remove my sin, and I will be clean; wash me, and
I will be whiter than snow.

PSALM 51:7 GNB

As soon as you open the door of the washing machine, you know something's gone terribly wrong. What used to be white is now pink, from undershirts to athletic socks. The culprit? One new red bandana. It's amazing how something so small and seemingly insignificant can affect so much. But it does.

The same can be said about holiness. God is pure, spotless, holy. He's never been unloving, unjust, or untrue. But the children He created, from Eden to Israel, turned their backs on holiness. They chose to go their own way, to do their own thing, to do what felt good regardless of the circumstances. They traded purity for sinfulness, and it, like the red bandana, began to "bleed" color on everything it touched.

God longed to be close to those He loves, but He couldn't sacrifice His holiness to draw near to them. After all, being holy isn't something God does. It's something God is. Someone had to pay the price for the wrongs that had been done. It was the only way that the people God loved would have the chance to be holy, to be close to God, once more.

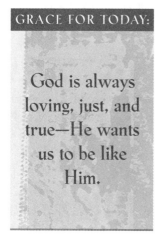

GRACE FOR TODAY:

God is always loving, just, and true—He wants us to be like Him.

Jesus chose to pay that price. Through His death on the Cross you became holy and pure in God's eyes. The word "holy" means "set apart for something special." That's true about you. Jesus' gift has set you apart for something special, for something better. Though God's grace keeps you "holy" even when you blow it, choosing to do what's right will make you a truer, purer reflection of God's image to the world.

WHAT'S YOUR MOTIVE?

Each man should give what he has decided in his heart to give.

2 CORINTHIANS 9:7

The notice posted on the school's bulletin board caught your attention. The Benevolence Society is planning an outing into the inner city to take food and clothing to the homeless and is asking for volunteers.

This is just the kind of thing you enjoy, and your heart of compassion urges you to become involved. But lately, you have started to wonder about the "so-called" homeless street people you see begging on street corners all the time.

Are they really homeless, or are they running some kind of scam? you think. *Most of them look as healthy as I am.*

That's a good question. But leave it for God to deal with, and follow your heart of compassion by doing what you can to help. People run scams every day that bilk honest, hard-working people out of their time and money. But there are just as many people who are truly in need of help.

In the Bible, the Good Samaritan stopped along the roadside to help a man he saw was badly injured. He never stopped to reason whether or not the man was faking injury, nor did he ask how the man got hurt. Instead, the Good Samaritan took the man to where he could get medical attention, paid the doctor bill in advance, and then made arrangements to pay any additional fees that might have been required. He saw someone in need, and he helped.

His help was based on love and compassion. As you allow the Holy Spirit to lead you, your decisions will be based on love, and you will feel good about saying yes.

GRACE FOR TODAY:

God's Holy Spirit will not let us be taken advantage of.

HELPING HANDS DESERVE APPLAUSE

"The more lowly your service to others, the greater you are.
To be the greatest, be a servant."

MATTHEW 23:11 TLB

Michael Johnson is, perhaps, the greatest sprinter the United States has ever produced. He holds world records in both the 200 and 400 meters, and, when he was in his prime, he was virtually unbeatable.

After retiring from competition, Johnson could have spent the rest of his life reaping the benefits, both financial and social, of his stellar career. Instead, he has dedicated much of his time to assisting the career of Jeremy Wariner, a promising young sprinter who won two gold medals at the 2004 Olympic Games in Athens, Greece.

Ironically, Johnson is assisting the man who might someday shatter his records, records that haven't been seriously threatened in several years. At the close of his sophomore collegiate season, Wariner had already run a 44-second flat 400 meters. Johnson didn't even break the 45-second barrier until his senior year.

Johnson is carrying on the tradition of novelist Sherwood Anderson, who, back in the early 1900s, coached and mentored several of America's most acclaimed novelists, including Ernest Hemingway, John Steinbeck, and William Faulkner. In all, Anderson's pupils included four Pulitzer Prize winners and five National Book Award honorees. Ironically, many of Anderson's students achieved far greater fame than he did.

In contemporary society, superstars in their various fields grab the headlines. But no one can become elite in their chosen field alone. Have you ever considered that one of your life missions might be to mentor and encourage others, helping them achieve a level of success higher than your own? The rewards you earn for such an effort might not burn as brightly as you would like, but they will likely last longer. And they will bring you the deep sense of satisfaction that comes from following Jesus' example of serving, rather than seeking to be served.

It is a noble and godly task to help others fulfill their dreams. Are you up to that task?

GRACE FOR TODAY:

God's grace is like a fine perfume or cologne: Every time we pour it on others, it ends up splashing on us.

WHAT'S YOUR GOAL?

When you decide to take a trip, you start out in one place with a goal to end up someplace else. You know where you're headed, and in most cases you have a pretty good idea of how much time it will take to get there. If not, then a road map will always fill in the gaps.

The same is true when it comes to your spiritual walk with God, only you are not sitting in the driver's seat.

When you become a Christian, God places His Holy Spirit inside you and begins a process that moves you from one degree of maturity to the next. If you allow Him and will listen to His instruction the Spirit will not only guide you in particular situations and circumstances, but will also help you understand God's Word along the way. He will lead you step by step to reaching the destination God has established for you.

On the other hand, when you have your own ideas and plans, the tendency is to try and come up with ways to make things happen. What usually follows is that you end up facing obstacles that either block your path, delay your arrival, or keep you from your destination altogether.

God does not get confused. His instructions are clear and definite. Stay focused on God and His leadings. Learn to distinguish His voice from your selfish desires, so that when He gives you instruction you will know it is Him talking, and you won't take off in the wrong direction.

I am the LORD your God, who teaches you what is best for you, who directs you in the way you should go.

ISAIAH 48:17

An Encouragement to Pray

By Charles Stanley

Some people question whether we should ask God for material things. The answer is simple. Wise parents do everything in their power to satisfy their children's needs. This goes for material needs as well as nutritional and spiritual needs. The material gifts we give our children are proof that God wants to give to us in the same way, but to a greater degree. Do we have a privilege that God has deprived himself of? No! In fact, there is no way we can outgive God, materially or any other way.

Another hang-up people have is thinking they are unworthy for God to answer their prayers. But the basis of all God's answered prayer is His love for us. Calvary settled the question of worth once and for all. According to His love, we are worthy of the greatest gift He had to give—His Son. After that, anything else we ask for is secondary.

Why do we have so much trouble believing God for the minor things in life? It is Satan who says, "Who do you think you are, to ask God for anything?"

To this question there is only one answer: "I am a child of the King. I am so worthy in the eyes of God, He sent His only begotten Son to die for me. If He died for me, certainly He will give me whatever I need."[26]

—∞—

HOLY FATHER: BY YOUR GRACE, YOU HAVE GIVEN ME EVERY GOOD GIFT, ESPECIALLY THE GIFT OF YOUR SON. NOT ONLY HAVE YOU GIVEN TO ME, YOU HAVE ALSO MADE ME WORTHY TO RECEIVE YOUR GIFTS. WHAT A WONDERFUL FATHER YOU ARE! AMEN.

[Jesus said,] "Ask and it will be given to you; seek and you will find; knock and the door will be opened to you. For everyone who asks receives; he who seeks finds; and to him who knocks, the door will be opened."

MATTHEW 7:7-8

LITTLE WHITE LIES

Let your conversation be always full of grace, seasoned with salt, so that you may know how to answer everyone.

COLOSSIANS 4:6

L ittle white lies. The Bible doesn't say much about little white lies. In fact, the Bible doesn't color code lies at all—a lie is a lie is a lie—period. But, as politically correct and polite people, we've accepted "the little white lie" as an okay part of speech. So when your best friend puts on a hideous outfit and asks you, "Do you like this on me?" Your "little white lie response" is: "Sure. Looks great!" But, in all honesty, she looks like a giant, purple grape. Or, when your dad wants to know why you were late for curfew last night, you slightly bend the truth and say, "There was a train stalled on the tracks, which cost me like fifteen minutes at least." In reality, you paused for thirty seconds as the train's caboose passed you by. You were late because you left your friend's house later than planned.

GRACE FOR TODAY:

God will help us tell the truth— just ask Him. He honestly loves us!

Lying may be common practice for many, but lying is never your ticket out of a mess. In fact, it's your all-access pass into more lies. Lying is exhausting, and it's also a sin. So stop telling lies—white or otherwise. Simply speak the truth in love, and if you mess up, remember God's grace is there for you. And that's no lie!

MORE THAN MEETS THE EYE

"People judge by outward appearance, but the LORD looks
at a person's thoughts and intentions."

1 SAMUEL 16:7 NLT

W hen it comes to clothing, some brand names convey an unwritten message about the people wearing them. One label shouts, "Go ahead, break the rules!" while another whispers, "Princess wannabe." Add a particular haircut, style of jewelry, or even a certain facial expression, and you can easily wind up labeling people, instead of clothing— jock, skater, loser, stuck up, computer geek. The list goes on and on, just like it has since the beginning of time.

The names of the labels may have changed, but the meanings behind them stay the same. There have always been the "haves" and the "have-nots," the popular crowd and the outcasts. But, when God looks at people, He doesn't see labels. He sees hearts, longing for His love.

Learning to see people the way God does is a big step toward really loving them. It begins with empathy—being able to put yourself in their place for a moment. It isn't easy. Sometimes it's hard to get beyond a style or attitude that's really different from your own. But, there's so much more going on inside than what's revealed on the outside.

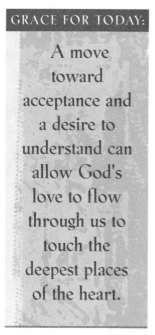

GRACE FOR TODAY:

A move toward acceptance and a desire to understand can allow God's love to flow through us to touch the deepest places of the heart.

You'll never know the whole story, the truth behind why people choose to act the way they do. But, God does. Ask Him to help you see the similarities you have with others, instead of focusing on your differences. An unspoken change in your attitude— a move toward acceptance and a desire to understand—can help others feel more comfortable and open with you. It can allow God's love to flow through you to touch the deepest places of another person's heart—places only God can see.

LOOK BEFORE YOU LEAP

Evil communications corrupt good manners.

1 CORINTHIANS 15:33 KJV

B eing part of the group was something you had looked forward to ever since your first year in high school. But now that they have asked you to hook up with them, you're not so sure joining it's the right thing to do. The wild parties. The drugs. It's not the kind of lifestyle you're use to. And it's certainly not something that your parents or God would approve of.

Then why go there?

It is never a good idea to compromise your beliefs and values just for the sake of being accepted. That's what God meant in the Bible when He warned that Christians are not to copy the behavior and customs of the world. (See Romans 12:2 NLT.)

Saying no to something you desperately want is not always the easiest thing to do. But walking away from it can be effortless and painless when the rejection is for all the right reasons.

God doesn't want your desire to belong to cause you to lose your good reputation. If it's wrong, don't be a part of it. You have already been accepted into the most important group of all—the family of God. God's love for you and His acceptance of you are permanent. You will never be rejected.

Instead, consider if this could be an opportunity to tell others about the love of God, and how He saved you from the very things they are struggling with. Not only could you be saving yourself from potential trouble, but you could be about to save someone's life.

GRACE FOR TODAY:

God's love for us, and His acceptance of us are permanent. We will never be rejected.

Being a Bad News "Bearer"

God will help you deal with whatever hard things come up
when the time comes.

Matthew 6:34 MSG

B ad news is inevitable in life. And sometimes that bad news will directly concern you: You didn't get into the college you were aiming for. You didn't make the cut for the sports team. Your "crush" started dating one of your best friends. Your parents are considering a separation.

Life has a way of handing people nuggets of information, and there are two things we can do with them. One option is to place each new worry into a big box with all the other worries—a box that you fear will overflow or perhaps even burst at its seams as its contents build up day after day. You can shake the box and hear all the worries rattling around, intermingling to form one giant mass of stress.

How about another option? You can put all your concerns in a jar labeled "Prayer." When you do this, you are, in essence, giving your worries to God. You are saying, "Father, I acknowledge that you are in control of my life. This problem is too big for me, but it's not too big for you. Not everything that comes into my life is good, but you can bring good from any circumstance."

Then, instead of fixing your attention on a big box of worries, you can focus instead on God's grace and goodness, as you trust Him to deal with your worries and guide you through times of doubt and pain.

You provide the prayer—both the calls for help and the gratitude when that help comes. God has the tough part—solving problems, quieting restless hearts, bringing peace to troubled minds. But that's okay; He's more than up to the task.

Grace for Today:

No matter what our troubles in life, God is an expert
in dealing with them.

LET HIM BLESS YOU

You want that position as head cheerleader, and you feel you deserve it. But you are hesitant to pray to God about it because you feel that somehow you have failed Him, and He won't answer your prayer.

Maybe you have been guilty of talking about someone and spreading rumors when you didn't know the truth. Or perhaps you yelled at someone or allowed your bad temper to get the best of you.

Surely, God is not going to bless me when I still have these kinds of problems, you reason.

Your problem is not just in the fact that you gossip, or that you have a quick temper. God can and will help you to get rid of those issues. The thing hindering you most is that you are basing what God will do for you on your own performance—the good you do. You think: *When I become perfect, then He will help me.*

Don't fall into that trap.

God created you, and He knows your abilities and understands your limitations. He does not expect you to do everything perfectly, nor does He look for you to be faultless. He also is not waiting for you to become good and perfect before He will bless you.

God is not motivated to bless you because of works—those things you do when others are looking so they can be impressed. But He is pleased when He sees you willing to be obedient to what He's asked you to do. God blesses you because He wants to, and because He loves you—no matter what.

GRACE FOR TODAY:

God's mercies never take a vacation. They are renewed every morning and ready to be dispensed.

He saved us, not because of the good things we did, but because of his mercy.

TITUS 3:5 NLT

154

GOD'S ANSWERS

By Charles Stanley

When God answers our prayers, He either answers with yes, no, or wait. When He answers yes, we are prone to shout, "Praise the Lord!" We tell everybody what a great thing God has done for us.

But when God says no, we have a hard time finding reasons to praise Him. We look for the sin in our lives that kept Him from granting our requests, because surely if we had been living right He would have answered yes. But not one shred of scriptural evidence shows that God will say yes to all our prayers just because we're living right. God is sovereign. He has the right to say no according to His infinite wisdom, regardless of our goodness.

But God only says no and wait when it is best for us. (See Romans 8:28.) He does it many times for our protection. Sometimes God wants to answer our prayer yes, but the timing is not right.

We don't like waiting around, especially when it looks like a unique opportunity might slip away. We don't like to hear God say no, especially when everything in us says yes, yes, yes!

But deep in our hearts we really want God's perfect will for our lives. And we must remember that God's answer is always His ultimate best for us. If He says no, then the answer is no. God is more interested in our character, our future, and our sanctification than He is in our momentary satisfaction. His answers are always an act of grace, motivated by His love.[27]

—⁂—

HEAVENLY FATHER: I WANT YOUR PERFECT WILL FOR MY LIFE—EVEN WHEN IT MEANS YOU MUST SAY NO TO SOMETHING I'VE ASKED OF YOU. I KNOW THAT YOUR PLAN FOR MY LIFE IS FAR BETTER THAN MY OWN. HELP ME AS I RESOLVE TO WALK IN THAT DIFFICULT TRUTH. AMEN.

In his heart a man plans his course, but the LORD determines his steps.

PROVERBS 16:9

MEMORABLE WISDOM

For the LORD grants wisdom!
From his mouth come knowledge and understanding.

PROVERBS 2:6 NLT

Author and humorist Martha Bolton has a book titled, *If the Pasta Wiggles, Don't Eat It.* Besides being funny, that's good advice. It's almost as good as the advice, "Don't eat yellow snow," or "Don't spit into the wind." All of these little tidbits of information will save you some embarrassing and disgusting circumstances down the road.

Many call this kind of wit "Proverbial wisdom," which refers to the Book of Proverbs in the Bible. If you've never read the Book of Proverbs, you need to jump right in! It is jam-packed with wisdom—practical stuff that will help you live a better life. Here are a couple of tidbits to whet your appetite:

God and His Word have never been more relevant than they are today.

"Whoever trusts in his riches will fall, but the righteous will thrive like a green leaf" (Proverbs 11:28).

"A cheerful heart is good medicine, but a crushed spirit dries up the bones" (Proverbs 17:22).

"Wine is a mocker and beer a brawler; whoever is led astray by them is not wise" (Proverbs 20:1).

Some people feel that the Bible is outdated with useless information, but it's not! The Bible is more relevant today than ever before. The Lord knew you'd need a roadmap to get through this life, so He left you the Bible. If you don't read the map, you just might take a wrong turn. So dive into the Word. Start reading a chapter of Proverbs every day. If you do, you'll finish in a month because there are only thirty-one chapters in that book. Jump into wisdom today!

HONEST AND TRUE

Good people are guided by their honesty.

PROVERBS 11:3 NLT

When Captain Fudge returned from a voyage at sea, it was rumored he carried with him more lies than cargo. The merchant ship commander was known for his wild imagination and even wilder tongue. Exaggeration, tall tales, and even outright lies filled his conversations, earning him the nickname, "Lying Fudge." The Captain's reputation was so well-known that if one member of the crew caught another in a lie, he'd say, "You're fudgin', aren't ya?"

Today, people "fudge" on their taxes. They fudge about their age. They fudge on exams. They fudge about what they did Saturday night. "Fudgin'" is just as common as it was back in the 1700s. But, with God there is no "fudge factor." He is honest, accurate, and true in everything He says and does. That's one reason you can trust Him.

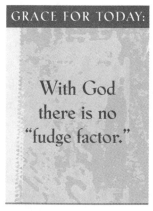

GRACE FOR TODAY:

With God there is no "fudge factor."

When you choose to live an honest life, you not only please God, but become more worthy of others' trust. You also find yourself set apart in this world. That's because plagiarizing a few sentences, giving bogus excuses, downloading music off the internet without paying for it, or exaggerating a story to keep your audience interested is such an accepted part of today's culture. But, God's way has never fit in with the crowd. It's always been counter culture. Just take a look at Jesus.

Then, take a look at your own life, honestly. Consider how well you keep promises, tell the truth, and steer clear of cheating. If there's any area where your conscience feels a twinge of guilt, ask God to help you to change your ways. The less fudge factor you have in your life, the sweeter it will be.

THE BIG GIFT BOOK

If we know that he hears us—whatever we ask—we know that we have what we asked of him.

1 JOHN 5:15

As a child, there was nothing more exciting for you than when Christmas time rolled around. Just turning the pages of the gigantic Christmas toy catalogs, and anticipating the gifts you might receive, would give you goose bumps.

Do you get that same feeling when it comes to reading your Bible? The Bible is like God's great big "gift book" to you. But unlike that holiday catalog you've been used to reading, the Bible will not leave you wondering if you will get what you want. Instead, it is a book of assurance—filled with promise after promise of things God says He will give you because He loves you.

There is no wishing, and you don't have to wonder. If He said He would do it, you can count on it. And the best part about it is you don't have to wait for a certain time of the year to receive what God has to offer you. If you are a Christian, the gifts and promises of God are yours for the asking—right now.

How cool is that?

Everyone loves to receive gifts. And you already have the greatest gift of all in Jesus Christ. But there's more on the way.

Be thankful that with God, you don't have to wish, hope, or wonder if He will do a certain thing or give you a particular desire of your heart. Get out your Bible and find out for yourself what He has in store for you on His gift list. You can take Him at His Word.

GRACE FOR TODAY:

Jesus Christ is the only gift that keeps on giving.

HELP FIGHT TRUTH DECAY

A good name is to be chosen rather than great riches,
Loving favor rather than silver and gold.

PROVERBS 22:1 NKJV

Three young scholar–athletes were visiting a large university. Each hoped for a scholarship that would pay for his education and perhaps position him for a long, profitable career in the National Football League.

During a day of meetings with coaches and the academic faculty, one of the three emerged as the clear favorite of the group. He had a higher grade point average, better test scores, and everyone was impressed with his eloquence, quick mind, and winning personality.

A small group of university staff took the young man to lunch, planning to tell him during the meal that he would be offered a scholarship. The student took his place in the school's cafeteria line. The coach watched the young man select his food, including a small square of butter. Just after placing the 25–cent square of butter on his tray, the student quickly grabbed a dinner roll and hid the butter from the cashier at the head of the line.

The dismayed coach related the episode to the rest of the staff. That afternoon the young man entered the head coach's office full of optimism. He sensed that the day had gone well for him. He imagined playing football on national television, being a big man on campus, and the money he would make upon graduation.

However, rather than offer him a scholarship, the head coach told him, "You're not the kind of young man we want at this university. Honesty and trust are vital to us, and earlier today, you demonstrated that you have a problem with honesty—at lunch."

"But, Coach," the student protested.

"Honesty is a character trait, young man," the coach countered. "Those who are honest in life's little things are honest when it comes to the big stuff too. It's the same way with dishonesty."

GRACE FOR TODAY:

God blesses honest people—and that's the truth!

LIVE GOOD, LOOK GOOD!

The images are all around you—in magazines and on TV. Even walking through the mall you notice the thin mannequins in the storefront windows.

Years have passed, yet the once-popular phrase "It's in to be thin" seems to still be a driving force when it comes to today's diet crazes and clothing styles.

If only I could control my eating habits, I could look like that, you think. *Why do I have to eat so much anyway?*

You have to eat food in order to survive. That's the way God made your body. For that matter, you also need air to breathe and water to drink. The desire to eat is triggered by hunger, a God-given function created to keep us alive. But some people are overweight because they abuse what God has given them.

First, you need to find out why you are overweight. It may be due to a medical problem. A doctor would be able to help you. Eating is a necessary part of life, but God never intended for our food cravings or our physical appearance to dominate our lives and rule over us. Some only count carbohydrates and watch their caloric intake out of pride. They want to look good to please themselves or to receive attention from others.

God, however, is more interested in how your heart—your spirit—looks. He said there are far more important things to life than the food you put in your stomach and how you look on the outside.

Yes, eat, drink, and exercise wisely for your health's sake. Look good for God because you are His child as well as His witness. He will help you bring everything under control so that you are happy and healthy.

> **GRACE FOR TODAY:**
> God wants us to look good, but it should begin on the inside—with our hearts.

I discipline my body like an athlete, training it to do what it should.

1 CORINTHIANS 9:27 NLT

GOD'S GRACE CHANGES US

By Gene Getz

" **A** s apostles of Christ we could have been a burden to you," but, said Paul, that was not true. Rather, "we were gentle among you, like a mother caring for her little children" (1 Thessalonians 2:7).

What a contrast! Could this be the same man who several years earlier was "breathing out murderous threats against the Lord's disciples," and now was using a nursing mother to illustrate his style of ministry (Acts 9:1)? What an example of God's grace! Paul was a changed man—a man of sensitivity and compassion.

It intrigues me that a man so tough, so rigid and unbending reflected this kind of gentleness. No relationship better personifies gentleness than a mother who is nursing a baby. Yet Paul was not ashamed to identify with this analogy. This confirms the depth of change that had taken place in him.

This does not mean that Paul was unwilling to be frank, straightforward,

and uncompromising. He never hesitated to confront wrongdoers—especially those whose motives were totally selfish. (See Titus 1:10–16.) But Paul resorted to this methodology when he saw no hope, or when he saw Christians being deliberately led astray be false teachers. He believed that his initial approach should be a gentle one.

By the time Paul arrived in Thessalonica, he learned a great deal about gentleness. And this Timothy observed in Paul's own ministry. With gentleness and tenderness he encouraged these Christians in their new life in Christ.[28]

—⁂—

FATHER GOD: CHANGE ME BY YOUR GRACE. MAKE OF ME THE PERSON YOU CREATED ME TO BE—A PERSON WHO IS PLEASING TO YOU AND OF SERVICE TO OTHERS. AMEN.

By the grace of God I am what I am,
and his grace to me was not without effect.

1 CORINTHIANS 15:10

WAITING ON GOD

Be still before the LORD and wait patiently for him.

PSALM 37:7

" **P** atience is a virtue." You've probably heard that expression a gazillion times in your life, but just how patient are you? Many people pray to God in this way, "God, please grant me a healthy dose of patience—NOW!"

We are an impatient society. We have instant oatmeal, instant tea, instant coffee, minute rice, etc.—and we like it. We like being able to drive through, speak into a microphone, tell the person on the other end what we want to eat, and have our hot food handed to us in a matter of minutes. We like to walk up to an ATM, punch in a few numbers, and walk away with our cash. We like being able to type in a few letters and be linked to a worldwide web of information. We like quick gratification. We want quick results.

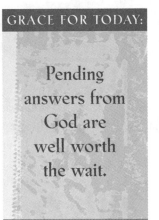

GRACE FOR TODAY:

Pending answers from God are well worth the wait.

Unfortunately, God doesn't always work that way. You can't pray, "God, I'll have a new red Hummer with an awesome sound system to go, please." Sure, He does answer prayers immediately with instantaneous results. It happens, but more often you have to wait. Sometimes, God's answer may be "not now." And, sometimes His answer is "no."

During those waiting times, have patience. Don't get mad at God. Don't whine and complain. Instead, praise God for your answered prayer. Thank Him for ordering your steps and supplying all of your needs. Thank Him for growing you up in the area of patience. Trust Him, knowing that whatever He has for you will be well worth the wait.

GIVE IT ALL YOU'VE GOT

Whatever you do, work at it with all your heart, as though you were working for the Lord and not for people.

COLOSSIANS 3:23 GNB

What might the world be like if God believed that "good enough" really was good enough? Creation would have taken place in four days instead of six, so God could enjoy a long weekend. Birds' wings would continually fall off from overuse. The law of gravity wouldn't be a law. It would simply be a suggestion. Every so often things would float up instead of falling down—including you. That is, if God got around to finishing the people He started.

Knowing God does everything with excellence is not an interesting bit of trivia. It's essential to understanding who God is. Your heavenly Father is a God who cares about details. He finishes what He starts. He leaves no loose ends. He never settles for "good enough."

Of course the fact that God is God also means that His "excellence" equals perfection. The same isn't true for people here on earth. They try and fail and learn and grow and try again. And they still may not get it quite right. Perfection is something only God can achieve.

GRACE FOR TODAY:

We serve a God who cares about details.

However, excellence is always within your reach. Excellence is simply doing the very best you can with what you have wherever you are in life. It doesn't mean that you always succeed or never make mistakes. It just means that you put your whole heart into doing whatever God has set before you. That includes everything from finishing a term paper to cleaning the kitchen to comforting a friend.

Having excellence as your aim, simply because it makes God smile, may lead you to do lots of things that others never see or appreciate. But God sees. And He knows how little things can make a big difference. Just consider His excellent molecule.

READ THE MAP

Study this Book of the Law continually. . . . Only then will you succeed.

JOSHUA 1:8 NLT

I know that building is around here somewhere. Maybe I came off the highway one exit too soon.

"Somewhere" is right. But the real question is: "Where?"

More than likely you would know where, and you would not have gotten lost had you taken the time to read a road map.

The same is true when it comes to our personal lives, where the roads we travel often lead to uncertainties. Almost daily, we are faced with situations too tough for us to handle or questions too hard for us to answer: Should I date this guy? Am I the best one suited for team captain? Is this really the right college for me?

How we arrive at answers to these and other important questions will play a major part in being successful when it comes to reaching our true goals and destinations.

Guessing which direction to take is risky because there is a possibility you will get lost or cruise off course along the way. A better solution is to let the Bible—God's Word—be your road map.

When you follow His directions, instead of being led by your own desires, the Lord promises that you will not get lost. Despite the twists and turns, no matter the detours, regardless of the side roads, you will always reach your intended destination.

Trust the Lord to direct your path. He has already mapped out the sure plan for your success. Follow it.

GRACE FOR TODAY:

God gives us all the instruction we need through His Word.

Superficial Beauty Is Pretty Ugly

I have learned, in whatsoever state I am, therewith to be content.

Philippians 4:11 KJV

A Russian boy, haunted by feelings of ugliness, gazed into his mirror and studied his reflection—wide nose, thick lips, tiny gray eyes, and oversized hands and feet. The boy was so distraught about his appearance that he begged God to work a miracle and turn him into a handsome man. He vowed that if God would transform him, he would give his Creator all that he currently possessed and all that he would earn in the future.

That Russian boy was Count Leo Tolstoy, who grew up to become one of the world's most acclaimed novelists. He is best known for epics like *War and Peace* and *Anna Karenina*.

At one point in his life, Tolstoy wrote about how he had ultimately learned, over the course of the years, that the physical beauty he once craved is not the only beauty in life. Ultimately, Tolstoy grew to regard the beauty of a strong, loving character as the most pleasing in God's eyes.

Many people today spend vast sums of money on physical appearance. Designer clothes. Tanning sessions. Laser hair removal and microsurgical hair implants. Regular Botox injections. Plastic surgery. Liposuction.

Character, in contrast, can't be bought, injected, worn, or implanted. It is a matter of living according to God's rules, being guided by His Spirit. It's a matter of doing what is right, and standing up for what is right. It's a commitment to developing the qualities you can't see by gazing into a mirror.

Grace for Today:

The beauty of a godly character will never fade. That means we can be truly beautiful forever.

DON'T CROSS THE LINE

A group has decided to skip school on Friday to hang out at the beach and has asked you to come along. "Just tell your parents you'll be going on an all-day field trip," they suggest. "We'll be back before school gets out, so no one will ever know."

Correction. Someone WILL know.

God knows all, and He sees everything. He recognizes that this is a trap the devil has set for you. And just like your schoolmates, He will be watching to see how you will respond. Thankfully, God's Holy Spirit is working on the inside to help you recognize this is wrong. You allow the Spirit to lead you and choose not to go along with them just because it sounded good. You recognize

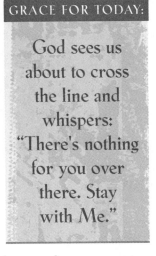

GRACE FOR TODAY:

God sees us about to cross the line and whispers: "There's nothing for you over there. Stay with Me."

temptation, despite its disguise.

There will be times when you are tempted to compromise or straddle the fence when it comes to making choices. Just remember, there is no such thing as a gray area where living godly is concerned. Either something is black, or it is white. It is either cold or hot. Right or wrong.

God is excited to see you call wrong for what it is—wrong. He is proud of you when you choose what is right, even if it means losing a friendship. And as much as you would like to join in for the sake of being accepted as part of the crowd, the compromise is not worth sacrificing your relationship with God.

Stay alert; be in prayer so you don't wander into temptation without even knowing you're in danger.

MATTHEW 26:41 MSG

HONORING GOD

By John MacArthur Jr.

We ought to keep our bodies in subjection to insure that we are honoring God. That includes controlling the way we dress and the things we do with our bodies. This principle covers the whole area of the lust of the flesh, and not just sexual things. A person can dishonor God by overdressing to attract attention. Gluttony also puts one in the position of dishonoring God and committing sin because it is obvious to everyone that the glutton cannot control the desire to eat. Nothing that gratifies the body to the dishonoring of God can have a place in the will of God.

Robert Murray McCheyne spoke at the ordination of young Dan Edwards in the 1860s. He said something like this: "Mr. Edwards, . . . do not forget the inner man, the heart. The cavalry officer knows that his life depends upon his saber, so he keeps it clean. Every stain he wipes off with the greatest care. Mr. Edwards, you are God's chosen instrument. According to your purity, so shall be your success. It is not great talent; it is not great ideas that God uses; it is great likeness to Jesus Christ. Mr. Edwards, a holy man is an awesome weapon in the hand of God" (See 2 Timothy 2:21). McCheyne was right, and God's will is that you be holy—sanctified.[29]

—∞—

DEAR LORD: THANK YOU FOR YOUR GRACE THAT COVERS ALL MY MISTAKES AND POOR CHOICES. THANK YOU FOR YOUR HOLY SPIRIT THAT HELPS ME LIVE A LIFE THAT'S PLEASING TO YOU. AMEN.

God hasn't invited us into a disorderly, unkempt life but into something holy and beautiful—as beautiful on the inside as the outside.

1 THESSALONIANS 4:7 MSG

BULLDOG DETERMINATION

Let him ask in faith, with no doubting.

JAMES 1:6 NKJV

Almost every rags-to-riches story has one thing in common—the person who comes through a winner didn't become a winner without an unfailing determination. Country singer Jimmy Wayne is one of those determined winners. Growing up in North Carolina, he lived either on the streets or in foster homes because his mother was in prison. Even as young as twelve, he was determined to help his mama, so he found ways to make money. Then he'd send her money orders in prison.

GRACE FOR TODAY:

God-given dreams are worth pursing with everything within us—and then a little more.

When his teacher whipped him three or four times a week, saying she was giving him what he didn't get at home, he shrugged it off. Now in his thirties and doing quite nicely in the country music world, he still has the report card in which she wrote: "Has not completed all his work in writing and needs extra help in it." Funny, that's how Jimmy Wayne makes his living now—writing songs.

Jimmy had a determination on the inside of him that pushed him forward. No matter how terrible his circumstances looked, he believed he'd emerge a winner. You have to know that for your life, too.

You can become so determined that nothing anyone says or does is able to cause you to waiver. People will try to discourage you from pursuing your dreams. There will be roadblocks along the way. Still, you must remain determined to go the distance. Keep your focus. Stay the course. Trust the Lord. Live your own rags-to-riches story. Nothing is impossible with Him.

OWNERSHIP OVERLOAD

[Jesus said,] "Real life is not measured by how much we own."

LUKE 12:15 NLT

At first glance, you might say Francesco had everything a teen could ever want. His father was a wealthy businessman who spoiled his son with privileges and possessions at a time when others often went hungry. Francesco spent his days partying with friends and spending money on whatever was "in" at the turn of the thirteenth century. But it still wasn't enough. Francesco wanted to be worshipped like a prince.

He decided to become a knight in the religious crusades, which meant he needed a suit of armor and a horse. But Francesco wouldn't settle for any suit of armor. He wanted his trimmed in gold—which, of course, his father quickly provided. When Francesco left his hometown, he boasted to everyone that he'd return even richer than before, perhaps as a prince.

But that night in a dream, Francesco heard God telling him to return home. The dream was so vivid that Francesco immediately did what he believed he was told. When he returned, the village called him a coward, and his father disowned him for wasting so much money on a suit of armor he never used. Francesco retreated to a cave and cried out to God over the life he'd lived.

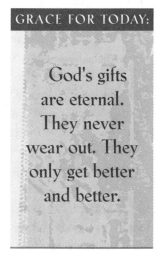

GRACE FOR TODAY:

God's gifts are eternal. They never wear out. They only get better and better.

But Francesco left that cave a richer man than he'd ever been before. Francesco became known as Saint Francis of Assisi, a person who believed that worshipping God and loving others were the only things he needed in this world.

Owning things isn't bad. But when your possessions begin to own you, they can drown out the sound of God's voice in your life. Allow God to loosen your grip on any "thing" you feel you could never live without. In God's kingdom, you're already royalty—and have everything you need.

STOP TRYING!

I will put my Spirit in you so you will obey my laws and
do whatever I command.

EZEKIEL 36:27 NLT

As a Christian you hope that the kids in your neighborhood and your school have observed your good conduct. You have done your best to obey all the things your parents taught you, being careful to keep the smallest detail. You didn't smoke. You didn't drink. Why, if there was a school social you did not dance because you thought it was not the Christian thing to do.

Before others, you were the "perfect" Christian. But on the inside, there was a secret longing to do the very things you had been programmed to stay away from.

Now, a feeling of guilt has you crying out to God and promising never to disappoint Him again by longing for things that are "bad."

God's love for you is not based on whether you think good thoughts or bad, or if you do right or wrong. Sure, He expects you to make right decisions and to think about things that are true, honorable, and right. But that's why you have been given His Holy Spirit.

Wrong thoughts or deeds do not automatically alienate you from God, neither will He condemn you for committing them. When you mess up, He wants you to come to Him. It is commendable that you want to please God in every way possible. But don't be so hard on yourself that you are less forgiving of yourself than God is. Your relationship with God is not about following the rules and regulations, but truly wanting to know Him better.

GRACE FOR TODAY:

God wants us to know Him better—with that focus,
we can always follow the right road for our lives.

A FRIEND IN HIGH PLACES

I can do all things through Christ who strengthens me.

PHILIPPIANS 4:13 NKJV

I f you have had an astronomy class in your academic career, you probably have some idea about the vastness of space. For example:

Astronomers have discovered galaxies that are billions and billions of light years away from ours. When you gaze up at the stars at night, do you realize that the light you are seeing from some of them is actually thousands of years old? Some stars are so old, in fact, that by the time their light reaches us, they have already died or collapsed.

We tend to think of our sun as a major entity, but it's actually rather mediocre, as stars go. For example, the star Eta Carinae outshines the sun the same way a raging forest fire outshines a lone birthday candle.

The universe is populated with neutron stars so dense that one teaspoon of its matter weighs tons—as much, in fact, as 3,000 aircraft carriers!

Who wouldn't marvel at the power of a God who created a universe so vast and spectacular? But, have you stopped to realize that all of that power is available to you? The Bible says that the same extraordinary power God used to raise Jesus from the dead can be tapped into by His followers.

So don't let life's challenges overwhelm you. Next time you gaze up at the stars, remember that you truly have a Friend in high places. Face today's problems with today's God-given strength and wisdom. Don't spend time or energy worrying about future troubles. Some of them won't even come about. And with the others, God will provide for you when the time is right. Remember that God's guidance is a light unto our feet, not a high-intensity spotlight that penetrates miles into the future.

GRACE FOR TODAY:

The God who established the universe wants to establish our lives' path, one day at a time, one step at a time.

FRETTING: BEST USED WITH GUITARS

A businessman once made a "Worry Chart," on which he recorded all of his various troubles and woes. After a year of this worrisome task, he decided to tabulate the results. Know what he discovered?

The businessman found that forty percent of his anxieties turned out to be things that either didn't happen or were unlikely to happen in the future. Thirty percent of his worries centered on decisions he had made—and could not "unmake." Twelve percent were based on people's criticism of him, and ten percent concerned his future health—including getting an ulcer from too much worrying! And only about half of this ten percent were items over which the man had any control.

When the tabulating and analyzing was done, the businessman concluded

GRACE FOR TODAY:

From God's perspective even the biggest challenges we face are attainable because He knows we can.

that only about eight percent of his past year's worries had been legitimate.

What are your worries as you sit reading this book today? Whatever they are, consider converting your worry time to prayer time. Seek God's perspective, God's wisdom, God's peace. It's amazing how much stress can be alleviated when God's people talk with Him about their concerns, give them over to His care.

One final thought: Don't add worrying about how to pray to your list of concerns. If you can't find the right words to express your troubles, your emotions, to God, be at peace. He knows your heart and mind and hears you even when you don't speak. You can just sit quietly and soak up His goodness.

Therefore I tell you, do not worry about your life, what you will eat or drink; or about your body, what you will wear. Is not life more important than food, and the body more important than clothes?

MATTHEW 6:25

PLANNED NEGLECT

By John MacArthur Jr.

T he more you study the Word of God, the more it saturates your mind and life. Someone asked a concert violinist in New York's Carnegie Hall how she became so skilled. She said that it was by "planned neglect." She planned to neglect everything that was not related to her goal.

Some less important things in your life could stand some planned neglect so that you might give yourself to studying the Word of God. Do you know what would happen? The more you would study the Word of God, the more your mind would be saturated with it. It will be no problem then for you to think of Christ. You won't be able to stop thinking of Him.

To be Spirit-filled is to live a Christ-conscious life, and there is no shortcut to that. You can't go and get yourself super-dedicated to live a Christ-conscious life. The only way you can be saturated with the thoughts of Christ is to saturate yourself with the Book that is all about Him. And this is God's will, that you not only be saved but that you also be Spirit-filled.[30]

—⁓—

HEAVENLY FATHER: THANK YOU FOR SHOWING ME WHEN I HAVE BECOME TOO CONCERNED WITH OTHER THINGS AND FORGETFUL OF YOUR WORD, WHICH OPENS TO ME THE UNDERSTANDING OF YOUR GRACE IN MY LIFE. HELP ME TO LEARN AND PRACTICE THE PRINCIPLE OF PLANNED NEGLECT. AMEN.

[Jesus said,] "Others, like seed sown on good soil, hear the word, accept it, and produce a crop—thirty, sixty or even a hundred times what was sown."

MARK 4:20

HOPE HAPPENS

God will help you overflow with hope in him through
the Holy Spirit's power within you.

ROMANS 15:13 TLB

W hen you were younger, did you ever wake up in the middle of the night and find your own bedroom terrifying? Did unfamiliar shapes, shadows, and sounds cause you to freeze in fear, seemingly unable to move? Were you shocked at how a once-familiar place, your own room, could be transformed into a chamber of horrors?

GRACE FOR TODAY:

With God's love active in our lives, hope happens here; hope happens now.

But what happened when morning came and the rising sun poured in its light? The shadows disappeared, and the once-terrifying shapes became familiar again. The troll crouching in the corner was just a mound of dirty laundry. The huge stranger lurking in the closet was just a coat on a hanger.

And the sounds—the clicks, groans, and rumbles—weren't nearly so terrifying in the bright light of day, were they?

That's the way God's hope is. It floods into your world, warming and illuminating everything in its path, chasing away cold, evil, and despair.

Hope is a gift that God loves to give. He enjoys surprising us by fulfilling our hopes—and even granting us more than we could ever hope for or imagine. He let an old man named Simeon fulfill a lifelong dream by holding the Christ child before he passed away. He granted another old man, Abraham, a son when he and his wife were well beyond childbearing years. He turned Joseph from a slave to a mighty ruler.

Who knows how God might fulfill and surpass your hopes? It might surprise you, but it will happen. So never, never, never give up hope.

HANDLE WITH CARE

Out of the abundance of the heart the mouth speaks.

MATTHEW 12:34 NKJV

You can start a wildfire without a match in your hand. All you have to do is open your mouth. The Bible says that words can rage out of control like a fire, cut like a sword, pierce like an arrow, poison like a snake, or destroy like a wrecking ball. But it also says words can comfort, heal, encourage, instruct, praise, and build. The choice is up to you.

Every conversation you have and every comment you make has power. It may not feel that way. After all, talking feels almost like a reflex. You think, "I'm not giving a prepared speech for forensics class. I'm just chatting with a friend." But the truth is that playing with words is as dangerous as playing with a knife.

A knife can be used to make a sandwich or inflict a fatal wound. It just depends on how you use it. Before your parents let you hold a knife in your hands, they made sure you knew how to use it carefully. But God allows words to be handled by toddlers—and teens—as well as adults. He knows that as you mature, you have the opportunity to learn how to use words wisely and well. And with God's Spirit in your life, you have a built in Guide to help you know when to speak and when to hold your tongue.

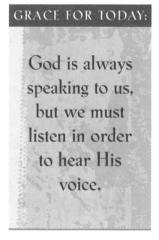

GRACE FOR TODAY:

God is always speaking to us, but we must listen in order to hear His voice.

Listen for that Guide. To hear His whisper, you may have to respond a bit more slowly, taking time to put thought into what you're going to say. As God changes your heart, making it more like His, you'll notice your words will be changing too. They'll become something that draws others closer to God and to you.

LEAST OF ALL

By God's special favor and mighty power, I have been given the wonderful privilege of serving Him.

EPHESIANS 3:7 NLT

Y ou are surprised and shocked to learn that someone with far less experience
than you has been chosen for a position you were hoping for.

He is nowhere near as qualified as I am, you complain to yourself. *They'll see they were
wrong. That guy is sure to fail.*

Fortunately, God does not resort to that kind of thinking when it comes to deciding who is best suited for the job. His system of choosing has nothing to do with how
strong, how intelligent, or how good looking a person might be. In fact, it really does-
n't matter to Him whether or not you have any experience in the area He assigns you
to.

The Bible says God makes a habit of choosing ordinary people—those who aren't
necessarily trained professionals, but who are willing to trust and obey Him. Then, He
works alongside them and causes them to do extraordinary things.

Before being critical of someone else, think about yourself for a moment. How
qualified were you to be called a Christian when God saved you? What had you done
that would have convinced Him that you deserved His love and mercy?

Others may not have seen you as a likely candidate for salvation, but God did.
That's how love and mercy work.

In our sinful state, none of us deserved the love and kindness of God. Yet, He gave
it to us. And now that we are serving Him, He will use us in ways we never imagined.

GRACE FOR TODAY:

God chose each one of us because He wanted to,
not because He had to.

HARMONY IS HEAVENLY

Live in harmony with one another.

1 PETER 3:8

I f you were given millions of dollars and told to start your own company, what kind of people would you hire? Which of your friends, classmates, or teammates would you want on your team? Businessman Andrew Carnegie, founder of Carnegie Steel, was able to assemble the greatest private-enterprise leadership team of his day. And to achieve this feat, he looked far beyond his immediate circle of friends and acquaintances.

Carnegie searched the world for the top women and men in their various fields of expertise. At one point, he found a chemist in Germany, a man who was known as the best of the best. Carnegie lured the chemist away from his current job by doubling his salary, giving him a new house, and providing the security of a five-year employment contract.

However, after only three months, Carnegie called the chemist into his office and fired him. He bought out the rest of the man's contract and paid his moving expenses back to Germany.

Why would a smart businessman like Carnegie forfeit his substantial investment and remove an elite scientist from his company? Because, as Carnegie and the chemist's new coworkers quickly discovered, the man was impossible to get along with. He constantly argued with his colleagues, hindering the company's progress and making lives miserable in the process.

Explaining his decision, Carnegie strongly declared, "I will not have anyone work for me, especially in a leadership position, who does not have the quality of being able to get along with others."

If you will be a peacemaker at home, at school, and everywhere else, you have the Lord's promise that you will be blessed.

GRACE FOR TODAY:

The peace of God sings a song of life, and the harmony is beautiful.

SEEING IN THE DARK

One night, a group of people staying in a remote tropical resort were evacuated from their building. All of the power was shut off due to a gas leak, and it was imperative for everyone to get as far away from the resort as possible—and as quickly as possible.

As the guests clustered outside, an assistant manager ordered, "It's pitch black out tonight, so everyone stay together and follow me. We must go right away; it would be too dangerous and time-consuming to go back into the building and try to find a flashlight."

"But we can't see anything," one guest protested. "Our eyes haven't adjusted to the dark yet—they're useless."

"It's okay," the assistant manager replied. "Let me be your eyes. I have been outside on my break; I can see in this darkness. Besides, I know this country well. I can lead you to safety. Just stay close to me; stay close to the sound of my voice."

The guests obeyed—although many of them were afraid and confused for the entire journey—but eventually arrived safely to another resort. The guide in this story didn't get rid of all the thick jungle foliage. Nor did he rid the area of wild animals and poisonous spiders and snakes. But he did make sure he led his charges to their destination.

Jesus is like the guide in this story. He doesn't give us the gift of a danger-free, obstacle-free life. Instead, He gives us the gift of himself. He promises to serve as our guide on every step of life's journey.

GRACE FOR TODAY:

God doesn't smooth out all of life's bumpy terrain, but He does lead us over it.

The LORD will guide you continually, watering your life when you are dry and keeping you healthy, too. You will be like a well-watered garden, like an ever-flowing spring.

ISAIAH 58:11 NLT

FREE FOR ALL

By John Wesley

The grace or love of God, that our salvation comes from, is free in all, and free for all. It is free in all to whom it is given. It does not depend on any power or merit in us; no, not in any degree, neither in whole, nor in part. It does not in anyway depend either on the good works or righteousness of the receiver; not on anything they have done, or anything they are.

Receiving God's love and grace does not depend on a person's endeavors. It does not depend on their good temper, or good desires, or good purposes and intentions; for all these flow from the free grace of God; they are the streams only, not the fountain. They are the fruits of free grace, and not the root. They are not the cause, but the effects of it.

Whatever good is in us, or is done by us, God is the author and doer of it. Thus is His grace free in all, that is, no way depending on any power or merit in us, but on God alone, who freely gave us His own Son, and with Him freely giveth us all things.[31]

—⁓—

FATHER GOD: THANK YOU FOR SAVING ME WHEN I COULD NOT SAVE MYSELF. I KNOW THAT I DON'T DESERVE YOUR LOVE AND GRACE BUT YOU HAVE GIVEN IT TO ME DESPITE MY UNWORTHINESS. I WILL CALL UPON THAT GRACE EVERY DAY AS I WALK OUT MY SALVATION. AMEN.

God is able to make all grace abound to you, so that in all things at all times, having all that you need, you will abound in every good work.

2 CORINTHIANS 9:8

JOY INFUSION

Do not be grieved, for the joy of the LORD is your strength.

NEHEMIAH 8:10 NASB

The Bible tells us that the devil comes to kill, steal, and destroy; and one of the things the devil loves to take from Christians is their joy. He knows the joy of the Lord is our strength. He will try to do everything he can to steal your joy. That's why you have to identify your joy stealers and limit their entrance into your life. For instance, if crowded rooms annoy you, then you should avoid situations that involve large crowds. If there is a certain person who aggravates you, then you should limit your time with that person. (And, if you have to be around that person, pray for an extra dose of patience and kindness.)

GRACE FOR TODAY:

God has an endless supply of joy awaiting us, and the devil can't steal it if we won't let him.

God want to give you a daily infusion of joy. It's easy when you keep your heart and head full of the Word of God. Meditate on scriptures that deal with joy such as: "You will show me the path of life; In Your presence is fullness of joy; At Your right hand are pleasures forevermore" (Psalm 16:11 NKJV).

There are some natural things you can do that will also help keep your joy at an optimum level. Make sure you get enough sleep each night. Exercise on a regular basis. Eat a nutritionally–balanced diet. Drink plenty of water. Don't overload your schedule with too many activities, which can lead to stress. Surround yourself with positive people. Last, make time to laugh each day. If you're running low on joy today, it's time for a joy infusion.

THE INVITATION OF BEAUTY

Let the beauty of the LORD our God be upon us.

PSALM 90:17 NKJV

God is strong and powerful. He's a Warrior who fights for you, a King who rules over all of creation. His voice thunders. His breath bestows life. His word stands immoveable. He's so immense He can hold the oceans in the palm of His hand or measure the heavens with His fingertips. But, God is more than just mighty. He's also beautiful.

God's beauty isn't something people talk much about. Maybe it's because beauty doesn't seem all that important or necessary. Beauty doesn't help defeat enemies, heal broken hearts, or draw us closer to God. Then again, maybe it does.

Think back to a time in your life when you were struck by the incredible beauty of God's handiwork—a dazzling sunset, a galloping stallion, the smile of someone you love. You're drawn to beauty because it reflects the nature of the one who made it. When beauty captures your eye, and your heart, you do what you were designed to do. You worship God.

Not everyone is aware that God is the one they are responding to when they appreciate beauty. Some people just know that beauty lifts their spirits. It makes them forget their problems for awhile. It helps give them the strength to stop, take a deep breath, and go back to fight whatever personal battle they may be dealing with at the moment.

GRACE FOR TODAY:

Beauty is God's fingerprint on all He's made.

Beauty matters. It has a gentle power and strength that brute force cannot equal. Look for it today in your surroundings and in the faces of those around you. Then praise God, the most beautiful of all, for sharing it with you.

AVOID THE SNARES

A man's mind plans his way,
but the Lord directs his steps and makes them sure.

PROVERBS 16:9 AMP

Taking on new challenges has never been a problem for you. After all, you've always looked to God for help, and He has always given you the strength to get through—no matter how big or how small the assignment might have been.

But for some reason, taking on the responsibility of organizing the senior prom has not been so easy. Nothing you do seems to turn out right. Even the members of the planning committee seem to oppose you at every turn.

Sometimes, in our zeal to show God how good we are at handling things, we go overboard. We think God is handing out the assignment, when in reality we are tempted by pride. The devil will use that to expose our weaknesses and inabilities and, at the same time, cause us to see ourselves as failures.

The result is that we sink into despair and want to quit altogether.

Remember, you are God's workmanship. His masterpiece. He knows your limitations and would never ever set you up to fail. Taking on responsibility is just like giving your word. Your reputation is on the line.

Before you agree to accept responsibility, take a moment to pray and ask God if this is something He wants you to do. If you have peace about it, then go ahead. God will be right there to back you up.

If not, then offer a polite "no." There will be plenty of other opportunities.

GRACE FOR TODAY:

Every plan God has for us is assured success.

HUMBLE PIE: A HEAVENLY DESSERT

Whoever wishes to become great among you shall be your servant.

MATTHEW 20:26 NASB

To some teens, life is all about popularity, material possessions, and living large. They strive to have the most influential friends, wear the hottest designer clothes, and drive the most expensive cars. They want to be named sports MVP, selected for lead roles in the school play, or voted homecoming king or queen.

There's nothing wrong with achieving success in what we do or having good things, as long as these things are kept in perspective. It's possible for people's possessions to start possessing them! And it's important to remember that God's standards for success differ markedly from those of the image seekers.

The Bible is filled with principles like these:

The people who always want to be first will end up being last—and those who willingly take the behind-the-scenes roles, do the "grunt work," will someday be honored for their humility and lack of greed.

Small seeds can grow into great trees.

One lost, forlorn sheep takes priority over the whole flock.

The Bible encourages people to "walk humbly"—not strut around with the attitude "I'm better than everyone else; I'm special!" If you walk humbly, being grateful for what you have and keeping an eye out for those who might need help or encouragement, you will become increasingly in tune with God's character.

How do you want to be remembered after you graduate from high school and move on to college or to a job? Don't you want to be remembered as the person who always had a smile for a discouraged classmate, was eager to volunteer for community service projects, cared more about shining the spotlight on others than hogging it for yourself?

The decision is yours.

GRACE FOR TODAY:

God pours out His grace on us so that we can pass it on to others.

ENOUGH IS ENOUGH

Imagine the following question showed up on a final exam at school: I will be completely happy as soon as _____. How would you answer that one?

"As soon as I have a high-paying job?"

"As soon as I am famous?"

"As soon as I am physically perfect?"

"As soon as I fall in love with someone who loves me back?"

"As soon as I can get out of my hometown and live somewhere cool?"

Now, here's another question for you: What if your answer to the question above never comes? Do you think you would be plagued by discontent if that blank up there remains blank? If your answer is yes, please consider this: You have a God who always cares about you, always listens to you. You have access to His Holy Spirit—and to a home in heaven with your name on it.

All your sins can be forgiven and forgotten. In times of trouble, you have God's promise that He will never leave you or forsake you.

The Lord has promised that He will give us life, and give it to us abundantly. If the missing object of happiness above is part of God's abundant-life equation for you, it will be yours. But if it isn't, don't let yourself be locked in the cold room of discontent.

In other words, if your ship doesn't come in, don't whine, "Where's my ship?" Instead, ask yourself, "Why am I looking for a ship in the first place? Maybe the true key to my happiness is right here on dry land."

> GRACE FOR TODAY:
>
> **What we have because Jesus is our friend and savior is far greater than anything we might not have in this life.**

The LORD is my Shepherd; I shall not want.

PSALM 23:1 NKJV

THE PEACE THAT GUARDS OUR HEARTS

By John MacArthur Jr.

John Bunyan's allegory *The Holy War* illustrates how God's peace guards the believer's heart from anxiety, doubt, fear, and distress. In it Mr. God's-Peace was appointed to guard the city of Mansoul. As long as Mr. God's-Peace ruled, Mansoul enjoyed harmony, happiness, joy, and health. However, Prince Emmanuel (Christ) went away because Mansoul grieved Him. Consequently, Mr. God's-Peace resigned his commission, and chaos resulted.

The believer who doesn't live in the confidence of God's sovereignty will lack God's peace and be left to the chaos of a troubled heart. But our confident trust in the Lord will allow us to thank Him in the midst of trials because we have God's peace on duty to protect our hearts.

During World War II, an armed German freighter picked up a missionary whose ship had been torpedoed. He was put into the hold. For a while he was too terrified to even close his eyes. Sensing the need to adjust his perspective, he tells us how he got through the night: "I began communing with the Lord. He reminded me of His word in the 121st Psalm: "He who keeps you will not slumber. Behold He . . . Will neither slumber nor sleep' (vv. 2-4, NASB). So I said, 'Lord there isn't really any use for both of us to stay awake tonight. If You are going to keep watch, I'll thank Thee for some sleep!'"[32]

He replaced his fear and anxiety with thankful prayer, and the peace of God that resulted enabled him to sleep soundly. You too will enjoy peace and rest when you cultivate the habit of looking to God with a grateful heart.[33]

—⁊⁊⁊—

HEAVENLY FATHER: BY YOUR GRACE YOU HAVE PROVIDED PERFECT PEACE FOR MY TROUBLED AND CHAOTIC HEART. I THANK YOU FOR YOUR UNINTERRUPTED, WATCHFUL CARE THAT ALLOWS ME TO REST PEACEFULLY. AMEN.

The peace of God, which transcends all understanding, will guard your hearts and your minds in Christ Jesus.

PHILIPPIANS 4:7

GO FOR IT!

When I am weak, then I am strong.

2 CORINTHIANS 12:10 NLT

When Marla Runyan was thirty-one years old, she became one of America's greatest success stories, finishing third at the Olympic trials in Sacramento, California, in July 2000. Was it her fast time? No. Was it her running style? No. Was it her determination? You bet. Marla made the U. S. Olympic team even though she was legally blind.

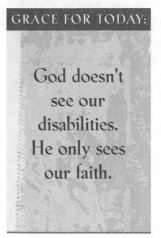

GRACE FOR TODAY:

God doesn't see our disabilities. He only sees our faith.

Marla has been blind since she was nine, yet she's never let her disability stop her. She has participated in sports since she was a child, focusing on track and field for the past fourteen years. When Marla made the Olympic team, she became an inspiration for millions of other people with disabilities. Almost immediately, she began receiving e-mails and cards from people around the world—especially others who suffered from the same disease she suffers, Stargardt's. Marla didn't plan on being anyone's role model—she just wanted to compete. She just wanted the chance to go for her dreams, and that's exactly what she was given.

Maybe you are different from others. Maybe you're crippled by fear of failure. Whatever your disability, it's no problem for God. He says in the Bible that you are more than a conqueror in Him. So, start acting like it! Go for your dreams. Don't be hindered by anything. Instead, let God turn your inability into a positive. Remember, He is made strong in our weakness. He doesn't need your ability; He only needs your faith and availability. You can do all things through Him!

Little Deeds Can Fill Great Needs

Whoever is kind to the needy honors God.

Proverbs 14:31

E lizabeth Fry looked like a teenage rebel to many people in her conservative Quaker church. Her purple boots laced in red stood out among the drab black and gray outfits the other girls wore. Little did those around her realize that it was Elizabeth's life that would soon stand out, an example of God's love in action that would change the lives of thousands.

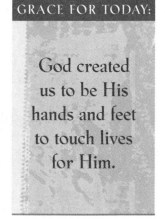

GRACE FOR TODAY:

God created us to be His hands and feet to touch lives for Him.

When she was eighteen years old, Elizabeth felt that God wanted her to devote her life to helping those in need. She'd heard stories about Newgate Women's prison in London, but nothing prepared her for what she saw with her own eyes. Over three hundred women and children were crowded into two small wards. They slept on bare stone floors. Many of the children had no clothing and were covered with filth.

Elizabeth worked for prison reform, providing clothing, Bible studies, and educational programs that helped restore the prisoners' self-respect. Throughout her life, Elizabeth championed many other social programs, such as helping women on death row, establishing a homeless shelter, opening schools, and improving hospital conditions. Along with helping others, Elizabeth also gave birth to twelve children of her own. During the 1800s, it was unusual for women to play important roles outside their own home, but Elizabeth not only helped change her community, but won its respect.

God used the teen in the purple boots to change countless lives. He can use you, too. It doesn't matter if your efforts help one person or one thousand. Every person is of worth in God's eyes. Share the love and the gifts God's given you with those in need. Who knows? God may want you to be the answer to one of His children's prayers.

How's the Fruit?

When the Holy Spirit controls our lives, he will produce . . .
love, joy, peace, patience, kindness, goodness, faithfulness, gentleness,
and self-control.

GALATIANS 5:22-23 NLT

The words came so fast you could hardly remember what was said. But more surprising was the fact that your best friend had verbally attacked you in front of everyone in the classroom.

Immediately, you feel anger set in, and you start thinking of what you can say in return. But the words will not come.

First, you remember where you are. Then, more importantly you remember who you are—God's child who is like a spiritual tree that grows fruit of the Spirit. Right now, others are about to sample the fruit from your spiritual tree by watching and waiting for your response. What will your fruit taste like?

Jesus faced worse abuse than what you have just experienced, yet He never fought back with words. Rather, He chose to forgive those who opposed Him and show them love.

God expects the same response from you, and He will help you.

As a Christian, you can expect to face spiritual warfare of one kind or another. That's a main priority with the devil. He loves to try to discredit God's children—especially in front of others because he knows they will be watching to see what kind of show you will put on.

If it's a show they want, then give them one.

Instead of retaliating with a barrage of abusive words that will make you look as silly as your attacker, give your observers and the devil a clear picture of the fruit of God's love in action. Pray for them, and then show love by forgiving the offense against you.

GRACE FOR TODAY:

God's love in us produces good fruit!

CAN YOU GO THE DISTANCE?

Let us run with perseverance the race marked out for us.

HEBREWS 12:1

The twentyfirst century is an age of immediate gratification. We have instant cappuccino, microwave dinners, and instant messaging. First-class mail, once the fastest way to send information, is now dubbed "snail mail."

There's a drive-through for nearly every product or service and same-day delivery for nearly everything we might want to purchase.

However, there's no Instant Formula, no "Sixty-Second" approach to true success in life (despite what you might hear on those late-night info-mercials. Many people have chased get-rich-quick schemes, only to "get disappointed"-quick. Others have trusted "fast-n-easy" plans to get fit and lose weight—and realized that the only thing that got lighter was their bank account.

Becoming proficient in any discipline takes time. So does improving your level of health and fitness. You must invest time into learning new skills and refining old ones.

So don't let anyone deceive you with too-good-to-be-true claims. Don't try to climb the ladder to success too quickly. Because if that ladder isn't secure—and you don't proceed carefully—you might slip and fall.

Life's most worthwhile goals aren't achieved overnight. Accomplishing them is a process, not an instantaneous transformation. So learn to enjoy the process. Enjoy those working toward similar goals. Appreciate the people who are helping you toward your goals. Relish the confidence you build day by day, week by week, as you become better and better in your chosen endeavors.

Life is a marathon, not a 40-yard dash. It's not a race won by the flashiest and quickest. The ultimate victory will go to those who just keep on running.

GRACE FOR TODAY:

God's love and mercy never give up on us!

THE UNCOMMONLY GOOD COMMON LIFE

Most likely, you began today in unspectacular fashion. Your own private robot didn't roll into your room and wake you by playing a selection of your favorite songs on its on-board, state-of-the-art sound system.

You probably didn't begin the day with a brisk workout and yoga session with a live-in personal trainer—followed by a massage from your masseuse. A private chef didn't cook your favorite breakfast, complete with fresh-squeezed orange juice and imported Swiss hot chocolate and pastries flown in from France.

And, when it was time to head to school or work, chances are that you left a house, dorm, or apartment—not a mansion. And your mode of transportation was not a stretch limo piloted by your personal chauffeur.

GRACE FOR TODAY:

The difference between an ordinary life and an extraordinary one is the "extra" care we take to appreciate God's blessings.

In short, your day—like your life—has probably been rather common. But that doesn't mean it has to be mundane or ordinary. In every day, God provides dozens of small blessings for those with eyes to see them, hearts to appreciate them. The warmth of a friend's smile. The camaraderie of sharing a meal or a favorite TV show with family members. The beauty of a sunset. The glory of a sunrise. The comfort of crawling into a warm bed after a busy day.

So the next time your life seems too dull, too common, look past the surface elements of life to the hidden blessings. A common life can be uncommonly good. You just need to live it the right way.

My grace is sufficient for thee:
for my strength is made perfect in weakness.

2 CORINTHIANS 12:9 KJV

OUR BEST GIFTS

By Matthew Henry

The first appearance of God to Moses found him tending sheep. Formerly Moses thought himself able to deliver Israel, and set himself to the work too hastily. Now, when he is the best person on earth for it, he knows his own weakness. This was the effect of more knowledge of God and of himself. Formerly, self-confidence mingled with strong faith and great zeal, now sinful distrust of God crept in under the garb of humility. But all his objections are answered by God with, "Certainly I will be with you. That is enough."

Moses continued going backward to the work God designed for him because there was much cowardice, laziness, and unbelief in him. We must not judge people by the readiness of their talk. A great deal of wisdom and true worth may be with a slow tongue. God sometimes makes choice of these people as His messengers, who have the least advantages of art or nature, so that His grace in them may appear the more glorious. Christ's disciples were no orators, until the Holy Spirit made them such. God condescends to answer the excuse of Moses. Even self-diffidence, when it stops us from or slows down our duty, is very displeasing to the Lord. But while we blame Moses for shrinking from this dangerous service, let us ask our own hearts if we are not neglecting duties easier and less perilous. The tongue of Aaron, with the head and heart of Moses, would make one completely fit for this errand.

God promises, I will be with your mouth and with his mouth. Even Aaron, who could speak well, yet could not speak to purpose, unless God gave constant teaching and help. For without the constant aid of Divine grace, the best gifts will fail.

—⟡—

DEAR LORD: I'M SO GLAD THAT YOUR GRACE EXTENDS TO THE WORDS OF MY MOUTH. HELP ME SPEAK BOLDLY FOR YOU. AMEN.

If you could find someone whose speech was perfectly true, you'd have a perfect person, in perfect control of life.

JAMES 3:2 MSG

MOUNTAIN MOVING FAITH

The mountains melt like wax before the LORD,
before the Lord of all the earth.

PSALM 97:5

F or more than thirty years, John Amatt has led expeditions to remote regions of Northern Norway, Peru, Nepal, China, and Greenland—and has explored areas of the Arctic on more than six occasions. In 1981, he was the leader of the first Canadian mountaineering expedition to Western China, which conquered the 24,757-foot Mount Muztagata—the highest peak in the world to have ever been ascended and descended entirely on skis. John has also climbed Everest—a feat very few ever realize. Since that accomplishment, he has been a motivational speaker, encouraging others to "Climb Your Own Everest."

GRACE FOR TODAY:

No mountain is too big when God is on our side.

What is your Everest today? Are you facing something that seems overwhelming? Are you battling a serious illness? Are you hooked on drugs? Whatever your mountain is, God is well able to cause that mountain to crash into the sea. He is bigger than any mountain in your life. Sure it may look bad now, but like the old expression goes, "It's always darkest before the dawn." If you're a Christian, you've got the God advantage. You have the all-powerful One on your side. It's a fixed fight, and you win!

Pastor Joel Osteen of Lakewood Church in Houston, Texas, often says, "Stop talking about how big your mountain is and start telling your mountain how big your God is." In other words, get a faith perspective. Your Everest is no match for your God. The Bible says that you are more than a conqueror. You are strong in the Lord. No matter what you're going through today, you can overcome it with God.

CONFIDENCE IN A KING

You have been my hope, O Sovereign LORD,
my confidence since my youth.

PSALM 71:5

H as your room ever been such a mess that you misplaced something valuable? That happened to the people of Israel. They neglected God's temple for so long they misplaced the scrolls of God's law. They not only misplaced them, they forgot about them altogether—until King Josiah came along.

Josiah became king when he was only eight years old. A pretty big job for a little kid, especially since his father and grandfather had been horrible kings who'd led the kingdom of Judah to worship idols, instead of God. But, Josiah was different. He wanted to do what pleased God, instead of himself.

When he was twenty-six, Josiah noticed God's temple needed repairs. During the work, the scrolls were rediscovered. Immediately Josiah had God's law read aloud to him. His heart broke over how far his kingdom had wandered away from what God asked them to do.

King Josiah called the kingdom together so everyone could hear the words of God's law. Then, he went into action. He not only cleaned up the temple, he cleaned up the whole kingdom. King Josiah had foreign idols throughout the kingdom destroyed. It was a risky move. The people could have turned against him, just like they had against God. But Josiah moved forward with confidence. His confidence wasn't based on his own abilities, but on God's character and plan.

GRACE FOR TODAY:

God's confidence is BIG in us to do all He's called us to do.

Where does your confidence lie? God's given you special talents. He's determined your IQ, and your economic and genetic background. You have the opportunity to use all of these gifts to the best of your ability. But they are not your most important asset. Place your confidence in God and His love for you, instead of your own capabilities. He's a King who will never lead you the wrong way.

TURN ON THE LIGHT

Let your good deeds shine out for all to see.

MATTHEW 5:16 NLT

The day you joined the football team was special enough. But it became even more special when you learned the team captain was a fellow Christian. Almost immediately, the two of you established a bond, sharing scriptures and talking about how good God has been to you and your family.

Now, you're picking up little signals through things he does and says that your friend may not be walking as close to God as he led you to believe.

You may be disappointed that your friend is not what you believed him to be. But don't be too surprised. Many people claim to have a strong relationship with God after they become Christians. But in reality, their relationships are based on head knowledge—what they have read, been told, or taught—rather than what they have experienced for themselves through the presence of the Holy Spirit.

When you became a Christian, God gave you His Spirit to help deal with temptations. But the Holy Spirit will only work for you if you let Him. It is up to you to decide which will control your life, the Spirit or the flesh.

You don't have to give up relationships with friends because they are not strong Christians like you. Instead, pray for them, and use what you know to help them. Let your light shine so that it helps them see clearer. Pray and ask God to show them how to pay closer attention to the Holy Spirit, so that they will be quick to turn away from those things that are stunting their spiritual growth.

GRACE FOR TODAY:

The Holy Spirit helps us take control over the flesh.

Don't Battle Your Critics; Humor 'Em!

A discerning man keeps wisdom in view.
Proverbs 17:24

The famous British Prime Minister Winston Churchill had just finished a rousing speech. Upon his final words, the crowd who had gathered to hear him erupted with a thunderous ovation. However, when the clapping and cheering ceased, one man, unimpressed by Sir Winston's rhetoric, blew him "the raspberry."

The rest of the audience froze in suspense, awaiting the powerful statesman's response to the rude heckler. Would he scream at the man, publicly humiliate him? Would he have him thrown out? Churchill looked at his tormentor, then spoke, "I know," he said good-naturedly. "I agree with you. But what are we among so many?"

Churchill's humble and humorous reply was a hit with the throng, and a tense situation was quickly diffused.

Like Sir Winston, you might occasionally face insults or criticism from a jealous or mean-spirited classmate or rival. In such cases it's tempting to become angry and lose your composure. And in today's power-is-everything world, conventional "wisdom" tells people to be defiant in the face of criticism, to fight fire with fire. Unfortunately, this approach usually leads to someone getting burned.

Don't forget the power of humility and humor to relax a tense situation. The Bible promises that a soft answer turns away wrath. (See Proverbs 15:1.)

Certainly, there will be times when you must forcefully defend yourself or a friend. Be watchful, however, for those times when a clever, self-deprecating comeback can disarm even the most hostile of foes, the harshest of critics.

Grace for Today:

Because we have God's love, we are rich— rich enough to be able to afford some jokes at our own expense.

PUTTING DISAPPOINTMENT IN ITS PLACE

What do you do with the inevitable disappointments that life hands you? Many people internalize them, let them into their hearts, where they fester and cause worry, pain, and despair.

Others are wiser, sharing disappointments with friends, relatives, or a pastor or counselor. People like these can be great sounding boards— and great resources for solutions to problems. But they aren't the best resource.

Do you make a habit of taking your disappointments to God? He should be your first option, not your last resort. Maybe you are hesitant to share your disappointments with Him. He is, after all, dealing with wars, pollutions, famine, crime, AIDS, and terrorism. You might think, "I feel guilty about complaining about my stupid problems, in the face of all the important prayer requests God must be getting."

If you feel this way, give God a chance. He might just surprise you with how much He cares about even the little things. He cared enough about a wedding going well that He turned water into wine. He cared enough about lots of stomachs rumbling that, on at least two occasions, He provided food for people who had come to listen to Him. He even cared enough about his disciple Peter's tax problem to give him a coin.

Think about the really good fathers you know. Don't they care about their children's minor bumps and bruises and small problems—as well as the major injuries and serious life difficulties? Would they want their kids to hide their small struggles and keep them internalized? Of course not. God is the same way. Problems big and small—He wants them all!

GRACE FOR TODAY:

God would be disappointed if we didn't bring our disappointments to Him.

Are any of you in trouble? Then you should pray.

JAMES 5:13 NIRV

ABSOLUTELY NOTHING!

By Richard Baxter

B e at peace. God's love is constant. It cannot be torn from you and it will never change except to grow stronger and stronger as you return it with love of your own.

You shall be eternally embraced in the arms of the love that was from everlasting, and, will extend to everlasting. This is the same love that brought the Son of God's love from heaven to earth, from earth to the Cross, from the Cross to the grave, from the grave to glory. It is the love through Christ that was weary, hungry, tempted, scorned, scourged, buffeted, spit upon, crucified, pierced; which did fast, pray, teach, heal, weep, sweat, bleed, and die. This love of God will eternally embrace you.

Let this be your everlasting comfort and peace, if God's arms have once embraced you, neither sin nor hell can grip you. You do not have to deal with an inconstant human, but with Him with whom there is no variableness nor shadow of turning. (See James 1:17.) His love to you will not be as yours is on earth to Him, seldom, and cold, up, and down. He will not cease nor reduce His love, for all your hostility, neglect, and opposition. How can He cease to love you, when He has made you truly lovely? He even keeps you so stable in your love to Him, that you can challenge all that will try to separate your love from Christ—tribulation, distress, persecution, famine, nakedness, peril, and sword. How much more will He himself be constant!

Indeed, you should be "convinced that nothing—nothing living or dead, angelic or demonic, today or tomorrow, high or low, thinkable or unthinkable— absolutely nothing can get between us and God's love because of the way that Jesus our Master has embraced us" (Romans 8:38–39 MSG).

—⁂—

HEAVENLY FATHER: THANK YOU FOR EMBRACING ME WITH YOUR LOVE AND GRACE. AMEN.

The mountains may depart and the hills disappear,
but my kindness shall not leave you.

ISAIAH 54:10 TLB

EXTREME MAKEOVER!

Anyone who belongs to Christ is a new person.
The past is forgotten, and everything is new.

2 CORINTHIANS 5:17 CEV

There are about a gazillion "make-over" shows on television these days. From "Extreme Makeover" to "Ambush Makeover," this reality TV concept has really caught on in America. Ever wonder why? Probably because most every person—if given the opportunity—would love to change something about himself or herself. In fact, sometimes people want to change their image so badly, they turn to self-destructive behavior to accomplish their goals. Did you know that anorexia nervosa affects one teenager in every two hundred among teens ages sixteen to eighteen?[34]

Teen girls are the most vulnerable to this disorder, because many aspire to become model thin.

It's time to stop striving for "the perfect body" or the "model-like face" and be happy with who God made us. Of course, it's perfectly fine to do the best you can with what you've got—keeping in shape, eating right, grooming properly, etc. But, don't become obsessed with your outward appearance. Want some true beauty tips? Gorgeous actress, the late Audrey Hepburn, once wrote these beauty secrets:

*For attractive lips—Speak words of kindness.

*For lovely eyes—Seek out the good in people.

*For a slim figure—Share your food with the hungry.

*For beautiful hair—Let a child run his fingers through it once a day.

*For poise—Walk with the knowledge you'll never walk alone.

That's good advice. Ask God to give you the Master Makeover—from the inside out. Ask Him to develop the fruits of the spirit in your life: love, joy, peace, longsuffering, kindness, goodness, faithfulness, gentleness and self-control. (See Galatians 5:22.) If you do, you'll become a beautiful creature on the inside, which is sure to spill over onto your outer appearance, as well.

BEAUTY FROM ASHES

Forgive anyone who does you wrong, just as Christ has forgiven you.

COLOSSIANS 3:13 CEV

On the evening of August 5, 1945, eight–year–old Thomas Takashi Tanemori dreamed of butterflies. The next morning, his hometown of Hiroshima was destroyed by an atomic bomb. Six members of Thomas' family, including his parents, died in the devastation. Now an orphan, Thomas lived on the streets, scavenging for food amid the ashes of what used to be home. Holding on tightly to his anger and resentment, Thomas grew up a bitter young man.

Years later, Thomas was asked to speak in San Francisco at an event held in remembrance of the fortieth anniversary of the bombing. He prepared a message that hadn't changed in forty years, one fueled by hatred and dreams of revenge. But on his way to the ceremony a beautiful butterfly landed on the windshield of his car, taking him back to another time and another dream.

Thomas had heard of God's love, but he'd never felt it, until now. Suddenly, the picture of a worm leaving its old life behind to become something new and beautiful like a butterfly filled his heart with hope. That day, God changed Thomas' message of hate to one of forgiveness. Thomas later became a minister, helping others discover how forgiveness can transform a life.

GRACE FOR TODAY:

God is good at helping us let go so we're ready to embrace the next good thing He has for us.

God has the power, and the desire, to help you forgive anything that's weighing you down. Big or small, any offense you're holding onto can rob you of joy. God wants to help you break out of the cocoon of bitterness and be fully free. If any person or situation comes to mind that stirs up anger or resentment in your heart, bring it to God. Ask His help in letting it go. Your feelings may not change overnight, but you can be sure the transformation has begun. Beautiful things lie ahead.

LEARN TO LIKE IT

Whatever your hand finds to do, do it with all your might.

ECCLESIASTES 9:10

Twice, your mom has asked that you take out the garbage. And each time, you've nodded your head only to turn back to the TV and continue playing your video game. Understandably, taking out the trash is one job nobody wants. But somebody has to do it, and in this case that somebody just happens to be you.

You can murmur and complain about how much you hate it, but what would that accomplish? First, the garbage is still there, and you're still the one who has to carry it out. Second, if you leave it there too long then the foul odor will give you something really worth complaining about.

Why not use the time it takes to carry out the garbage to talk with God? You might even think about the effort involved in carrying out the trash, and consider how God helps you to accomplish the task.

You have to use your arms, your hands, and your legs. You even need the use of your brain to tell you where to deposit the bags. God gave you all of those body parts, plus wisdom and ability, just so you could perform a menial task like taking out the trash.

What a perfect time to acknowledge that, and to tell Him thanks. It is also a perfect time to think about all the other blessings He gives to you. By the time you're done thinking on His many blessings, the irritation you felt initially will have turned into great joy. And the task you were grumbling about will have been completed.

GRACE FOR TODAY:

God has given so much to us—there's always reason to celebrate.

10 Rules for a Successful Today

So watch your step. Use your head. Make the most of
every chance you get. These are desperate times!

EPHESIANS 5:15-16 MSG

1. Today I will not strike back. If someone is rude, impatient, or cruel to me, I will
not respond in the same manner. Hate and anger only breed more of the same.
2. Today I will ask God to bless my enemies. If I encounter a longtime school rival
or difficult customer at my job—or anyone who treats me harshly or unfairly—I
will quietly ask God to bless them.
3. Today I will be thoughtful about what I say. I will choose words with care, making sure I don't spread gossip or malign anyone's character.
4. Today I will go the extra mile. I will find a way to lighten another's load. I will
find ways to make life more pleasant for everyone I encounter—within and beyond
my home.
5. Today I will forgive. I will forgive the people who hurt me or anger me. I will
strive to put offenses behind me, in the past where they belong.
6. Today I will do something nice for someone, but secretly. I will reach out anony-
mously to bless the life of another person. My reward will be the smile of surprise, not a personal thank-you.
7. Today I will treat others as I wish to be treated. I will practice the golden rule.
8. Today I will lift the spirits of someone who is discouraged. My smile, my words,
and my actions can make a difference to someone who is struggling in life.
9. Today I will nurture my body. I will eat healthy foods. I will exercise and get to
bed on time. I will be grateful for, and respectful of, the body God has given me.
10. Today I will grow spiritually. I will find time to pray and meditate. I will set aside
the busyness of life to thank God for His blessings and rejuvenate my spirit.

GRACE FOR TODAY:

God's grace provides true contentment in life as we
spend more time counting our blessings than adding up
our troubles.

A HOLY TERROR

Everyone experiences fear—even sheer terror—sometimes. Jesus was no exception. When He was facing the brutal reality of the crucifixion, Jesus felt a level of terror and anguish that few will ever know. But it's important to note what He did with that fear. He took it to God, the Heavenly Father of us all. He took to heart the words of the psalmist who wrote, "When I am afraid, I put my trust in you" (Psalm 56:3 NLT).

Jesus was honest with God. He even asked that, if it were possible, that He wouldn't have to endure the crucifixion. But at the same time, he acknowledged that He wanted God's will, not His own, to be done. What a great model for people to follow!

Today, when people face fear, they tend to go everywhere else but the prop-er destination. Some use drugs or alcohol to deal with fear. Others rely on their own resources, their own insufficient strength. For yet others, the latest bestseller, written by the hottest advice guru, is the most popular solution.

In a few cases, people don't deal with their fear at all. They put on "No Fear" t-shirts and try to convince everyone, including themselves, that they are super-humans who don't feel fear. (When, in reality, they are too afraid to even admit they're scared!)

Jesus was wiser, more honest, and He set the perfect example for us. The first one to hear our fear should be our loving, all-powerful Father in heaven.

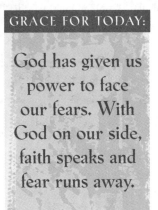

GRACE FOR TODAY:

God has given us power to face our fears. With God on our side, faith speaks and fear runs away.

Give your burdens to the LORD, and he will take care of you.

PSALM 55:22 NLT

ASK WHAT YOU WISH

By R. A. Torrey

The whole secret of prayer is found in these words of our Lord. Here is prayer that has unbounded power: "Ask whatever you wish, and it will be done for you." There is a way then of asking and getting precisely what we ask and getting all we ask. Christ gives two conditions of this all-prevailing prayer. The first condition is, "If you abide in Me."

Now for us to abide in Christ is to bear the same relation to Him that branches bear to the vine. That is to say, to abide in Christ is to renounce any independent life of our own, to give up trying to think our thoughts, or form our resolutions, or cultivate our feelings, and simply and constantly look to Christ to think His thoughts in us, to form His purposes in us, to feel His emotions and affections in us. It is to renounce all life independent of Christ, and constantly to look to Him for the inflow of His life into us, and the outworking of His life through us. When we do this, and as much as we do this, our prayers will obtain what we seek from God.

This must necessarily be so, for our desires will not be our own desires, but Christ's, and our prayers will not in reality be our own prayers, but Christ praying in us. Such prayers will always be in harmony with God's will, and the Father hears them always.

—m—

HEAVENLY FATHER: I CAN'T IMAGINE THAT YOU—THE CREATOR OF THE UNIVERSE—WOULD WANT ME TO "ABIDE" WITH YOU. IT IS AN HONOR TO KNOW THAT YOU WANT ME TO BE IN YOUR PRESENCE. THANK YOU FOR YOUR GRACE THAT MAKES BEING NEAR YOU POSSIBLE. AMEN.

[Jesus said,] "If you abide in Me, and My words abide in you, ask whatever you wish, and it will be done for you."

JOHN 15:7 NASB

MORE THAN ENOUGH GRACE

The LORD your God will go ahead of you. He will neither fail you
nor forsake you.

DEUTERONOMY 31:6 NLT

I n 1932, Tommy A. Dorsey was a young husband and soon-to-be new father. He and his wife, Nettie, were living in a small apartment in Chicago. It was a muggy August day when Tommy kissed Nettie goodbye on his way out the door to sing at a large revival meeting in St. Louis. He hated to leave her, but he was the featured soloist.

The next night, he sang his heart out. The people kept urging him to sing again and again. Truly, he was walking in God's calling for his life. When he finally sat down to hear the message, he was handed a Western Union telegram with the words, "YOUR WIFE JUST DIED." Nettie had died giving birth to a baby boy. Later that night, the baby died too. As Tommy collapsed from all of his grief, he felt as though God had betrayed him. He didn't want to sing gospel songs anymore.

GRACE FOR TODAY:

Even in a tragic situation, God can birth something beautiful.

That next Saturday evening, Tommy sat at the piano and as he played, he felt the peace of God come over him in a way he'd never felt before. He began playing a melody that just fell into place. It was the melody for the famous hymn, "Precious Lord."

The words go: "Precious Lord, take my hand, Lead me on, let me stand. I am tired, I am weak, I am worn, Through the storm, through the night, lead me on to the light. Take my hand, precious Lord, lead me home."

Even in a tragic situation, God can birth something beautiful. Maybe you're going through something terrible right now. If so, hang on. God promises to never leave you. He will give you plenty of grace to make it through this difficult situation.

GARBAGE COLLECTORS

Forget about what's happened; don't keep going over old history. Be alert, be present. I'm about to do something brand-new.

ISAIAH 43:18-19 MSG

I t's Friday night, and you invite your closest friends over to just hang out for awhile. As soon as they arrive, you lead them to your room and slowly open your closet. Crammed inside is a wall of "stuff" reaching from floor to ceiling. Trying not to cause a sudden avalanche, you carefully take out each item. As you pass each trinket, one by one, around the room, you go over its significance, just like you have so many times before.

" . . . and here's a History quiz I flunked in eight grade. You wouldn't believe how unfair that teacher was! And this piece of masking tape? I used it to hold my gym shoe together last semester. And would you look at this? Half a taco from the school cafeteria. I think it's from my freshman year . . . ."

By this time, your friends are thinking, *Why would anyone want to look at a friend's old garbage?* But people do it all the time. They sift through trash from the past, over and over again. Old hurts, angry words, moments when they've experienced rejection or humiliation.

God wants to help you let go of any old garbage you've gotten into the habit of hanging onto. He wants to do something new and dynamic with your life. But He needs all of your heart to make it happen. Going over and over wounds from the past does nothing to heal them. It only keeps the wounds open and bleeding.

Let God help you clean out the closet of your heart. Go through any wrongs you've been holding onto—one last time. Forgive what needs to be forgiven. Attend to any relationships that need repair. Then, allow God to replace old painful memories with new ones, ones filled with cause for love and thanks.

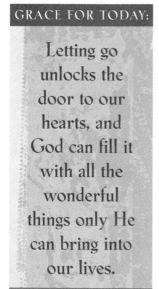

GRACE FOR TODAY:

Letting go unlocks the door to our hearts, and God can fill it with all the wonderful things only He can bring into our lives.

READ YOUR MAIL

Open my eyes to see the wonderful truths in your law.

PSALM 119:18 NLT

D ing!
You glance at the clock, and break out in a smile. It's 8:15 P.M. and an e-mail from your best friend has just arrived. She lives halfway around the country, and she's been gone now for nearly four years, but the friendship you developed way back in grade school has stood the test of time. It has proven how friendships can become so meaningful that two people can truly become inseparable.

And today, twelve years later, you are still as close as two people could be.

You smile as you open the e-mail and begin reading, thinking about the first time you met. How neat it is, you think, that something as simple as e-mail can be such a powerful tool when it comes to helping people to stay in touch.

The same could be said about the Bible—God's personal e-mail to you.

Like the electronic message, the Bible is a direct link to keep you in touch with the One who is closer and more personal than your best friend. Unlike e-mail, your contact is not limited to the Internet. God's Word is with you all the time, ready to be opened and read anywhere.

When you read the Bible, it is just like having a conversation with God. He talks to you through His Word, and you respond to Him with prayer. If you have questions, His Word has the answers. That's a friendship you can count on.

You've got mail waiting for you right now. Go ahead and open it. You won't be disappointed to read what your friend has to say.

GRACE FOR TODAY:

God always has a message ready and waiting for us to read.

Jesus' "One" Wish

Every kingdom divided against itself is brought to desolation, and every city or house divided against itself will not stand.

MATTHEW 12:25 NKJV

J esus' last formal prayer before He died on the Cross was for unity within the body of Christ. As He awaited the most terrible ordeal a human has ever faced, Jesus took the time to pray that "those who will believe in me . . . may be one as we are one" (John 17:20–22).

Sadly, today that body has been wounded and disjointed—not so much from outside assaults, but by quarrels from within.

Churches split and splinter with regularity. And many authors and artists are attacked, for their alleged "incorrect" beliefs and motives. All the while, the world that Christians are called to witnesses to is watching.

Think about your life. Are there religious cliques at your school—even within your church? Have you found yourself being criticized for the kind of music you listen to (e.g., "There's no way rock music can be Christian!"), the denomination you belong to, or the TV shows you watch?

Imagine the impact Christians could have on the world if we quit fighting among ourselves. For Christians to effectively witness to a lost world, we must stop fighting among ourselves. You can't pull a truck out of a ditch with one tiny thread—or even hundreds of individual threads. However, if you weave the threads together, they can become a rope that is strong enough for the task at hand.

In the same manner, it's time for Christians to lay aside their differences, join forces, and pull together.

GRACE FOR TODAY:

God created us to be individuals coming together as one family celebrating our differences.

AN END TO THE
SOB STORY

When you were a small child, whom did you run to when you fell down and hurt yourself? Who wiped away your tears when someone said something so cruel to you that you couldn't help but cry? Who was your refuge when, despite your best efforts, you didn't win the race, earn the A, or find the lost toy? Perhaps it was your mother or grandmother who was always handy with a tissue or a kind word. Or maybe it was your father or a big brother who lent you a handkerchief or brushed away your tears with a large but tender finger.

Writing in the book of Revelation, the Bible's grand finale, the apostle John promises that someday God himself will wipe away your tears. Think about that for a moment: The same hands that stretched out the heavens, scattered the stars across the sky, and formed mountains will someday gently touch your cheeks and brush away your tears forever.

And when those final tears disappear, so will the fear, despair, and pain that accompanied them. One of the coolest things about heaven is that it's a place of perfect happiness. There will be room for friendship, worship, celebration, and joy.

But, as big as heaven is, it can't hold everything. There will simply be no room for tears. It's doubtful, though, that anyone will miss them.

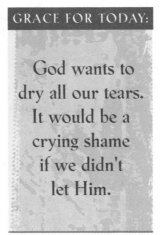

GRACE FOR TODAY:

God wants to dry all our tears. It would be a crying shame if we didn't let Him.

God will wipe away every tear from their eyes.

REVELATION 21:4 NKJV

THE POWER OF FORGIVENESS

By Dwight L. Moody

Several years ago the Church of England sent a devoted missionary to New Zealand. One Sunday, after a few years of toil and success, he was holding a communion service in a district with many new converts. As the missionary was conducting the service, he observed one of the men, just as he was about to kneel at the rail, suddenly start to his feet and hastily go to the opposite end of the church. After a while he returned and calmly took his place.

After the service the clergyman took him to the side and asked the reason for his strange behavior. He replied, "As I was about to kneel I recognized in the man next to me the chief of a neighboring tribe, who had murdered my father and drunk his blood; and I had sworn by all the gods that I would slay that man at the first opportunity.

The impulse to have my revenge, at first almost overpowered me, and I rushed away, as you saw me, to escape the power of it. As I stood at the other end of the room and considered the purpose of our meeting, I thought of Him who prayed for His own murderers, 'Father, forgive them, for they know not what they do.' And I felt then that I could forgive the murderer of my father, and I went and knelt down at his side."

—∞—

DEAR FATHER: I SAY I'M GOING TO FORGIVE SOMEONE, BUT THEN SOMETIMES I DON'T MEAN IT COMPLETELY. I KNOW YOU HAVE FORGIVEN ME BY YOUR GRACE, EVEN WHEN I KNEW I NEEDED TO BE FORGIVEN. I NEED YOUR GRACE TO HELP ME FORGIVE OTHERS, ESPECIALLY WHEN THEY DON'T SEEM TO KNOW THEY'VE DONE ANYTHING WRONG. AMEN.

"When you assume the posture of prayer, remember that it's not all asking. If you have anything against someone, forgive—only then will your heavenly Father be inclined to also wipe your slate clean of sins."

MARK 11:25 MSG

COURAGEOUS CHRISTIAN

Yea, though I walk through the valley of the shadow of death,
I will fear no evil: for thou art with me.

PSALM 23:4 KJV

I n an article titled, "The Real Story of Flight 93," *Newsweek* magazine retells the gripping story of that fateful 9–11 flight—the one that terrorists hijacked and intended to crash into the White House or the U.S. Capitol. As you probably know, that flight didn't make it to Washington, D.C. Instead, a group of passengers led by courageous Todd Beamer attacked the hijackers, and some say they probably forced the plane down in a Western Pennsylvania field. While all of the details aren't known, one thing is for sure—Todd relied on his faith in Jesus Christ and acted heroically in his last moments on earth.

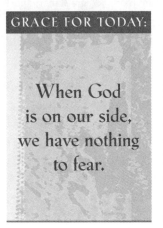

GRACE FOR TODAY:

When God is on our side, we have nothing to fear.

When faced with an absolutely horrifying situation, Todd knew where to turn. We know from GTE Supervisor Lisa Jefferson, whom Todd ended up connecting with on his cell phone, that Todd prayed the Lord's Prayer in those last minutes, and then led the other passengers in the Twenty-third Psalm before uttering those famous words: "Are you guys ready? Let's roll!" We know from the cockpit voice recorder that Todd and his group wrestled with the hijackers, thwarting their ultimate plan. He lived a Christian life, and he died a hero. You can't do much better than that.

What would you do if placed in that same situation? Would you turn to God for strength as Todd did? Would you act heroically—pushing your own fear aside? Thankfully, we'll probably never have to go through something as unimaginable as Todd Beamer and the others on that flight encountered, but we have opportunities to stand up for our faith every day. We have chances to act courageously on God's behalf. The next time you're given the opportunity, remember you don't have to go it alone. As God was with Todd, He is also with you.

SECURE CONNECTION

Think about things that are pure and lovely and admirable. Think about things that are excellent and worthy of praise.

PHILIPPIANS 4:8 NLT

W hen it comes to protecting your computer, you know the rules. Don't open e-mail attachments from anyone you don't know or trust. Use a firewall. Update your virus protection software regularly. If you don't, your computer is liable to pick up something you don't want, something that could cause it to malfunction or "corrupt" important files.

But did you know the same applies to your mind? There's a lot of valuable stuff in there. Things that are true, noble, good, lovely, excellent, and worthy of praise. But all of these good things can be corrupted when you open your mind to what doesn't belong there.

Choosing to open yourself up to movies, books, web sites, and even conversations that you know God wouldn't approve of can be more dangerous than it appears. That's because words and images "attach" themselves to your thoughts, popping up later when you don't want them to. Once there, they're almost impossible to erase. Your best defense is never opening yourself up to them in the first place. To help you understand what to "open" and what to turn your back on, God offers a great protection program.

GRACE FOR TODAY:

The more we fill our minds with good things, the easier it is for God to guide us.

God's Word is your virus protection software. Regularly reading the Bible and spending time really thinking over the truth of what you've read will help alert you to anything that doesn't sound quite right. It will help you sort out what's helpful from what's harmful.

God's Spirit is your firewall. Your mind, along with your body and your spirit, is very important to God. He wants you to use it well, to fill it with things that will help you enjoy life and your relationship with Him. God's Spirit is always there, helping guide your thoughts in the right direction.

WATCH THE SIGNS

Pay attention, my child, to what I say. Listen carefully.

PROVERBS 4:20 NLT

Y ou sink in your seat as the car screeches to a halt. Then you offer a silent prayer of thanks to God as your dad leans forward and looks in both directions.

The flashing red lights and the blaring sound of the horn warning that a train is approaching are a strong reminder of yesterday, when you almost did something in chemistry class that could have been disastrous.

Fortunately, you sensed something was wrong when you smelled gas. Lighting a match might have caused an explosion resulting in serious injury to you and your classmates.

Sometimes, God will put people in your path to help you recognize when something is wrong—that you are about to do something that could be dangerous. But at other times He will speak directly to you.

You may not see flashing red lights, or hear blaring horns that signal you have entered a danger zone and are about to make a wrong decision. But God has given you a special warning device, an inner voice called a conscience, which is led by the Holy Spirit to alert you when danger is near. He speaks to you in such a way that you know God is trying to get your attention. He wants to alert you of potential danger and help you to make a right decision.

When you pay attention to that small voice, the warning sign, you have time to decide which direction to take. You know to proceed with caution.

Listen to your conscience. Pay attention to the signs, and you will avoid the pitfalls.

GRACE FOR TODAY:

God not only warns of danger, He also protects us from it.

THE FEAR OF FALLING

God is our refuge and strength.

PSALM 46:1 KJV

Katie Brown weighs only ninety-five pounds, and she is just a bit over five feet tall. She stands a lot taller than that, however, once she's nimbly scaled a hundred-foot climbing wall (that's equivalent to a ten-story building).

Katie is a "difficulty climber," an endeavor in which she's a world champion and multiple gold medalist at the "X Games"—which you may have seen televised on networks like ESPN2.

As you might imagine, it's intimidating for a small person to attack climbing walls and cliffs that are twenty times her height, but Katie says that extreme faith can bring her peace, even in extremely dangerous challenges. "I know that I couldn't have done what I've done without being a Christian," she explains. "My faith in God doesn't get rid of my healthy fear of climbing extreme heights, but it does help me deal with it. It takes away a lot of the pressure, because you know that God's not going to condemn you if you don't win. So there's nothing to worry about. When I see others competing, I wonder how I could compete if I didn't have faith in God."

The "walls" you face in your life might not be physical. They might be emotional or relational. And it's okay to feel intimidated or frightened by the walls in your life. As Katie notes, it would be unhealthy not to appreciate the significance of a major challenge.

But, like Katie, you can rest secure in the truth that God will not condemn you if you can't get to the top of your wall—or if it takes you hundreds of attempts. God is more concerned with your faithful effort.

GRACE FOR TODAY:

If we will only attempt to walk toward Him, He is pleased even with our stumbles.

C.S. LEWIS

IN THE MAZE—DAZED & CONFUSED

One of Colorado's many ski resorts offers its guests a challenge beyond those they might find on the slopes—a large maze. The maze is composed of row after row of high walls, leading to one dead end after another. The maze is so complex that the resort offers a prize to anyone who can complete it within an allotted time limit.

Above the maze sits a dining area, where a person's friends or relatives can try to guide him through the labyrinth: "You're going the wrong way—you'll never get through if you keep going that direction!" "Keep turning right, and you'll be okay!" "You need to backtrack; you're headed for a dead end!"

Of course, the people inside the maze don't particularly want to hear any advice. They think they can figure things out, if they just trust their instincts and sense of direction. It almost never works. Others try to ask their fellow maze-navigators for advice, but find that everyone inside the maze is, for the most part, equally lost and confused.

Finally, after the time limit has elapsed and the prize forfeited, the maze-runners will look up forlornly for guidance from their family or friends who have the better vantage point. Then they'll turn up their palms, shrug their shoulders, and say something like, "Where am I, and how do I get out of this place!?"

Many people today are like those lost souls in the maze. They think they can figure out life for themselves. They are too proud to seek help from someone with a better view. But in reality, they are lost—and getting "loster."

God is above the confusing labyrinth we live in from day to day. His perspective is better than ours, and He sees exactly where we need to go and what we need to avoid. All we need to do is quit looking at the confusion in front of us and look to Him instead.

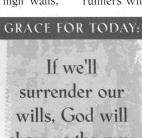

GRACE FOR TODAY:

If we'll surrender our wills, God will show us the way.

Your word is a lamp for my feet and a light for my path.

PSALM 119:105 NLT

WHAT SHALL WE PRAY?

By Dr. Charles Stanley

When we go to God, instead of asking, "Lord, please do this and that," let's ask Him to show us how to pray. Let's ask the Holy Spirit to pray through us from beginning to end. Then we can be assured of praying according to His will. We will pray for things we would never think to pray for otherwise. As we pray, God will show us a side of prayer we have never seen.

When our hearts are clean, and we have committed ourselves to obey Him, yet we haven't a clue as to what to pray; God takes the responsibility for showing us. He may use Scripture or He may use circumstances. If our request isn't in keeping with His will, He will redirect our attention on Him; and we will lose interest in what we were asking for. Regardless of how He shows us, we must believe that He will. Often we will have to wait. But it is during these times of waiting that we begin to really know God.

As we find God's will in our prayers, He confirms it by filling our hearts with the peace of the Holy Spirit. We can know without doubt that we are on His track in our prayers. When this is true, we can pray with the assurance that Christ is praying with us to the same end. Peace in our hearts is God's seal of approval on our prayers.[35]

—∞—

HEAVENLY FATHER: SHOW ME HOW TO PRAY FOR MYSELF AND ALSO FOR OTHERS. I DON'T WANT TO JUST SAY WORDS; I WANT MY WORDS TO MATTER.

Do not worry about anything, but in everything by prayer and supplication with thanksgiving let your requests be made known to God. And the peace of God, which surpasses all understanding, will guard your hearts and your minds in Christ Jesus.

PHILIPPIANS 4:6–7 NRSV

NAYSAYERS SCHMAYSAYERS!

Jesus beheld them, and said unto them, With men this is impossible;
but with God all things are possible.

MATTHEW 19:26 KJV

W hen Lisa Fernandez was twelve, a coach told her she'd never make it as a
pitcher because she wasn't the right size or build. She didn't let that discourage her, though. She proved him wrong in a big way when she led the U.S.
women's softball team to a gold medal victory at the 1996 Olympic Games. Lisa did-
n't let the naysayer coach trample her dream of becoming the best softball pitcher she
could be. She worked hard, practiced long hours, and
achieved her ultimate goal.

GRACE FOR TODAY:

**Whatever we
can dream—
God's dream for
us is a little
bigger.**

As Christians, we have to possess that same
tenacity and steadfastness that Lisa had concerning her
dream. We have to have a dogged determination—no
matter what others say. You can almost bet that if God
places a dream in your heart, someone will come your
way and speak against it. See, the devil isn't going to
roll out the red carpet and say, "Welcome to your
dreams." He wants to discourage you before you even
start down the road that will lead to God's plan for your
life. But he can't stop you if you won't let him. Ignore
the naysayers. Press forward toward the dream that
God has given you. As they say in sports, keep your eye on the ball. Keep your focus.
Meditate on your ultimate goal. Like Lisa, ignore the negative comments.

Maybe God has put a big dream in your heart—so big that you can't even imagine it coming true. Maybe you're feeling overwhelmed by the enormity of it. Don't
worry. You don't have to make it come to pass. All you have to do is trust God, follow Him, and watch the miracle unfold.

KNOW WHO YOU'RE
FIGHTING

Resist the devil, and he will run from you.
Come near to God, and he will come near to you.

JAMES 4:7–8 CEV

You have an enemy. When you read these words, perhaps the face of someone who used to be a friend but dumped you for one reason or another, comes to mind. Or maybe the word "enemy" is tied to the name of someone you hardly know, a person who doesn't like the way you dress or talk or walk or breathe—for some reason they can't quite figure out. Maybe it's someone you've offended. Maybe it's someone who's offended you. Or perhaps you feel this statement is totally untrue, that so far you've lived your life "enemy free."

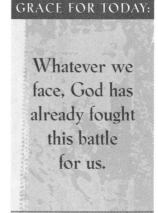

GRACE FOR TODAY:

Whatever we face, God has already fought this battle for us.

The day you chose to love God, you also gained an enemy. It's someone who hates God and everything precious to Him, including you. You can't see him or feel him, but he's just as real as the atoms and molecules you can't detect with the human eye. And he's trying to pick a fight with you every single day by tempting you to do things that would pull you away from God.

But the good news is you don't need to be afraid. With God on your side, you're stronger than your enemy could ever be. Anytime you're pulled in a direction you know you shouldn't go, all you need to do is remember that God's already fought this battle for you. Ask for His help. Then turn around and walk the other way.

As for any of those other people who may have come to mind? They're not your enemies. They're fighting the same battle you are. Perhaps they're simply unaware of who they're really fighting. Don't let your one real enemy get between you and those God has asked you to love. Forgive, reconcile, pray, and move on.

RESTORED RELATIONSHIPS

Nothing in all creation will ever be able to separate us
from the love of God.

ROMANS 8:39 NLT

R oger had meant well when he promised Mike he would drop off the two tuxe-
does they had rented for the senior prom. Unfortunately, a prior commitment
kept Roger from keeping his word. Remembering the suits a couple of weeks later after
carting them around in the trunk of his car, Roger had dropped off the tuxedos but failed
to pay the charges for not returning them on time.

Now, Mike had a large bill staring him in the face and was angry with Roger.

Nigel reminded Mike of how forgetful their friend Roger can be at times, and the
busy schedule he keeps. He also told him about Roger's financial situation. There was
no way Roger could pay the late charges.

To protect his friends' relationship, Nigel had used some of his own savings to pay
all the late charges.

Nigel's gesture may remind you of Jesus Christ, and how when mankind had no
relationship with God because of sin, Jesus stepped in and fixed it. God was not pleased
that He could not fellowship with mankind—his very own creation. He wanted the
relationship to be renewed, and allowed His only Son, Jesus Christ, to pay the debt of
sin with His own life. Now, because of His loving sacrifice, your relationship with
God, your Heavenly Father, is restored.

God, who loves you so much, is always concerned when your relationship with
Him is strained. He would never allow a debt to come between you and Him, or His
love for you.

GRACE FOR TODAY:

God has removed the debt,
so that there will be no guilt.

Travel Light, Travel Right

The world and its desires pass away, but the man who does
the will of God lives forever.

1 John 2:17

W hat's on your life's Wish List right now? What do you wish you had, but
don't possess? For many, money and material possessions top the list.
Americans have a possession obsession: We want bigger, better TVs, faster comput-
ers, and MP3 players with more memory and longer battery life.

For others, status and success are the ultimate prize. Some want to be the next pop
star, game-show champion, or winner of a new face and better body.

Seeking "the good life" isn't inherently bad—as long as this quest is secondary to
"the God life." Unfortunately, the drive for material possessions and physical attractiveness can become an all-consuming goal—a shallow, self-gratifying obsession with
no eternal significance.

God's Word teaches us to travel light. In fact, Jesus instructed His followers to
take with them only the bare necessities when they set out on a journey. He reminded
them not to be distracted by the glitter of money or the aura of fame and power.

In truth, the light of God's divine love is so brilliant that it makes everything else
dull in comparison. God's light is the one we should run to, because only in that light
can we find true happiness and fulfillment. So don't misplace your hope in things that
don't last—or have no lasting value. Put "loving and serving God" atop your list of life's
priorities. Because of all the treasures life has to offer, God tops them all.

Grace for Today:

The light of God's divine love is so brilliant that it
makes everything else dull in comparison.

LASTING IMPRESSIONS

Here's a little quiz for you, one that will test your memory as well as your knowledge of pop culture:

1. Name the "Best Comic Actor" from the past three Emmy Awards.

2. Name the last five Heisman trophy winners.

3. List the last five people who have been dubbed by *People* magazine as the "Most Beautiful" in the world.

How did you fare? Even if you're a pop-culture maven, you probably came up with only a name or two. Isn't it amazing how quickly we forget even high-profile award winners? How quickly spotlights fade, applause dies, and achievements get lost amid the furor over the latest Next Big Thing!

Now, here's another quiz. Maybe you'll fare better on this one.

1. Name the three people you'd turn to first in times of trouble.

2. List the five people who have had the greatest influence on your life.

3. List your five favorite teachers or coaches of all time.

4. Name the three people you trust the most—with your secrets, your mistakes, your dreams.

5. Select the three people whom you enjoy spending time with the most.

How did you do this time? The names came easier this time, didn't they? In fact, the hardest part might have been narrowing down some of the lists to only a few people.

The people who truly make a difference in life aren't the celebrities, the mega-superstars. They are the "regular people" that God places in our lives to enrich us, not with their celebrity credentials, but with their care and concern. Be thankful for these kind of people—and strive to be one yourself. You could end up on a lot of lists.

> **GRACE FOR TODAY:**
>
> God makes our lives rich by filling them with people.

We all have happy memories of the godly,
but the name of a wicked person rots away.

PROVERBS 10:7 NLT

GOD INSCRIBED YOUR NAME

By Charles Spurgeon

G od was thinking about you long before your mother held baby you in her arms for the very first time:

God thought of you before you had a being, when the sun, moon, and stars slept in the mind of God like unborn forests in an acorn cup, and the old sea was not yet born. God thought of you long before this infant world lay in its swaddling bands of mist. It was then that God inscribed your name upon the heart and upon the hands of Christ indelibly, to remain forever. (See Ephesians 1:4.) Doesn't this make you love God?

When the time comes for you to die, you need not be afraid, because death cannot separate you from God's love. When you shall come into the mysteries of eternity, you do not need to tremble. You never hear Jesus say in Pilate's judgment hall one word that would let you imagine that He was sorry that He had undertaken so costly a sacrifice for us. When His hands are pierced, when He is parched with fever, His tongue dried up like a shard of pottery, when His whole body is dissolved into the dust of death, you never hear a groan or a shriek that looks like Jesus is going to go back on His commitment. It was love that could not be stayed by death, but over-came all the horrors of the grave.

Go forth today, by the help of God's Spirit, vowing and declaring that in life—come poverty, come wealth, in death—come pain or come what may, you are and ever must be the Lord's.[36]

—∿—

DEAR FATHER: THANK YOU FOR YOUR GREAT LOVE THAT HOLDS ME TO YOU NO MATTER WHAT. YOUR GRACE IS MORE THAN I CAN KNOW OR UNDER-STAND. AMEN.

Like an open book, you watched me grow from conception to birth; all the stages of my life were spread out before you, the days of my life all prepared before I'd even lived one day.

PSALM 139:16 MSG

THE CHOSEN

You are a chosen generation, a royal priesthood, a holy nation, His own special people, that you may proclaim the praises of Him who called you out of darkness into His marvelous light.

1 PETER 2:9 NKJV

P astor W.C. Martin and his wife Donna of Texas decided it was time to make a difference in the world, so they began opening their home to children who were "in the system," being shuffled from institution to institution. Many were abused, unwanted, and troubled children—the ones that are hard to place for adoption. They took in dozens of these children over several years, giving them a home full of love and hope. Later, the Martins introduced the joy of foster parenting to the members of their church, and more than twenty families also opened their homes. Ultimately, eighteen children were permanently adopted.

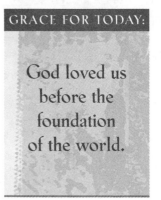

GRACE FOR TODAY:

God loved us before the foundation of the world.

Since 1977, more than seventy children have been placed with families in the area, changing lives through love. Their center, the W.C. & Donna Martin Center in Texas, even won the 2001 Caring Institute Award. Of course, their real reward is knowing that so many children were given a second chance.

Maybe you were once a foster child, or maybe you know someone who was placed in a foster family. Many children suffer as they are shuffled from home to home, but those who are adopted by a loving family gain stability, security, and hope. They can feel quite special knowing they were especially chosen to be in their family.

You can feel special today, too, because you were chosen to be part of God's family. When you accepted Jesus as your Savior, you were adopted into the best family—God's family. He adores you. You are the apple of His eye. He is proud of you. In fact, you're His favorite child.

GOD DOESN'T GIVE WHITE ELEPHANT GIFTS

Every good and perfect gift comes down from the Father
who created all the lights in the heavens.

JAMES 1:17 CEV

I t's your birthday, and the moment you dread each year is here—great-aunt Gertie's gift has arrived. This year, she's included a pair of footed pajamas (three sizes too small), a chartreuse knit hat (that you wouldn't wear even on a dare), and a can of peanut brittle (even though you happen to be highly allergic to nuts). While Aunt Gertie may send you a birthday gift because she loves you, her choice of what to give communicates another message—she doesn't really know you.

God knows you more intimately and loves you more deeply than any aunt, uncle, father, mother, sister, brother, or best friend ever will. That makes Him an incredible gift-giver. Not only does He know the perfect size, He has perfect timing. He gives you just what you need when you need it most. Because He cares about you so much, He doesn't settle for just giving you what you need. He throws in lots of extra, unexpected presents for no special reason other than to say He's thinking of you.

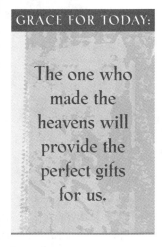

GRACE FOR TODAY:

The one who made the heavens will provide the perfect gifts for us.

God gives you gifts every day of your life. He even gave you a few before you were born. The talents and abilities He entrusted to you at birth were picked out especially for you. He knew they would fit you and your life just right. When you use them, it's like saying "thank you" to Him. It shows how much you enjoy what God's chosen for you.

Another way to show your gratitude is by simply telling God how much you appreciate the gifts He's brought your way. By taking a few moments each day to send a verbal "thank you note" to God, you'll not only delight His heart, but also recognize what an awesome gift-giver He really is.

SPICE IT UP

You will fill me with joy in your presence.

PSALM 16:11

How much quality goes into the time you spend with God? For many, that special time with God means little more than a daily routine that includes reading a few scriptures and saying a quick prayer. Then, they're off and running!

It is so easy to fall into such routine when spending time with God that you lose the excitement. Scriptures that used to speak life to you now have little meaning. The prayers that once brought answers now seem to get no further than the ceiling. Often, your mind tends to wander when you read the Bible, or you drift off to sleep. Consequently, you find yourself facing challenges without sensing the close presence of God.

God wants you to enjoy your relationship with Him. Remove the limits when it comes to how you spend time with Him. Spice things up a little. Try writing God a letter, just like you would if you wanted to contact a friend in another state. Let Him know how much you love and appreciate Him for all He has done for you.

Sing worship songs to Him. Pretty soon, you will sense His presence and know that He is receiving your praise. Maybe you can take a walk in a park, or hike a nature trail. Visit a museum or stop off at the zoo. You'll find God, and the beauty of His creation, in all those places.

There are lots of ways and places to spend time with God. And He will be just as ready to talk to you then as He was when you were locked in the privacy of your bedroom.

GRACE FOR TODAY:

God wants to be involved in every area of our lives, not just part of our routines.

Inside Every "Don't" Is a "Do"

Your word is a lamp to my feet and a light for my path.

PSALM 119:105

W hy did God give us a list of rules to follow? Why is the Bible so full of "Thou shalt not's"? A mother doesn't let her toddler touch a hot stove. A father doesn't let his child run out into traffic. A doctor insists on having a patient's medical history before prescribing medication.

A toddler wants to touch the stove because the orange glow is alluring. A child wants to play on the street because being confined to the yard is boring. And a sick person wants the medication "right now" to make him or her feel good again. At the moment each of these people collides with a brick wall called "Rules," the first instinct is to get around, over, under, or through that troublesome wall.

Little thought is given to the fact that the rules are meant to protect, to ensure safety and happiness. Similarly, abiding by the commandments of our Creator ensures our protection, fulfillment, peace, and well-being. The quality of our lives is a product of our choices, and we don't always have the information, wisdom, or perspective to make the best choices. That's precisely why the God who loves us and yearns to see us succeed has given us rules to live by.

The commandments that begin with "Don't" or "Thou shalt not" are positive. For example, "Don't covet" is another way of saying DO appreciate what you have. Be grateful for it. Get true joy from it by avoiding comparing your stuff with someone else's. "Don't kill" means DO value and treasure life—yours and that of others. DO realize that God created every person with the capacity to do good in the world.

If you have been viewing the Ten Commandments or other biblical rules as a big stick God uses to beat His creation into submission, it's time to shift your perspective. God is for you, not against you.

GRACE FOR TODAY:

God provided rules to help us achieve the "abundant life" Jesus promised.

ALMOST NOTHING GETS DONE ON "SOMEDAY"

D o any of these statements sound familiar to you?

"Someday I'll take my little sibling to the movies."

"Someday I'll volunteer to do some community service."

"Someday I'll start attending youth group regularly again."

"Someday I'll call or e-mail my old friend, as soon as things get less busy."

"Someday I'm gonna say something nice to that student everyone ignores."

Good intentions are fine, but there is a problem with "someday" statements. Sometimes, someday never comes. Opportunities vanish. Little brothers and sisters grow up. Long-lost, friends move (again), and you lose contact with them.

Heaven knows that teen life can be busy. But, it's your teen life, and it's up to you how you will spend it. Don't let opportunities to reach out and touch the lives of others slip through your fingers. Make an effort. Set priorities. Give yourself some deadlines if you must. Send that letter or e-mail. Make that phone call. Buy that gift. Put your name on that "Volunteer" list—get committed. Do something kind for that little brother or sister or cousin or neighbor while he or she is still little.

Don't look at time as a prison. Think of it as a gift from God. Then, as you sort through your life's priorities, think of how God would want you to use His gift of time. Would He want you to seize those opportunities to do good, or to neglect them?

> GRACE FOR TODAY:
> God tosses lots of opportunities to enrich other's lives, and when we take them, we'll be blessed as well.

Don't brashly announce what you're going to do tomorrow; you don't know the first thing about tomorrow.

PROVERBS 27:1 MSG

CREATOR AND PRESERVER OF THE WORLD

By John Wesley

God sees and knows the properties of everything created and all the connections, dependencies, relationships, and ways in which one of them can affect another. (See Hebrews 4:13.) God knows how the celestial bodies above influence the inhabitants of the earth beneath. The exact influences that fire, hail, snow, winds, and storms have on our planet, God knows. God knows what effects may be produced in the bowels of the earth and what effects every mineral or vegetable may have upon human beings. God knows all the animals and insects and all the qualities and powers given them, from the highest to the lowest.

God looks upon human beings over the whole face of the earth and knows all the hearts of them and understands all their thoughts. What any human being thinks, speaks, does, and feels, God knows. God sees all their sufferings with every attending circumstance.

Is the Creator and Preserver of the world unconcerned for what is seen, sitting at ease in the heaven without regarding the poor inhabitants of earth? No! God made us and cannot regard us as unworthy of Divine interest or concern. God is concerned every moment for what befalls every creature, more especially what befalls any human being.

It is hard to comprehend, no, it is hard to believe it, considering the complicated wickedness and misery we see on every side. Believe it we must, or else make God a liar. We must humble ourselves before God, then, and acknowledge our ignorance. How can we expect to comprehend the ways of God? Can a worm comprehend a worm? How much less can we suppose that finite human beings can comprehend God?[37]

—⁓—

HEAVENLY FATHER: YOUR INTEREST AND CONCERN FOR ME ARE THE RESULT OF YOUR LOVE AND GRACE IN MY LIFE. I WILL NEVER KNOW WHY YOU CHOOSE TO LOVE ME SO, BUT I THANK YOU FOR IT. AMEN.

The LORD has made the heavens his throne; from there he rules over everything there is.

PSALM 103:19 TLB

FALSE FACES

The LORD said to Samuel, "Do not consider his appearance or his height, for I have rejected him. . . . Man looks at the outward appearance, but the LORD looks at the heart."

1 SAMUEL 16:7

Costume parties are a blast! It's fun to dress up like somebody else, disguising our true identities. Wearing a mask allows you to act like someone else—at least for a little while. It's great fun for special occasions, but some people wear masks all the time. People wear "masks" for a variety of reasons, but mostly because they are not comfortable with who they really are, so they pretend to be someone else.

GRACE FOR TODAY:

God loves who we really are— not just the person everyone else sees.

Mask-wearing is not a new phenomenon. Back in Bible days, the most famous "mask-wearers" were the Pharisees. They wore a mask of "Hey, look at me! I am perfect. I never sin. I am better than everyone else." In reality, they were as flawed, if not more flawed, than many of their Gentile neighbors. Jesus, of course, saw right through their masks. He knew that behind their masks of purity were corrupt hearts that didn't know God. That's why He said this to them: "Woe to you, scribes and Pharisees, hypocrites! For you are like whitewashed tombs which on the outside appear beautiful, but inside they are full of dead men's bones and all uncleanness" (Matthew 23:27 NASB).

So, what kind of mask are you wearing today? Do you put on your "Joe Christian" mask on Sunday, but during the week that mask stays in the closet? Or, are you one of those "holier than thou" types who wears the "Church lady" mask and condemns all of her friends? If you're wearing a mask today, throw it off. Let Jesus do a work on the inside of you, which will alter your very being. As you allow Him, He will change you to be more and more like Him. Now that's Someone worth impersonating!

BEYOND COMPARE

Be content with who you are, and don't put on airs.
God's strong hand is on you.

1 PETER 5:6 MSG

I n school you're taught the value of being able to contrast and compare. It helps you weigh one thing against another, deciding which is more important, the best buy, or the wisest choice. But when it comes to people, the tendency to "contrast and com-pare" only causes pain.

That's because people are a one-of-a-kind creation. You can't compare apples with oranges—or Amys and Andys with Oprahs and Ozzies. Comparing another person's physical characteristics, talents, or blessings with yours only messes with your self-image, stirring up jealousy and pride. It also accuses God of playing favorites.

You are not an accidental combination of genes and chromosomes. God had a specific purpose in mind when He carefully created you. You have the choice of what you'll do with what you've been given, but that's between you and God. His plans for your life can look totally different from those He has for your best friend.

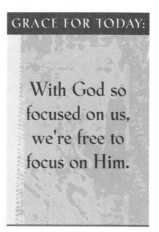

GRACE FOR TODAY:

With God so focused on us, we're free to focus on Him.

Get in the habit of focusing on your own life. There's so much to see and learn. Look at how much you've matured inside and out over the last year. Allow God to help you enjoy how He's put you together. Spend time with Him rejoicing over the hard things He's brought you through. Together, celebrate every step forward you take with Him.

One of those steps forward will be learning to take your eyes off of yourself more often so you can focus more fully on God. The more you focus on Him, the more you'll begin to notice a family resemblance growing between His character and yours.

YOU'RE HIRED!

He is faithful and just to forgive us and to cleanse us from every wrong.

1 JOHN 1:9 NLT

"You're fired!"

The words brought an unsettling feeling as you looked at the expression on the young woman's face.

Sure, it was just another one of those TV reality shows, and the woman wasn't really being let go from her real job. Still, the thought of being told you are no longer wanted or that your services are no longer needed because you made a mistake is not comforting.

Aren't you glad God is not so quick to kick you out of His family because you have made mistakes or messed up? He does not hand out pink slips. When you do wrong, He desires to restore you to fellowship with Him rather than get rid of you.

When God created you, He knew there would be times when things would not go as planned and you would falter. That always happens when you don't pay attention to the Holy Spirit, who has been sent to guide you and keep you from making mistakes. But His mercy and grace are always there to say, "It's okay. I understand, and I forgive you."

As a Christian, you have everything you need to succeed—to carry out God's will and accomplish whatever He wants you to. (See Hebrews 13:21.)

If you slip up, don't let it destroy you. First, ask God to forgive you. Then, ask Him to show you where you went wrong and to help you never to do it again.

Someone once said: "Do what is right, do it because it is right, and then do it right." Doing what is right begins with being obedient to God's Word. When you do that, you leave little room for failure. In fact, you set the stage for a life that is filled with peace, joy and success.

GRACE FOR TODAY:

God is always ready to forgive our mistakes—and He'll never mention them again.

THE HARD WORK OF LOVE

"Though the mountains be shaken and the hills be removed, yet my unfailing love for you will not be shaken nor my covenant of peace be removed," says the LORD, who has compassion on you.

ISAIAH 54:10

What is love? Almost every pop song mentions the concept. It's a major theme of movies and TV shows as well. Unfortunately, much of what you see and hear in modern media isn't real love. The "love" many singers profess, for example, is often a selfish obsession, lacking real depth. Or, it's a whim, usually driven by physical appearance. "I love you, baby!" in a pop song, is better translated, "I am hot for you at this present moment—until someone more attractive than you comes into the picture."

God, the author of love, didn't design it to be a mere feeling. Love is a decision, an act of the will. Love is a struggle, something that requires constant effort. True love is caring about another person even if your love isn't reciprocated. Love is a commitment that doesn't fade, regardless of consequences. It's a sacrifice.

Real love is what Jesus displayed for the world when He chose to sacrifice himself for all of us. And He made this choice knowing that many would spurn or belittle His supreme sacrifice. Further, He knew that no one deserved this great gift of love. He knows the selfishness of the human heart. He knows every awful thing about every single person who has ever lived—or ever will live. Yet He still gave himself up.

The Lord of all creation, who knew you even before you were born, has decided to love you in spite of mistakes or of the indifference you might feel toward Him sometimes. God loves you. He is committed to you. He will faithfully forgive, unconditionally accept, and perfectly love you always. He makes the effort, every day.

So don't be swayed by the media depictions of fake love. You have the real thing, direct from the Source.

GRACE FOR TODAY:

Christ's love will carry us through whatever happens, even if today it feels impossible to make it to tomorrow.

TURNING STUMBLING BLOCKS INTO STEPPING STONES

Have you ever wondered why God allows so many stumbling blocks to be thrown into your path? Does He just enjoy seeing you trip over them—or is there something else in play here? Could those stumbling blocks be turned into stepping stones?

Kevin Smith wanted to be a filmmaker, but he didn't exactly have movie-studio executives pounding at his door. Trying to get a break in the film industry was frustrating, but Smith was determined. Finally, he sold his prized comic book collection and used a credit card to finance his first film. That film, with its paltry $27,000 budget, was such a hit at the Sundance Film Festival that he had people lining up to back his next effort. Ten years later, he is one of the film industry's most creative and intriguing figures.

Lee Trevino was an 8th-grade dropout, with few prospects for a bright future. But he dedicated himself to the game of golf and became one of the greatest players of his day. In fact, he was one of the few players who could give the legendary Jack Nicklaus a run for his money.

Jack Gantos began his writing career in prison. After being paid $10,000 to smuggle hashish from the Virgin Islands to New York City in a boat, he ran aground in Jersey—at a Coast Guard base. He was captured and sentenced to six years in prison. While there, he had time to re-think his life's direction. His acclaimed book *Hole in My Life* was based on his experiences.

What about you? Wouldn't you like to be able to add your story to the ones above? It can happen. It's all a matter of whether you decide to trip over those stumbling stones or climb them to reach new heights.

> **GRACE FOR TODAY:**
> Adversity will make us rely on God, and we'll be stronger, smarter, and more determined.

The fastest runner doesn't always win the race, and the strongest warrior doesn't always win the battle. The wise are often poor, and the skillful are not necessarily wealthy. And those who are educated don't always lead successful lives.

ECCLESIASTES 9:11 NLT

KINGDOM INHERITANCE

By Thomas Watson

A father may have lost his wealth and property and have nothing but his blessing to leave to his children. God, on the other hand, will leave an inheritance to His children, one that is nothing less than a kingdom! (See Luke 12:32.) This kingdom is more glorious and magnificent than any earthly kingdom. It is arrayed with pearls, precious stones, and the richest of jewels. (See Revelation 21:19.) What are all the rarities in the world, the coasts of pearl, the islands of spices, the rocks of diamonds in comparison to this kingdom? In this heavenly kingdom there is satisfying, unparalleled beauty, rivers of pleasure, and it lasts forever. "At Your right hand are pleasures forevermore" (Psalm 16:11 NKJV).

Heaven's eminence is its permanence, and God's children enter into this kingdom immediately after death. There is a sudden transition and passage from death to glory: absent from the body, present with the Lord. God's children will not wait long to receive their inheritance. Just a wink, and they shall see God.

How comforting this should be to God's children who are low in the world in rank and social status! Your Father in heaven, by permanent grant, will confer a kingdom upon you at death. It is such a kingdom as eye has not seen! He will give you a crown, not of gold, but of glory! He will give you white robes lined with immortality![58]

—∞—

DEAR FATHER: IT'S EXCITING TO THINK ABOUT THE THINGS YOU HAVE PREPARED FOR ME IN HEAVEN—BEAUTY AND JOY ENOUGH TO LAST FOR ALL ETERNITY. THANK YOU FOR ALL YOUR GRACIOUS GIFTS, ESPECIALLY FOR GIVING ME YOUR GRACE AND YOUR REMARKABLE KINGDOM. AMEN.

[Jesus said,] "Don't be afraid, little flock. For it gives your Father great happiness to give you the Kingdom.

LUKE 12:32 TLB

YOU FIRST

He who did not spare his own Son, but gave him up for us all—how will
he not also, along with him, graciously give us all things?

ROMANS 8:32

E xpectations were high for the young American swimmer named Michael Phelps. As a favorite in the 2004 summer Olympics, Phelps was attempting to do something no other athlete before him had been able to do—win a record eight Olympic gold medals. To do this, however, Phelps would have to rely on his teammates to pull their weight in the group relay events. In the very first team relay event, one of Phelps' teammates, Ian Crocker, swam a disastrously slow leg, and the team had to settle for a bronze. This one race cost Phelps the chance to break the record for winning eight gold medals.

> **GRACE FOR TODAY:**
>
> The true grace of Christ is reflected in His willingness to give himself for us.

Phelps continued on, however, and his performance in the rest of the events earned him a chance to compete in the coveted 400-meter medley relay. This final team event in swimming, everyone thought, would give Phelps the chance to take one final victory lap and show the world that if it hadn't been for his teammate, he would have easily broken the record and gone down in history. Perhaps that is why everyone was shocked when Phelps announced that he would give up his place to none other than Ian Crocker, the man who had "cost" him the record. When asked to explain, he simply said, "I wanted to give Ian another chance."

Such moments of selflessness reflect the true grace of Christ, who put aside His own life in the single most important act of selflessness so that you could be redeemed and enter into fellowship with God. As you go through your day today, think about the ways you can demonstrate the love of Christ by putting someone else first. Let God fill you with the joy of doing good for others so that you also can demonstrate His grace to the world.

Open Arms

You are a forgiving God, gracious and compassionate,
slow to anger and abounding in love.

Nehemiah 9:17

I t was almost sunset. The father squinted toward the horizon, hoping to see what he'd been looking for every day for more months than he cared to count. Today, he took a second look, straining to see if the figure moving along the edge of the fields was really a person or simply wishful thinking. A moment later, the father's feet began to move, faster and faster, more quickly than a man his age was accustomed to go. As tears of joy flowed down his face, the father's arms opened wide anticipating the long awaited embrace of the child he longed to hold close to his heart.

It was true his son had hurt him—more deeply than the father could express aloud. His son had demanded his inheritance while his father was still alive, then left without a word. His son had wasted every cent of the money and done things that would shame any family. But all of that was behind them now. His son had returned. The child the father loved was home at last.

The story Jesus told of the Prodigal Son is every-one's story. Every one of God's children has turned against Him. Every one has taken God's gifts and wasted them, done things God never intended His beloved children to do. But the story does not end there.

God is waiting for each and every one of his children with His arms open wide, ready to forgive. God's forgiveness is larger than the most horrible deed ever done. It's also once-and-for-all. No "I told you so" or "This is your last chance."

If you have turned your back on God in any area of your life, don't wait any longer. Run into His open arms. Feel the freedom of being totally and eternally forgiven.

> **GRACE FOR TODAY:**
> God's forgiving arms are open for every child who's looking for the way home.

HE HEARS YOU

The eyes of the LORD are on the righteous,
and his ears are attentive to their cry.

PSALM 34:15

"**M**y mom never listens to me!"

Your friend sounded pretty dejected as she shared her hurt.

"She's always so busy with her friends and that club she runs that I never get a chance to talk with her."

Hearing those words brought back some familiar memories for you. It was a similar story for you a year or so ago when both parents worked and, as the only child, you were always at home alone. When your parents were around, they were so consumed with work they hardly had time for you.

A friend from school told you about Jesus Christ, and how He was always there to watch over you and listen to you when nobody else was around. You became a Christian and found out that what they were saying is true. God is always there, no matter what time of day or night. And He wants to talk to you. He is genuinely interested in what you have to say.

With the busyness of life, it is easy to become so wrapped up in work that you overlook the things that are important—like relationships. Thankfully, God's love will not allow Him to overlook anyone. Everyone is important to Him.

Tell your lonely friend about Jesus Christ and how much He loves her. Offer to pray with her so she will come to know Him, then show her how she can talk to God anytime through prayer, knowing that He will listen.

GRACE FOR TODAY:

God is never too busy to listen to
what we have to say.

The Difference Between Why's and Wise

As the heavens are higher than the earth, so are my ways higher than your ways and my thoughts than your thoughts.

Isaiah 55:9

Have you ever tried to explain a complex subject or important rule to a young sibling or to a child you are baby-sitting? It can be frustrating. Sometimes, small children just don't seem to understand what their "elders" are telling them—especially when it comes to answers to that never-ending little-kid question, "Why?"

In our information-rich world, we have figured out so much, unraveled so many of life's tangled mysteries. But there is much more that we don't understand. And, just like a child who can't understand why she can't touch the moon—or why he can't eat candy for every meal—we question God about things that don't make sense to us. We demand to know "why" when life doesn't go according to our plan. At times like these, we forget that all that we know (or think we know) is a tiny droplet in the vast ocean of God's knowledge.

The Bible reminds us that God's ways are much higher than our ways, and we can comprehend only tiny shreds of His comprehensive master plan. Our responsibility is to follow Him, and everything will ultimately work out for good. This doesn't mean that everything that happens in life is good. But it does mean that even the most frightening, terrible stories can have happy endings when we place our trust in God and strive to obey Him.

So, learn to appreciate life's questions. You can learn much about yourself—and about life itself—from the questions that emerge day to day. And remember that God, the Master Architect of the universe, has chosen to reach past the sun, the moon, and the stars to take your hand.

Grace for Today:

Travel hand in hand with God, and your journey and your destination will be truly rewarding.

237

WATCHING OUT FOR YOU

It makes you angry that your parents always want to know everything about your friends. *Why is it necessary for them to know everything anyway?* you wonder. Why can't they trust you to pick your own friends?

Your parents love you. It is important that they make sure you don't make a wreck of your young life by choosing to associate with the wrong crowd.

God is your Heavenly Father. But He has given you earthly parents who love you a great deal. They have the awesome responsibility to watch over you—as you grow and mature into adulthood—and to see that you stay away from bad influences, including people who do not honor God and whose lifestyles are not pleasing to Him.

You may not see anything wrong with keeping that kind of company, but the Bible calls these people corrupt. If you allow them, they will destroy your good morals and your character.

God warns us to watch and pray so that we never stumble into things that would tempt us to compromise our faith in Him. When you meet someone new, don't just judge the person from the outside, or by what others say or think about him. Trust the Spirit to show you if there is anything hidden you need to know about him. Take time to get to know people before you decide to pal around with them.

GRACE FOR TODAY:

God will show us what company to keep.

Take them by the hand and lead them in the way of the Master.

EPHESIANS 6:4 MSG

GOD'S WARRIOR

By Charles Spurgeon

A primary qualification for serving God with any amount of success and for doing God's work well and triumphantly is a sense of our own weakness. When God's warriors march forth to battle, strong in their own might, defeat is not far distant. The follower of Jesus who reckons on victory thus, has reckoned wrongly, for it is "'not by might, nor by power, but by my Spirit,' says the LORD Almighty" (Zachariah 4:6). Those who go forth to fight, boasting of their prowess, shall return with their colorful banners trailing in the dust and their armor stained with disgrace.

Those who serve God must serve God in God's own way and in God's strength, or God will never accept their service. That which humans do, unaided by divine strength, God can never own. The mere fruit of the earth God casts away. God will only reap that corn, the seed of which was sown from heaven, watered by grace, and ripened by the sun of divine love. God will empty out all that you have, before God will put His own into you. The river of God is full of water, but not one drop of it flows from earthly springs. God will have no strength used in God's battles but the strength that God imparts.

Take courage. There must be a consciousness of weakness before the Lord will give you victory. Your emptiness is but the preparation for your being filled. Your casting down is but the making ready for your lifting up.[39]

FATHER GOD: I'M YOUNG AND INEXPERIENCED, AND I CAN'T SEE THAT I WOULD BE MUCH HELP TO YOU IN A BATTLE. BUT I WILL TRUST IN YOUR STRENGTH AND TAKE ON YOUR POWER. I WILL INVITE YOU TO FILL ME WITH YOUR HOLY SPIRIT. I'M WEAK, LORD, BUT YOU ARE STRONG. I AM MIGHTY IN YOU. AMEN.

Take all the help you can get, every weapon God has issued, so that when it's all over but the shouting you'll still be on your feet.

EPHESIANS 6:13 MSG

BE POWERFUL

For let not that man suppose that he will receive anything from the Lord;
he is a double-minded man, unstable in all his ways.

JAMES 1:7-8 NKJV

Preacher and Bible teacher Joyce Meyer always says, "You can be pitiful or powerful, but you can't be both." It's your choice. The devil will try to persuade you
into having a pity party on a daily basis. He will give you all sorts of reasons that you
should feel sorry for yourself. He will remind you of all
of your past failures and whisper things like, "You'll
never be successful. You don't have what it takes." Oh
yeah, the devil is the perfect host at pity parties. He has
thrown a lot of them over the years.

**The Bible
nowhere
indicates that
God withdraws
us from the
troubles of life
. . . but He gives
us power to go
on with the
battle.**

BILLY GRAHAM

When you feel yourself getting into the "pity party
mode," begin praising the Lord. Praise will change the
atmosphere. Start confessing God's Word over your
life. Say things like, "I am more than a conqueror. No
weapon formed against me shall prosper. Everything I
touch prospers and succeeds. I can do all things through
Christ who strengthens me." When you do that, you
give God something to work with.

Until we get to heaven, we're going to encounter
trouble. The Word even says so, but how we handle
that trouble will determine whether or not we're pitiful
or powerful. You can face that trouble—no matter what
it is—without fear. You can have peace in the middle of an intense storm in your life.
You can view each problem as simply a chance for God to work a miracle. You can be
pitiful or powerful—it's your choice. So, choose powerful! Allow God to completely
take control of your life today, and leave those pity parties behind.

THANKSGIVING THAT NEVER ENDS

No matter what happens, always be thankful, for this is God's will for you who belong to Christ Jesus.

1 THESSALONIANS 5:18 TLB

O nce a year, Christmas lights appear. They cover eaves and evergreens, gutters and gateways, Christmas trees and holly leaves. While some displays lean toward tacky, others take your breath away with their beauty. But all of them grab your attention when they first appear. When they go up after Thanksgiving, they herald the joy of the coming season—a celebration of the moment in time when God came down to earth wrapped in a baby's cry. After the first of the year, it's time for them to go back in the box for the next ten and a half months.

But what if everyone left their lights up all year round. Past Easter, through the Fourth of July and beyond, the outline of neon angels would shine and rooftops would twinkle. After awhile, the lights would no longer seem special or celebratory. As a matter of fact, the time would come when you'd hardly notice them at all.

The same thing can happen as you receive God's abundant gifts each and every day. You get so used to receiving them, you wind up taking them for granted. You hardly notice the food on the table, the roof over your head, or the amazing privilege of being able to move and breathe and love and talk to the God of the universe.

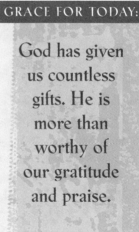

GRACE FOR TODAY:

God has given us countless gifts. He is more than worthy of our gratitude and praise.

It's important to stop and thank God for His countless gifts. He's certainly more than worthy of your gratitude and praise. But giving thanks is as much a gift to you as it is to Him. It helps you grow a grateful heart. The more your gratitude grows, the more blessed you'll feel—and the less of life you'll take for granted.

SPEAK WHAT YOU KNOW

Fire goes out for lack of fuel, and quarrels disappear when gossip stops.

PROVERBS 26:20 NLT

Y ou've heard the rumors just like everyone else. But so far neither you nor any-one else in class has seen any evidence that the school's football captain is using drugs.

It bothers you that people can be so quick to pass judgment on someone else, or run and tell when they don't know all the facts.

What right do they have to judge someone, especially when what they are saying may not even be true? you wonder. *How would they feel if the shoe were on the other foot and they were the subject of gossip? Don't they know how dangerous and destructive it is to spread gossip and lies?*

Sure they do. And so did you before becoming a Christian. You were all ears when someone came to you with gossip. And you could hardly wait to share what you had heard with others—whether you knew for sure that it was true or not.

Fortunately, God helped you to see how potentially destructive that could be. He showed you that gossip is a dangerous tool and that the result is always the same—someone ends up getting hurt. It also ruins friendships.

If hearing others gossip bothers you so much, then speak up. Tell them what a dangerous game they are playing and what bad effects it could have on someone's life.

Ask them how they would feel if someone were saying bad things about them.

Speaking the truth might not be the most popular thing to do, but it is certainly the right thing.

GRACE FOR TODAY:

When we speak the truth, God will back us up.

DON'T SUCCUMB TO THE CULT OF COOL

And do not be conformed to this world, but be transformed by the
renewing of your mind, that you may prove what is that good
and acceptable and perfect will of God.

ROMANS 12:2 NKJV

L emmings are small rodents who migrate in huge, furry masses. Sometimes, this
practice leads to disaster, as one lemming might unwittingly follow another as he
tumbles off the edge of a cliff or ledge.

Not surprisingly, then, no major sports team is dubbed "The Lemmings." After
all, who would want to be named after a critter that blindly follows its peers, even to
its own destruction?

Sadly, many teens today become lemmings in the all-consuming quest to fit in and
to be counted among the ranks of the cool. Being cool is more important yet harder to
define than ever. One thing we know about our ultimate role model: Jesus was not cool.

He was an outcast, a lowly Hebrew carpenter weirdo who hung out with those at
the bottom of the social food chain. Humans who, in reality, were not worthy to touch
the bottom of his sandals routinely treated Him like trash because of where He was
from and whom He hung out with.

Probably every young believer will eventually face a situation in which peers will
do their best to convince them to rebel against the Lord or disrespect Him in some way.

Jesus is the ideal model to look to when issues of peer pressure and the "cool factor" present themselves. Jesus never cared for the world's idea of status. He defined
greatness this way to His friends: Be a servant. (See Mark 9:35.)

GRACE FOR TODAY:

The model that Jesus gave us to follow is not only
more positive than the world's, it's consistent, unlike
the ever-changing tides of what's cool in pop culture.

TURN IT OFF!

After a hard day at school, a relaxed afternoon looking at television before getting down to homework sounds nice. Only there's one problem. There's nothing on TV you want to see.

When it comes to programming, the TV industry is not lacking. From reality shows, to how to get rich, to where to find a mate, TV has it all. But where is the quality TV—the kind that is not rippled with sex, drugs, or violence? These days you've got to look very hard to find it.

What has society come to when it warns against violence, but then blankets the TV screen with drug-pushing, pill-popping addicts who kill to get their next fix and the angry action "heros" who track down these killers to get revenge? Why are teens told to avoid sex when nearly every other TV show and commercial is replete with sexual innuendos? How can teenagers not be tempted to drink when their favorite music stars and actors are always pictured with a drink in their hands?

Television has long been jokingly referred to as the "boob tube." More than that, it is one big "booby trap." It is one of the biggest weapons the devil uses in his effort to lure you away from God and into sin. With all of its suggestive material, it leads you into areas of temptation that you would have never imagined.

If you know there is nothing on worth watching, leave off the TV. Find something that is wholesome and enjoyable to do. God will gladly help you.

GRACE FOR TODAY:

God is more than willing to help us make good choices about what we are watching.

Throw out anything tainted with evil.

1 THESSALONIANS 5:22 MSG

WHAT IS REPENTANCE?

By Dwight L. Moody

L et me say what it is not. Repentance is not fear. Many think they have to be alarmed and terrified, and in order to repent, they are waiting for some kind of fear to come down upon them.

Repentance is not feeling. I find a great many people are waiting to turn to God, but think they cannot do it until this feeling comes.

Repentance is not fasting and afflicting the body. A person may fast for weeks and months and years, yet not repent of one sin.

Neither is it remorse. Judas had terrible remorse, but that was not repentance.

Repentance is not conviction of sin. I have seen people under such deep conviction of sin that they could not sleep at night nor enjoy a single meal, and yet, they did not truly repent.

Neither is praying repentance. Many people say, "I will pray and read the Bible," and yet never repent.

It is not quitting one single sin. Forsaking one vice is like breaking off one limb of a tree when the whole tree has to come down.

What is repentance? It is "Right About Face!" It implies that a person walking in one direction has not only faced about, but is actually walking in an exactly contrary direction.[40]

—ᗰ—

FATHER GOD: GRANT ME A REPEN-TANT HEART BY YOUR GRACE—A HEART THAT HAS TAKEN A NEW DIRECTION HEADED STRAIGHT FOR GODLINESS. THANK YOU FOR FORGIVING ME AND MAKING MY LIFE PLEASING TO YOU. AMEN.

Repent, then, and turn to God, so that your sins may be wiped out, that times of refreshing may come from the Lord.

ACTS 3:19

WAITING IN FAITH

Moreover David was greatly distressed because the people spoke of stoning him. . . . But David strengthened himself in the LORD his God.

1 SAMUEL 30:6 NASB

W hen Chris Klug captured the bronze medal in the Giant Slalom event at the 2002 Olympic Games in Salt Lake City, his friends and family celebrated with him. He had not only placed well in the Games, but also accomplished something no American had ever done. He had become the first-ever American to compete in the Olympics after having undergone an organ transplant.

Chris suffered from a rare liver disease, one that affects only one person in 10,000, and had spent seven years on the waiting list for a new liver. He received that transplant in July 2000 and five months later, he was back in shape and ready to compete in the sport he loved. But during those seven years of waiting, don't you imagine Chris grew weary? He probably knew that many people die every year awaiting transplants. Still, he never gave up.

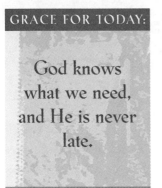

GRACE FOR TODAY:

God knows what we need, and He is never late.

You can't give up, either. No matter what you're going through, you have to hold on. When David and his troops returned to their home at Ziklag, he was at his darkest point in life. He had fought bravely for the Lord, yet when he and his men returned to camp, they discovered their town had been burned and their women and children captured. The men even talked of stoning David, but he didn't let it get him down. He encouraged himself in the Lord, and do you know what? In seventy-two hours, he had conquered the Amalekites and taken back the wives and children. Plus, David was then named king.

Your miracle may take seven years to manifest—like Chris Klug's. Or, you may only be seventy-two hours from your victory. Just know that you will triumph—in God's perfect timing. Wait in faith and expectancy. Encourage yourself in the Lord, and get ready for a miracle.

THE OPPORTUNE MOMENT

You are my God! Hour by hour I place my days in your hand.

PSALM 31:14-15 MSG

The Bible says that for God a day is like a thousand years. To you, a day is like, well—twenty-four hours. No more. No less. You can't subtract a few hours when you have the flu to save up and enjoy on a more pleasant day. You can't stretch a day past midnight to finish a paper without beginning to use up time from the day ahead. Once your twenty-four hours are spent, they're gone forever. There are no deposits and no returns.

Every single day is filled with unique opportunities that, like those twenty-four hours, happen only once in a lifetime. Those opportunities may seem small, almost insignificant, at the time—the chance to do your best on a history exam, to hug a friend who's hurting, or to tell someone about how God has changed your life. But as you learn in Physics, every action has a reaction. Everything you do has an effect in this world. What kind of effect do you want to have?

Jesus' time on this earth was limited. He had thirty-three years, only three of which He spent in the public eye telling others about God. Jesus knew His time was short, so He invested it on things that made a difference in light of eternity. He loved others well,

GRACE FOR TODAY:

God gives opportunities; success depends on the use made of them.

ELLEN G. WHITE

treating interruptions and uncomfortable situations as opportunities, instead of disruptions to His schedule. And no matter how busy He got, Jesus always took time out to pray, to realign His purposes and plans with His heavenly Father's.

Only God knows how many twenty-four hour days you'll have the privilege of using in this lifetime. By following Jesus' example, God will give you the grace to use them well.

A FRESH START

Renew a right, persevering, and steadfast spirit within me.

PSALM 51:10 AMP

T he whirling sound coming from the computer is a good sign. Then the monitor comes on, and you hear music from the speakers. A quick check after the computer finishes loading, and you find your files are still there. It's a good end to what could have been a disaster after the screen had frozen and you could not get the system to work.

All it took was a quick reboot. Strike a couple of keys, wait for the computer to shut off and start up again and "presto"—it's a new beginning. The computer has reset, and everything is back to normal.

That's similar to the way it is with Christians. Obviously, God does not see you as a computer. But He does have a way to restore you when you seem to get all out of whack.

God knows that living the Christian life is not easy. He understands that somewhere along the line we make mistakes—we say or do things we shouldn't. Then we feel guilty.

But God, your Heavenly Father, says He is always willing to forgive your wrong and forget that it ever happened. In fact, He forgives you the very moment you ask for forgiveness. He wipes your record clean and then gives you a fresh reboot so that everything can be back to normal again.

There may not be a "delete" button for you to push when you make a mistake, but you can always go to God for help. He forgives, forgets, and gives you a brand-new lease on life.

GRACE FOR TODAY:

Because of His grace, God gives us new beginnings.

ARE YOU LIVING ON-PURPOSE?

I have not yet reached my goal, and I am not perfect. But Christ has taken hold of me. So I keep on running and struggling to take hold of the prize.

PHILIPPIANS 3:12 CEV

What is your passion in life? What do you enjoy more than anything else in the world—the kind of thing you know you will never grow tired of? Maybe it's music, art, teaching others, or creative writing. If you have found your passion, you know there is a sense of wonder about it.

Former professional baseball player Dave Dravecky loved his sport so much that he confessed, "I would have played for nothin'." And today, he brings that same kind of passion to his callings as a writer and head of a ministry for cancer victims and amputees.

What about you? Are you pursuing your passion? Sure, there are required classes you must take, maybe a part-time job that you must do to earn money toward college. Are you participating in the extracurricular activities you truly love—or just the ones you think will make you more popular, or look best on a college application? And are you taking elective classes that ignite in you a sense of wonder and challenge you, or are you picking easy classes to pad your grade-point average? In other words, are you making a grade—or making a difference?

If much of your life is sheer drudgery, you might be missing God's purpose for you. Think of the first disciples Jesus called. They all left what they were doing to follow Him. Their hearts pounded with excitement and anticipation of the adventures ahead.

The Lord wants no less for you. His plan for you is to experience a vibrant life, in perfect harmony with the gifts He has given you. So don't let your life be a series of random events. Live it on purpose; live it with passion.

GRACE FOR TODAY:

God is specific about His plans for us to live a brilliant life.

YOUR FIRST REAL LOVE

The story your mother told sounded like something out of a fairytale.

From the day she first laid eyes on your father, she knew he was the one for her. Actually, it was love at first sight for the both of them. Though they were just young kids in junior high school, each had met their first love.

More than forty years later they still have fond memories of that special day. But now they also talk about another "first love." They mean someone else who takes on a different meaning. They share about their first meeting with Jesus Christ—who they both agree is their true first love.

No matter what age you are, falling in love for the first time is perhaps the most memorable experience one can ever have. It is a moment you will treasure for the rest of your life.

GRACE FOR TODAY:

God puts us first—we're in His thoughts and dreams every moment of the day.

That's how it should be when it comes to your relationship with God, who loved you so much that He sent His Son to die for you. Your love for Him should be the most important thing in your life—even more important than family, friends, and passions.

You tell your friends you love them. You even go out of your way at times to find ways to show them how much you care. What about God? What are you doing to show Him how much He means to you?

God already knows how you feel. But it never hurts to assure Him. Take time out to pray, tell God how much He means to you, and thank Him for loving you first. Then, let your lifestyle be a witness to others of that love.

First we were loved, now we love. He loved us first.

1 JOHN 4:19 MSG

GLORY IN GOD

By Thomas à Kempis

Put no trust in your own learning nor in the cunning of any person. Instead, put your trust in the grace of God who helps the humble and humbles the proud.

If you have wealth, do not glory in it. Do not glory in friends because they are powerful. But glory in God, who gives all things, and who desires, above all, to give himself.

Do not boast of personal stature or of physical beauty. These are qualities that can be marred and destroyed by a little sickness. Do not take pride in your talent or ability, lest you displease God to whom all the natural gifts that you have belong.

Do not think yourself better than others, lest, perhaps, you be considered as being worse before God, who knows what is inside of human beings.

Do not take pride in your good deeds, for God's evaluations differ from those of human beings. What pleases others often displeases God.

If there is good in you, see more good in others, so that you may remain humble. It does no harm to esteem yourself less than anyone else. But it is very harmful to think yourself better than even one. The humble live in continuous peace, while in the hearts of the proud are envy and frequent anger.[41]

—⚍—

DEAR HEAVENLY FATHER: I SAY THAT I WANT TO PLEASE YOU, BUT IT'S HARD TO KEEP THAT COMMITMENT. THE WORLD I LIVE IN IS SO MUCH ABOUT LOOKING JUST RIGHT AND LOOKING DOWN ON THOSE WHO DON'T. HELP ME TO REMEMBER THAT YOU ARE ALWAYS LOOKING AT MY HEART AND WHEN I'M ALL FULL OF MYSELF, WHAT YOU SEE IS NOT PLEASING TO YOU. HELP ME AS I STRIVE TO KEEP MY HEART FREE OF PRIDE AND FULL OF YOUR LOVE AND GRACE. AMEN.

Charm can mislead and beauty soon fades.

PROVERBS 31:30 MSG

ETERNAL OPTIMISM

Consider it all joy, my brethren, when you encounter various trials,
knowing that the testing of your faith produces endurance.

JAMES 1:2–3 NASB

D uring World War II, an older distinguished gentleman who lived in a hotel in the United States made friends with a little girl who lived in the same hotel. She was the daughter of a serviceman. She often played in the lobby because it was the only place she could play. The old man learned that the little girl's family had moved many times because of the war, but now the hotel was their home. One day as the man observed her playing in the lobby, he said to her, "What a pity that you and your family don't have a home." The little girl, without missing a beat, answered, "Oh, we have a home. We just don't have a house to put it in!"

Now that's the right attitude. That little girl is a "glass half full" person. She looks on the brighter side of things. That's how we should be. As long as we're here on earth, we're going to encounter circumstances that aren't always comfortable. In fact, there will be times when you'll wonder if God has forgotten about you. But, don't let circumstances rule your world. Instead, keep a positive outlook. Always look for the good in every situation. Become a "glass half full" Christian. If you're a negative person, ask God to help you become more like Him. He is the eternal optimist. He will help you see situations through His eyes. You might be surprised how differently the world looks through the Father's eyes.

GRACE FOR TODAY:

We can look on the brighter side of life because the Light of the World lives inside us!

COME TOGETHER

No matter how significant you are,
it is only because of what you are a part of.

1 CORINTHIANS 12:19 MSG

Y ou are an incredible drummer. Or, at least let's pretend you are. You've had a
pair of drumsticks in your hand since you were able to hold a bottle. It's your
dream to use your skills to honor God and entertain others. So you go on tour.
Unfortunately, after the first twenty-minute drum solo, you can tell the crowd's getting a bit restless. After all, drums may be the heartbeat of music, but they're tough to
hum along with. So you start a band. As you begin your first rehearsal, it dawns on
you: Teamwork can take you places you could never go on your own.

There's only so much you can do "solo" in this
life. It takes teamwork to perform an operation, stage a
play, or sing in four-part harmony. In the same way
that band members can take different instruments playing different notes and wind up with a masterpiece,
working together with others who have skills you don't
possess can allow you to accomplish something you
couldn't do alone.

But there's something else that takes teamwork to
a whole different level. That's having God on your
team. In the same way that it takes a talented songwriter to give a band something worthwhile to play, it
takes God guiding your efforts to make what you do
have a lasting impact.

GRACE FOR TODAY:

True teamwork
beats together
in time with
one heart—
God's.

With God as your melody, you can find harmony on any team. Concentrate on
doing your own part well, without hogging the spotlight or insisting others do things
"your way." Instead, work together God's way. Reach out to your teammates with love,
patience, and humility. Share the joy of victory. Console each other through defeat.
Encourage each other along the way. Give credit to God through it all.

HANG IN THERE!

God isn't late with his promise as some measure lateness.

2 PETER 3:9 MSG

I t had been a grueling run that had taken you over seven miles of trudging up hills, around curves and long stretches of road in the hot Texas heat. Several times you thought about quitting, but something kept you going.

For one thing, there was the cause for which you had chosen to run. The money your supporters had pledged would go a long way toward helping to feed the needy children overseas. Seeing how poor those kids were had touched your heart, and you wanted to do whatever you could to help them.

The other, even more important thing was that it reminded you of how God's love never gave up on you. Simply put, that's the love of God. You put others' needs first. Discomfort did not stop your determination to finish the run for the sake of the children.

The Bible says God is longsuffering, not willing that anyone should perish. That means He is patient—so patient, in fact, that He is willing to stay, even when you make mistakes. He waits until finally He gets through to you with His Word.

When you asked Him into your life, He gladly forgave all of your wrong, wrapped you in His arms, and said, "It's okay, my child. I forgive you, and I love you."

That's how God's love, now working on the inside you, will cause you to respond. When what you're doing is for the benefit of someone else, you will not quit. Instead, you will press on and see it through to the end.

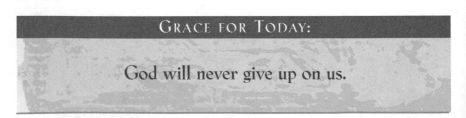

GRACE FOR TODAY:

God will never give up on us.

GOD'S CALLING—
IT'S FOR YOU!

The LORD God then said: I will look for my sheep and
take care of them myself.

EZEKIEL 34:11 CEV

The God of the entire universe longs to communicate with you! Let that truth sink in for a moment. It's amazing, but true.

Many of us would consider it the opportunity of a lifetime to, just once, talk with a favorite artist, athlete, or movie star. We would be eager to tell our friends about our "brush with greatness," knowing that they would be impressed—and probably jealous.

Unfortunately, we don't show the same zeal for communicating with God, who loves us, who is far more fascinating than any person we could ever encounter, and who longs to hang with us.

God created the universe and everything in it—including the celebrities we revere. He created us to have a relationship with Him. And the only way to have a relationship with anyone is to spend time with him. With God, this time can include prayer, meditation, reading the Bible or Christian books, listening to music, and worshiping by singing or even dancing.

Think about it: What relationship is more important than your personal relationship with God? Who is more worth knowing? After all, God created you, He loves you, and He has all the answers.

The Lord of all creation is waiting for you. You might not know Him well, but He knows you. He wants to hear from you. There is no risk. God will never betray your relationship with Him. So don't wait another second. Open your eyes; open your heart. God wants to communicate with you right now!

GRACE FOR TODAY:

God yearns to be close to us. He holds no grudges;
instead, He holds His people, close to His heart.

THE REAL DEAL

J enna was shocked and embarrassed as the cashier handed her back the money.

"What—do you mean it's no good?" she asked.

"It's fake," came the response. "It's counterfeit."

After quickly replacing the counterfeit twenty dollar bill with what turned out to be real money, Jenna left the store. Still stunned at what had just taken place, she felt herself become angry.

How could people be so dishonest, she thought. Just then Jenna thought about the devil, and what the Bible says about his many disguises. He is just as much a counterfeit as the phony money she had been carrying around in her purse. And because his disguises are usually so attractive, it can be just as hard to recog-

nize him as it is to detect fake money.

To recognize fake money, those in law enforcement and banking must spend hours studying the real thing. By the time they are done, they can spot the bad stuff at the blink of an eye.

The same should be true with the devil. His ways are not the same as God's. But he tries hard to make it appear that way.

Those who have a close, intimate relationship with God—who worship Him and keep Him first place in their hearts—will always be quick to recognize the devil. They won't act on what he says or cash in on his deceitful dealings.

Talk to God daily. Study His Word and hide it in your heart. Then, when the devil comes at you in any form, you will recognize him immediately.

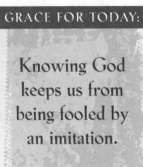

GRACE FOR TODAY:

Knowing God keeps us from being fooled by an imitation.

Do not believe everyone who claims to speak by the Spirit. You must test them.

1 JOHN 4:1 NLT

IN THE PRESENCE OF THE KING

By Francis de Sales

God's Presence is universal. There is no place in the world—not one—that is devoid of God's Most Holy Presence. Even as birds in flight continually meet the air, so also wherever we might go, we will meet with that Presence always and everywhere. This is a truth that all followers of Jesus readily admit, but all are not equally alive to its importance.

A blind person, when in the presence of a king, will preserve a reverential demeanor if told that the king is there, although they are unable to see him. But, practically speaking, what people don't see, they easily forget, and, therefore, readily lapse into carelessness and irreverence. In this same way, we do not see our God, although faith warns us that God is present. Because we are not seeing God with our physical eyes, we are too apt to forget God and act as though God is way far away.

While knowing perfectly well that God is everywhere, if we do not think about it, it is the same as if we did not know it. Therefore, before beginning to pray, it is always necessary to rouse your entire being to a constant, unswerving remembering and thinking about the Presence of God.

In Old Testament days, when Jacob beheld the ladder that went up to Heaven, he cried out, "Surely the LORD is in this place, and I was not aware of it" (Genesis 28:16). By saying this, he meant that he had not thought about it, because, surely, he could not fail to know that God was everywhere and in all things. Therefore, when you are preparing to pray, you must say with your whole heart, "God is indeed here."[42]

—///—

DEAR LORD: YOU HAVE PROMISED TO BE WITH ME—ALWAYS. BUT I OFTEN FORGET THAT YOU ARE THERE. GIVE ME A MOMENT-BY-MOMENT AWARENESS OF YOUR PRESENCE. AMEN.

The LORD is near to all who call on him, to all who call on him in truth.

PSALM 145:18 NRSV

HIS WAYS

You will keep on guiding me with your counsel,
leading me to a glorious destiny.

PSALM 73:24 NLT

Christian track star Vonetta Flowers was expected to be a medalist in the Summer Olympics of both 1996 and 2000, but injuries kept her from making the team both years. Vonetta couldn't understand why God would let this happen. Hadn't she already suffered enough adversity in life? She had grown up in one of the worst neighborhoods in Birmingham, Alabama, and had pushed through to become a seven-time All-American at the University of Alabama.

GRACE FOR TODAY:

God wants to draw out the champion in each of us.

Then one day, on the spur of a moment, Vonetta answered an ad placed from the U.S. Olympic Committee to try out for women's bobsled—and she was the best competitor by far. She started racing in the fall of 2000 as the pusher for veteran Bonny Warner. This pairing proved successful, as they finished in the top ten in all seven World Cup races in 2000-2001. And, the twosome placed eighth at the 2001 World Championships in Calgary, Alberta. Their medals are too numerous to name.

Vonetta was quoted as saying, "I always thought God had planned for me to win a medal, but I never dreamed it would be the winter games. It shows you never know what God has in mind. This is beyond anything I could have ever imagined."

Maybe you have a dream that hasn't yet been realized. Maybe you feel like God has totally turned His back on you, but He hasn't. He knows every tear you have ever cried. He knows your deepest desires. He knows everything about you—even the number of hairs on your head—and He loves you with an everlasting love. Keep believing! Remember, God's ways are higher than your ways, and His plan for your life is even bigger and better than you have ever imagined.

HIDE AND SEEK

Look to him, and be radiant; so your faces shall never be ashamed.

P<small>SALM</small> 34:5 <small>NRSV</small>

W hen Adam and Eve chose to disobey God, their first impulse was to hide. Not much has changed in human behavior since the days in the Garden of Eden. When little kids are caught doing something wrong, the first thing they do is try to run away. Adults are a little sneakier. They usually attempt to hide by passing the blame or telling a lie.

But in the same way that God had no trouble finding Adam and Eve hiding behind the bushes, He has no trouble finding you when a guilty conscience sends you undercover. Guilt drives you to want to hide. Grace is God seeking you out. Shame is something altogether different.

Guilt is a positive thing. It lets you know that you've wandered away from the path God has set before you. It's a glimpse of how holy God is and how imperfect you are. But once God's forgiven you, guilt should disappear. Its job is done.

If you still feel guilty after apologizing to God and others for what's happened, shame has taken over. Shame is not God condemning you. It just makes you feel that way. Feeling ashamed is like punishing your-self over and over for the same offense. A loving parent would never do that to a child. And God would never do that to you.

GRACE FOR TODAY:

God forgives us freely so that we can say goodbye to shame and guilt.

Shame can rob you of the joy and freedom of God's forgiveness. It can make you feel small and unworthy. It can cause you to hide from people, as well as God. The best way to get rid of it is to recognize it for what it really is—an outright lie. Anytime you feel ashamed, head straight to God. He wants to replace shame's lies with the truth of His steadfast love.

STAND OUT!

Do not be conformed to this world (this age), [fashioned after
and adapted to its external, superficial customs].

ROMANS 12:2 AMP

You love being a Christian. Living a life you know is pleasing to your Heavenly Father has brought you so much joy. Except when it comes to your relationship with your schoolmates.

Most of their activities are not the kinds of things you agree with, so you refuse to become involved. Consequently, instead of embracing you as one of the group, they think you're strange. It's tough trying to fit in, especially when you want so badly to be accepted.

When you asked God into your life, you made a decision to obey His Word no matter what persecution came your way. You made up your mind to do what is right, no matter what others around you were doing. Now, God expects you to stay true to that decision.

Part of pleasing God is living the right kind of life before others so that they may learn about Him. Much of what the world says is right or fun, God says is wrong. When you stand up for what God says is right and say no to things His Word says are wrong, then you are pleasing God. You are also sending a message to others that God isn't happy with them, or their actions.

God knows exactly how you feel, and He will help you get through the hurt and pain of being rejected. Jesus was ridiculed and rejected for the life He lived on earth. You can rest in knowing what He has in store for you far outweighs any amount of temporary happiness you could obtain from being part of the crowd.

Don't try to fit in when you know it could count you out with God. Do the right thing no matter what others say.

GRACE FOR TODAY:
God makes us feel welcome even when
others reject us.

GRIEF AND BELIEF

[Jesus said.] "God blesses those who mourn, for they will be comforted."

MATTHEW 5:4 NLT

We live in a fallen world and, as a result, we all experience pain. The hurt of a relationship destroyed or of a loved one lost will, most likely, affect every one of us at some point in life. Fortunately, God is Lord over all of it—the pain, the questions, the helpless feelings.

God never said our journey would be without stumbles, without heartaches, without deep loss. From our earthly perspective, the loss is sometimes all we can see. Yet, from His eternal, all-knowing perspective, it may not be a loss at all.

Your God knows when you are hurting, and He is there for you every second, through every tear.

Our duty as His followers is to seek God's will and purpose in everything. If we trust His plan, it is not necessary to wallow and feel sorry for ourselves. While we may see only a tiny piece of all that is going on, He sees it all—every effect, every ripple throughout eternity.

Someday, we will see His whole plan and how He orchestrated it all through history and through the moments of our lives—even the tough moments.

For now, we can rest in the understanding that God's plan is good and His promises are true. He will make good on His promise to work all things for our good if we love and serve Him. We know with absolute certainty that He will be our comforter and our deliverer in our times of utmost pain and grief.

God understands that this world can hurt sometimes. It's supposed to. This is not our home. Heaven is a real place, a place of complete joy, and we will see it soon enough. Then we will grieve no more.

GRACE FOR TODAY:

Rest in the knowledge that we cannot go anywhere—even the depths of despair—where God cannot reach us.

LIVE THE LIFE

Becoming a Christian is perhaps the most exciting thing that will ever happen in your life. At least that's how you felt when you asked Jesus into your life, and He dramatically transformed you. But getting others to understand how God has transformed you, and that He will do the same for them, is a different story.

Ever hear the old saying, "The proof is in the pudding"? The literal translation of that statement is that you can only know how good or bad pudding tastes if you eat some of it. Otherwise, you have to go by what others say, and unfortunately not everyone speaks the truth.

Jesus had an experience like this with one of His disciples upon returning to earth following His Resurrection. When Thomas was told by the others that they had seen Jesus, Thomas refused to believe them, and said, "I won't believe it unless I see the nail wounds in His hands, put my fingers into them, and place my hand into the wound in His side" (John 20:25 NLT).

Thomas needed some kind of physical, tangible proof before he would believe that something so wonderful, so miraculous could actually be true.

Your spiritual transformation is awesome, and marvelous. And because it is so far removed from what most people expect, they want to see some proof before they will believe.

Give them something to see—something to marvel over. Show them the dramatic transformation God has made in you by living a godly life and walking close to God. This doesn't mean we should pretend to be perfect. We all make mistakes and face problems, but as Christians we learn to admit our wrongs and to seek God for help. When others see what God has done in your life they will want to experience God for themselves.

> **GRACE FOR TODAY:**
>
> The best proof of the change God has made in us is our godly lives.

By opening up to others, you'll prompt people to open up with God.

MATTHEW 5:16 MSG

DOUBT NOT

By Charles Spurgeon

L et me forbid your fears with a few words of consolation. When Peter was in the water, he was where his master had called him to be. You, in your trouble now, are not only Christ's servant, but you are where Christ has chosen to put you.

I have heard of fiendish Sirens in fables who tempt persons into the sea to drown them. Is Christ a Siren? Will He entice His people onto the rocks where He shall destroy them? God forbid! If Christ calls you into the fire, He will bring you out of it. If He bids you walk the sea, He will enable you to tread it in safety. Doubt not, soul.

It is no austere, unloving heart who has summoned you to pass through this difficulty in order to gratify a capricious whim. Ah, no, it is Christ. Shall the heart that bled its life away on the cross to rescue you from death be hard and emotionless when you are overwhelmed in sorrow?

Peter is not the only one walking on the sea. His master is there with him, too. So Jesus is with you today in your troubles, suffering with you as He suffered for you. Oh, turn your eyes from the rough waves. Listen no longer to the howling tempest. Fix your trust on Him who even now cries out in the midst of the tempest, "It is I. Be not afraid."[45]

———

HEAVENLY FATHER: I AM SO GRATEFUL THAT YOU ARE WILLING TO WALK WITH ME THROUGH EVERY STORM IN MY LIFE. I SURE DON'T DESERVE YOUR PRESENCE IN MY LIFE. IT'S PART OF YOUR GRACE. I TRUST YOU TO HELP ME WHEN I CALL ON YOU. AMEN.

Listen now! The Lord isn't too weak to save you. And he isn't getting deaf! He can hear you when you call!

ISAIAH 59:1 TLB

TIME MANAGEMENT

May the Lord our God show us his approval and make our efforts
successful. Yes, make our efforts successful!

PSALM 90:17 NLT

A time management expert once said, "Time management is an illusion. You can't manage time; you can only manage what you spend your time doing." No truer words were ever spoken. Is your schedule jam-packed with way too much stuff? After-school jobs, homework, church commitments, athletic activities, and more can really fill up a to-do list. At some point, you have to realize that you simply can't do it all. There are only so many hours in a day, and trying to cram too much stuff into that twenty-four hour period can result in stress, aggravation, and exhaustion.

GRACE FOR TODAY:

God is the
Master at time
management.

Maybe you are busying your life with activity but not productivity. Maybe you're like the caterpillar. Noted French naturalist Jean Henri Fabre studied these furry little insects, in search of why they instinctively followed one another in mindless activity—no matter what. He ran an experiment in which he placed a number of these caterpillars in a single-file line around the circumference of a pot's rim.

Each caterpillar's head touched the caterpillar in front of it. Then, Fabre placed the caterpillars' favorite food in the middle of the circle created by the caterpillars' procession around the rim of the flowerpot. Thinking the caterpillar in front of him was heading toward the food, the caterpillars kept marching around the circle for days!

Those silly bugs walked in a circle for an entire week until they began dropping dead of exhaustion and starvation. Yet, they were only six inches from their favorite food. They were being active, but not productive; and it cost them their lives.

It can do the same thing to us. If you're feeling overwhelmed with life right now, take a moment and ask God to help you prioritize your to-do list.

UNDER THE SURFACE

The joy that the LORD gives you will make you strong.

NEHEMIAH 8:10 GNB

H appiness is like a sudden summer thunderstorm. It's loud and flashy, immediately grabbing your attention. It's a welcome break from the heat, but disappears before you know it. Once the clouds roll by and the sun comes out, all that's left are mud puddles and memories.

Joy is more like an underground river that never runs dry. No matter what the conditions are outside—rain, hail, snow, or drought—it keeps on flowing. It provides a constant source of refreshment for the soul.

While life in this world can bring brief showers of happiness, only God can provide a steady stream of joy. It's the kind of joy Jesus' disciples had as they sang at the top of their lungs at midnight, even though they were chained in jail. It's the kind of joy Daniel experienced as he shared a lion's den. It's the kind of joy that filled Jesus with courage and hope as He headed toward the Cross. Real joy is more than a giggle that leaves you giddy. It's a gift from God that gives you strength.

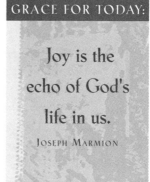

GRACE FOR TODAY:

Joy is the echo of God's life in us.

JOSEPH MARMION

Though the pursuit of happiness may be an "inalienable right" according to the United States Constitution, joy doesn't need to be pursued. It's there, as close as God's presence, ready to overflow onto any thirsty soul that is open to receive it.

Open your soul to God's gift of joy. Accept His forgiveness. Trust in His goodness. Celebrate His faithfulness. Express your gratefulness. The more you allow God to fill your life, the more joy will fill your heart.

WATCH YOUR WORDS

I will help both of you to speak clearly, and I will tell you what to do.

EXODUS 4:15 NLT

Pushing back from the computer, you stared blankly at the words on the screen. The message you had just finished writing had expressed your feelings. Finally, Lindsey would know just what you thought of her and how offensively she treats others.

But thankfully, you gave sending the e-mail more thought and decided that it was the wrong thing to do. Instead, you prayed and asked God to either handle the situation for you or to show you when and how to confront her lovingly.

Then you deleted the e-mail.

Not only was your decision to delete the e-mail the right thing to do, but deciding to hold your peace in a time of anger and frustration was wise. When you don't take time to think before you speak, anything could happen. Too quickly, you say what is on your mind, never once considering the effects your words might have. By the time you have given the matter more thought, your words have already gone to work.

God warns us in the Bible that the tongue is like wildfire—spreading out of control destruction with our words. The moment words are released, they go to work—blessing or cursing. We can speak good things and bless people. Or we can say unkind things and cause emotional wounds that may never heal.

God used words to create the heavens and the earth. When He was finished, He looked on His work with joy and called it good. Your words should always create the same results. Ask God to give you words of peace and love to speak to your friends when you're frustrated with them.

GRACE FOR TODAY:

When we allow God to speak for us, we won't speak out of turn.

WHO'S IN YOUR COMPANY?

He who walks with wise men will be wise,
But the companion of fools will be destroyed.

PROVERBS 13:20 NKJV

F ew of life's choices are tougher, or more important, than your choice of friends. After all, even Jesus spent time with people of low reputation—even to the point of being called a lowlife himself. Yet, the Bible is full of advice such as the proverb "Bad company corrupts good character."

So how do we follow Jesus' example and, at the same time, surround ourselves with the kind of people who positively influence us, rather than leading us into trouble?

First, we should spend as much time as possible with godly people who will encourage us to grow closer to our Creator. We all need people who provide a good example and can hold us accountable if our behavior starts to slide.

Second, as we befriend troubled people, we must be careful to do so on our terms, as much as possible. It's important to control the setting. An unsupervised party is not a good place to hang with troubled friends; neither is a car driven by someone who is intoxicated or under-age.

Finally, you must continue to monitor your friendships and be able to give a clear-eyed assessment of where they are leading you and vice versa. Are you influencing your friends for good? Are they asking more questions about God than they did days and weeks ago? Have they reduced bad habits, such as drinking, drugs, and Internet pornography?

Or, are you the one being changed? Has your language, your attitude, or your behavior changed for the worse? If that's the case, it might be time to "relocate" yourself to a new "company."

GRACE FOR TODAY:

God created us to lead—to influence others for Him.

DON'T GET EVEN

Y ou've just been told someone is going around saying bad things about you. Why they would do such a thing is beyond you. But you feel you can't just sit by and let your reputation be destroyed. You are hurt and angry, and the first thing that comes to mind is to retaliate and start a rumor about them.

Jesus never re-sponded to persecution by striking back; and you know that is not how God wants you to respond. But that is exactly how the devil would like to see you react.

Don't do it. Striking back or getting involved in senseless bickering only causes a lot of trouble for you and the other person. It can also destroy your Christian testimony.

Being the subject of lies and the object of ridicule are not pleasant. But

> **GRACE FOR TODAY:**
>
> The joy in knowing God will defend us greater than any false accusations.

fighting back, or giving an eye for an eye, makes you no better than your accusers. You can calmly tell them that it hurts you when they spread lies, and ask them to stop, but beyond that, it is God's job to take care of the problem and your job to pray for them.

God knows you are innocent, and He knows what you are going through. Let Him handle it. Then you can be free to walk in love and peace.

First, pray and forgive the person. Then, trust God to help you treat him or her with love so that you can avoid an angry confrontation that could have dis-astrous results. God has given you the Holy Spirit to help you in times like this. If you allow Him, He will strengthen you so that such abuse will not damage you.

"I will take vengeance; I will repay those who deserve it," says the Lord.

ROMANS 12:19 NLT

GOD IS OUR ROCK

By Charles Spurgeon

Many a giant rock is a source of admiration from its elevation, because on the summit we can see the world spread out below, like some small map. The mighty God is such a rock. God is our refuge and our high observatory from which we see the unseen and have the evidence of things not yet enjoyed.

If we are delivered and made alive in Christ, still our preservation is the Lord alone. If we are prayerful, God makes us prayerful. If we have graces, God gives us graces. If we have spiritual fruit, God gives us spiritual fruit. If we have repulsed an enemy, God's power strengthened our arm. Do we live to God a holy life? It is not us, but Christ who lives in us. Are we sanctified? God's Holy Spirit sanctifies us. Do we grow in knowledge? The great Instructor teaches us. "He alone is my rock and my salvation" (Psalm 62:2).

Can your salvation be by anything except by God? Are you strong enough to resist temptation without your God? A little servant-girl may cast a Peter down, and can cast you down, too, if God does not keep you. (See Luke 22:54–62.)

If God only is your rock, and you know it; aren't you bound to put all your trust in Him, to give all your love to Him? If God is all you have, surely, all you have shall be God's. If God alone is your hope, surely, you will put all your hope upon God. God has put all salvation in God, to bring all yourself unto God.⁴⁴

—∞—

DEAR GOD: THANK YOU FOR BEING A ROCK IN MY LIFE, LOVING ME, HELPING ME, PROTECTING ME, AND MAKING ME BETTER THAN I AM. I PRAISE YOU FOR YOUR GRACE. AMEN.

God is able to make all grace abound to you.

2 CORINTHIANS 9:8

LITTLE HELP FROM
YOUR FRIENDS

Moses' arms finally became too tired to hold up the staff any longer.
So Aaron and Hur found a stone for him to sit on. Then they stood
on each side, holding up his hands until sunset.

EXODUS 17:12 NLT

B ill Withers wrote and recorded "Lean on Me" which has this chorus: "Lean on
me, when you're not strong. And I'll be your friend. I'll help you carry on. For
it won't be long. 'Til I'm gonna need somebody to lean on." Many artists have re-
recorded this hit over the years. It's not only a catchy little tune, but also packs a powerful message.

Face it. We all need a little help from our friends sometimes. Even Moses (you
know, the "parting of the Red Sea" guy, Moses) need-
ed help from his pals. The Amalekites attacked the
Israelites at Rephidim. Moses said to Joshua, "Choose
some of our men and go out to fight the Amalekites.
Tomorrow I will stand on top of the hill with the staff
of God in my hands" (Exodus 17:9).

So Joshua went to battle as instructed, and Moses,
Aaron, and Hur went to the top of the hill. As long as
Moses held up his hands, the Israelites won, but
whenever he lowered his hands, the Amalekites began
winning. After a while, Moses' arms became tired, so
Aaron and Hur held his hands up—one on one side,
one on the other. That way, his hands remained steady
until Joshua overcame the Amalekite army. Together, Moses, Aaron, and Hur were
able to keep their side winning. (See Exodus 17:10-13.)

If Moses needed help from his friends, don't you think we probably need a little
help from our buddies once in a while? Don't try to go it alone. It's okay to admit that
you can't do everything by yourself. It's okay to show your vulnerability. If you don't
have any godly friends, ask God to place some in your life. And, remember, you can
always lean on God.

GRACE FOR TODAY:

God is a strong
pillar of strength
that will never
fail when we
lean on Him.

A MASTERPIECE IN THE MAKING

Our aim is to please him always in everything we do.

2 CORINTHIANS 5:9 TLB

I magine what it would be like trying to build a project in woodshop if your hammer had a will of its own. Every time you picked it up, the tool would begin to freak out with fear. When you attempted to drive a nail into a piece of wood, your hammer would sway to the left, then shift to the right, so it didn't have to feel the pressure of hitting the nail on the head. In spite of the fact that you only wanted to use it to do the job it was made for, your hammer didn't trust you. It felt so much safer just sitting around on the tool bench.

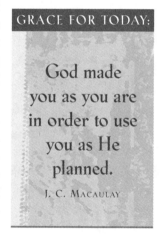

GRACE FOR TODAY:

God made you as you are in order to use you as He planned.

J. C. MACAULAY

You are much more complex—and valuable—than a common tool, but God did design you in a special way to do a specific job. However, He also gave you free will. That means you have a say in how you're going to complete the project you've been given. God may have made you with the skills and desire to become either a doctor or a teacher, but choosing which direction to go He leaves mainly up to you. That's because your primary purpose, the ultimate job you were designed for, is to give honor to God. You can do that as a doctor, a teacher, a missionary, a stay-at-home mom, an accountant, or an athlete.

The more you trust in the hand of the Master who holds you close, the more willing you'll be to risk tackling projects that may look difficult, or even impossible. God knows your limitations. But He also knows your potential. When you work together with Him, the end result is sure to be a masterpiece.

A SETTLED MIND

If you want to know what God wants you to do—ask him,
and he will gladly tell you.

JAMES 1:5 NLT

At first, you were confused and not sure about which direction to go. You gave the matter careful consideration and told yourself it was the right thing to do. Now, you're not too sure. You are concerned about what others will say. Will they agree with you, or will they be upset that your decision went against their wishes?

It is never possible to please everyone. But pleasing the crowd is not what God wants you to do. Especially when you know what you are doing is wrong.

God wants you to always do what is right whether it makes others happy or not. As a child of God, you have His Holy Spirit on the inside to lead and guide you into making right decisions. He tells you to do what is right, not what is popular.

The Bible says you have been given the mind of Christ. That means you think just like Jesus, who always followed the instructions given Him by His Father. As a child of God, you have a right to go to Him when you are confused and ask for guidance and to reveal whatever you need to know to make right decisions.

Don't compromise your faith because you want to be popular with the crowd. Do what you know is right, and then trust God to cause those around you to understand and agree with you.

Your Heavenly Father is as wise as He is powerful. Ask Him for wisdom; believe that He will give it to you. Then, allow that wisdom to speak to your heart so you always use good judgment.

GRACE FOR TODAY:

When God leads the way, success in every area of our lives is guaranteed.

ARE YOU GIFTED?

And that special gift of ministry you were given . . .
keep that dusted off and in use.

1 TIMOTHY 4:14 MSG

I magine receiving a gift from a wealthy woman who is renowned for her taste in selecting perfect (and expensive) presents for everyone on her gift list. Wouldn't this be a package you would be eager to open? A gift you would want to start enjoying right away?

Sadly, many people have received gifts from the perfect Giver, but they never bother to open them or use them for their intended purpose.

God has gifted each of us with abilities. And He never makes a mistake. His gifts are never the wrong size or style—or inappropriate in any way. No one has ever needed to return a gift from God.

If only we will open God's heaven-sent gifts, we can use them in a way that will benefit others and bring glory to Him. Do you know what your gifts are? (A sense of humor, a talent for art, the ability to encourage others?—just to name a few.) Are you using your gifts? Or are they lying dormant, gathering dust. If this is the case, it's time to tear into that aging wrapping paper.

Putting your God-given talents to work is one of the most satisfying things you will ever do. As you do what God created you for, you gain a deep sense of purpose and become closer and more grateful to the One who gave you your talents. Few things are as beautiful as Creator and creation working together. So don't neglect your gifts. Don't wish you had someone else's. Do all the good you can with what you've been given.

GRACE FOR TODAY:

The Life-giver knows best what gifts are most important for your life.

273

STAYING PLUGGED IN

What do video games, smoothie makers, electric guitars, and curling irons have in common? If they're not plugged into a power source, they lose their ability to do the job they were designed to do. The same goes for you.

You have access to the ultimate source of power—the God of the universe. But it's easy to get disconnected—You choose to skip reading the Bible when your homework stacks up. You turn to your best friend, instead of God, to talk to first about your problems. You sleep in, and miss church, when Saturday evenings run too late.

Unlike an electrical outlet, where power is immediately available when a blackout occurs, God's Spirit provides a back-up generator that keeps you going for awhile. But, the more time that passes when you're not connecting with God through prayer, worship, reading God's Word, and spending time with other people who believe in Him, the more spiritually ineffective you become. Doubts creep in. Joy and peace begin to fade. You don't talk to others about what God's doing in your life. You lose your ability to see God working behind the scenes when hard times come. You find yourself discontent with life.

If you feel your spiritual wattage draining away, don't waste any time. Plug back into God. His dynamic presence is always within reach, and His power is available. The more you provide a solid connection for God's power to flow through you, the more of an impact He can make on your life—and your life can make on the lives of those around you.

> ## GRACE FOR TODAY:
> ### We are the wire, God is the current. Our only power is to let the current pass through us.
> CARLO CARETTO

[Jesus said,] "The Holy Spirit will come upon you and give you power."

ACTS 1:8 CEV

THE GREAT RACE

By Brother Andrew

In any marathon, there are those who come in first place, second place, and so forth, but all of those who finish the race are considered winners and true athletes. All of them are worthy of reward. The reason why is because they finished the race that was placed before them. Many of those who have gone before us have finished their race. They fought physical and spiritual battles on our behalf. They suffered persecution and hardship, not willing to give up in the middle of their painful struggle. Because they kept running their race on our behalf, we enjoy many of the freedoms and liberties we have today.

God has also called us to run a race. But this race is not one that is won by those who are swift or strong. It is won by those who finish—whether they are swift, strong, weak, or slow. No matter how much or how little you have, God has given you enough to complete this Christian walk to the very end. You have the power to finish.

No matter how long the road ahead is, stay your course. Even when it seems that life is out of control, remember the One who is paving the road before you. Nothing in this world is impossible to you if only you believe, and keep on believing in Him. With every step of this marathon of life, the Lord is with you, strengthening and encouraging you. If you look to Him, you will finish this race. And at the finish line, God's reward will be waiting.

—⁓—

FATHER GOD: HELP ME TO FINISH THE RACE YOU'VE SET OUT FOR MY LIFE. I KNOW I CAN'T DO IT ON MY OWN. BUT I KNOW THAT YOU HAVE GIVEN ME YOUR GRACE. REMIND ME WHEN I'M FEELING TIRED AND DISCOURAGED THAT YOU ARE THERE TO HELP ME STAY ON MY FEET. AMEN.

Let us run with patience the particular race that God has set before us.

HEBREWS 12:1 TLB

IS THAT THE BELL?

We are citizens of heaven, where the Lord Jesus Christ lives. And we are
eagerly waiting for him to return as our Savior.

PHILIPPIANS 3:20 NLT

A re you living for the bell? School can seem to last an eternity—especially if you
have boring teachers. Who knew eight to three could last so long? If you're a
clock watcher, your heart probably races as the clock inches toward three every week-
day. Once the bell rings, there is such freedom. No more classes. No more hall passes. No more dress codes. At least not until the next morning when it all starts again.

As Christians, there is another bell we should
eagerly anticipate—the return of the Lord Jesus Christ!
Ministers have been preaching that Jesus is coming
again, and very soon, for years. Because of that, many
people find it difficult to believe that He really is going
to return for His children, but He is! That should excite
you! Just think, someday soon, we'll be able to meet
our Savior face-to-face and live in heaven with Him
for all eternity. In heaven, there will be no more sickness; no more confusion; no more poverty; no more
hunger; no more sadness; no more war; and no more
school! As you continue going about your everyday
life, you should keep that "ultimate bell" in the forefront of your mind. If you do, you'll
live your life differently.

GRACE FOR TODAY:

The heavenly
Father has great
expectation
in our
homecoming!

Suddenly, little annoyances won't bother you so much because you'll have your
eye on the big picture. Suddenly, you'll care more about your unsaved friends. You'll
want to share your faith with them at every opportunity. It's okay to be a clock watcher. Just make sure you're watching the right clock.

HOMEWARD BOUND

He puts a little heaven in our hearts so we'll never settle for less.

2 CORINTHIANS 5:5 MSG

A s a teen, you probably don't want to think about heaven just yet. You have so many wonderful adventures to look forward to right here on earth. Graduation, college, marriage, career, kids—who knows? Heaven is waiting somewhere off in the distance, a great retirement home where one day you'll meet God face-to-face.

But thinking about heaven is more than just a pastime for people who plan on arriving any day. It's a way of looking at life. God himself designed your heart with a built-in homing device. Just like ET, it keeps trying to "phone home." It drew you to search for God, even before you knew Him. And it will lead you to look for your true home everywhere you turn.

That's why people long to plan trips to an island "paradise" on vacation, build beautiful mansions, and live happily-ever-after lives. They are trying to create a little "heaven on earth." But this world will never be paradise. Just read the front page of your local paper. Things on earth have gone terribly wrong. They've taken a total "one-eighty" from what God first created in the Garden of Eden.

However, that's not the end of the story. God offers people an alternate ending to the one they chose when they turned their backs on Him. And this one does hold the fairy tale conclusion that feels so "right."

In the same way that looking forward to graduation can help keep you motivated through a really tough class, looking forward to heaven can help deepen your joy, even when life is hard. You're never too young to long for home.

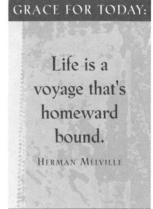

GRACE FOR TODAY:

Life is a voyage that's homeward bound.

HERMAN MELVILLE

IT'S NOT YOURS

Then you will understand what is right and just and fair—
every good path.

PROVERBS 2:9

The extra money is a welcome surprise, and a much needed one.
But then you realize there has been a mistake. You wrote down twenty-three hours when you filled out your time card at the end of the work period, but the person handling payroll had mistakenly paid you for twenty-seven hours.

As much as you would like to keep the extra, to do so would be wrong. Speaking up and pointing out the error is the only right thing to do.

As a Christian, you can expect God to bless you in many ways. But your conscience—His Holy Spirit leading you—will always let you know if something is really a blessing from Him, or if it is a trap the devil has set for you. One good way to judge if God is behind something that appears to be a blessing is to consider what kind of effect it will have on others and you.

The Bible says that God's blessings will cause a person to become rich, but will not result in sorrow or sadness. If something good happens to you, but it is likely to cause trouble for someone else, then most likely God is not the source of that good thing.

The person who mistakenly gave you too much money could get in trouble with the boss. They could be required to make up the difference by paying it back, or even be fired.

Don't be deceived by things that, on the surface, look to be from God. Take time to pray, and let God confirm what He is doing in your life.

GRACE FOR TODAY:

God's blessings always bring joy and increase.

Who Needs Enemies?

I tell you, love your enemies. Help and give without expecting a return.
You'll never—I promise—regret it.

O f all the Bible's commandments, perhaps none is tougher than "Love your enemies." Not just to tolerate them or do them a few favors to show what stellar people we are. No. Jesus said to love them. Those hateful, cruel, dishonest people. The fellow student who spreads hurtful rumors about you. The so-called friend who stabs you in the back. The teacher or coach who just won't give you a break.

Loving an enemy is a hard, often unpleasant task. That's why prayer is the first step in the process. Pray that you'll have the grace, the will, and the patience to show love; and pray that your enemy will accept your efforts.

You might also need to pray about your own bitterness. That way, even if your prayers don't change an enemy's ugly qualities, they will still change you.

As you pray for your enemies and make efforts to bring peace to your relationships with them, you might come to realize that these people are no less attractive to God—or loved by Him—than you are. Further, as you experience what hard work it is to love unlovable people, you might appreciate anew God's love for you.

Grace for Today:

God loves the unlovely—and His love is what
transforms us and makes us lovely.

TAKE CARE

L ouis IX of France said these remarkable words: "Take care not knowingly to do or say anything which, if everyone were to know of it, you could not own, and say, "Yes, that is what I did or what I said." That is a tall order, even for a king. Yet these words define the true nature of integrity.

Think about it. Living a life of integrity means being accountable for everything you say and everything you do, having nothing to be ashamed of, being ready to stand behind your words and actions unconditionally. That's not so difficult when it comes to the big things like killing and stealing. Most of us aren't criminals by the world's standards. But how do we do in the small things?

GRACE FOR TODAY:

God is ready and willing to help us as we choose a path of integrity.

Would you readily repeat to one friend what you just said about them to another friend? Do you tell your parents how things really are with you or how you want them to think they are? Do you sometimes lie about your motives or fudge the truth to make yourself look better than you really are? These are the true boundaries for a person who wishes to walk in integrity.

Problem is that few, if any, of us are capable of walking in true integrity. We aren't predisposed to it. We need God's help—wisdom to recognize the right thing to do, courage to do it, and grace and forgiveness when we don't. If you truly desire to be a person of integrity, God is willing and able to help you get there.

Show yourself in all respects a model of good works.

TITUS 2:7 NRSV

A THREEFOLD PROMISE

By Dr. Charles Stanley

God makes us a three-fold promise. First, He promises to listen if we pray according to His will. Second, He promises that we already possess what we have asked for. Third, He promises that we know that we have the petitions we desire. So when we pray according to His will, He hears us, we have what we ask for, and we know that we have what we ask for.

We must forget the notion that we cannot ask anything for ourselves. That is not what the Scriptures teach. These two verses [below] deal with our capacity to approach God openly, freely, confidently, and boldly with the assurance that He will hear and grant what we ask. As a result, we know that we will have what we ask for now.

But now back to this matter of praying in God's will. We say, "Oh, that's the catch." And in one sense, it is a catch. For many sincere, well-meant prayers have gone unanswered as a result of our praying out of God's will. Can we always know the will of God in our prayers? Yes, although not always at first. Sometimes when we go to God, we are in the dark—we don't know what to ask for. So in the beginning we do not know His will. But if we can understand and apply certain principles, ultimately we can know God's will as we pray.[45]

—⁂—

DEAR LORD: THANK YOU FOR ALLOWING ME TO COME INTO YOUR PRESENCE AND BRING MY PRAYERS TO YOU. OPEN MY HEART TO YOUR WISDOM SO THAT I MAY PRAY EFFECTIVELY, ACCORDING TO YOUR WILL. AMEN.

This is the boldness we have in him, that if we ask anything according to his will, he hears us. And if we know that he hears us in whatever we ask, we know that we have obtained the requests made of him.

1 JOHN 5:14-15 NRSV

GIVE THANKS

Thank GOD! Call out his Name! Tell the whole world who he is and
what he's done!

1 CHRONICLES 16:8 MSG

I n this fast-paced world, we rarely take time to appreciate others. When is the last
time that you received heartfelt thanks for something you've done? It's probably
been too long, and you're not alone. We aren't a very thankful people. Or, if we are,
we aren't very good at communicating that thanks.

Not only do we fail to appreciate our friends, families, and even strangers, but also
we fail to appreciate our Heavenly Father. Oh sure, we might say a few "Thank you
for saving me" mantras during our nightly prayer, but
that's hardly enough. You should look for opportunities
to praise God all day long.

GRACE FOR TODAY:

God never overlooks a thankful heart.

If you pull into the school parking lot and get a
really great parking space, give God thanks for saving
that spot just for you. If you do really well on a test,
thank God for giving you the mind of Christ so that you
can retain information and execute it well in testing situations. When you see a beautiful sunset, whisper,
"Father, thank You for putting on such a lovely show for
me." Look for ways to bless God; and while you're in
the thankful mode, look for ways to bless others, too.

Here's a goal. Try to tell at least one person a day something that you admire or
appreciate about him or her. If you're too embarrassed to say it to that person, then
drop a quick thank-you note in the mail. So many people feel unappreciated. So many
feel hopeless and depressed. Wouldn't it be an honor to be the bright spot in that person's day today? A two-second, "I really appreciate the way you care for the students
in this school," could mean so much to that teacher who has been overlooked for promotion. Just be aware, and be thankful.

MASTER PLAN

**Many are the plans in a man's heart,
but it is the LORD'S purpose that prevails.**

PROVERBS 19:21

Jacob had twelve sons, but seventeen–year–old Joseph was his favorite. And all Joseph's brothers knew it. Every time Joseph wore the colorful coat his father had given him, his brothers burned with envy. It was like their father was rubbing his favoritism in their faces. So Joseph's brothers devised a plan to get rid of Joseph. Though they intended to kill him, they ended up selling Joseph to a group of traders.

God brought about amazing circumstances that turned the brothers' evil plan into a wonderful one. Through it all, Joseph remained loyal, honest, and loving, in spite of how unfairly he was treated by others. The boy who was once a shepherd sold as a slave who became a prisoner and foreteller of dreams, finally wound up as Pharaoh's assistant.

Because of Joseph's high government position, he wound up saving his own family from starvation—including the brothers who had once plotted his death. Pharaoh had so much respect for Joseph that he gave him an Egyptian name that meant "God Speaks and Lives." Both Joseph and the God he worshiped received honor throughout Egypt and beyond, because of Joseph's integrity and dependence on God.

GRACE FOR TODAY:

Because God takes care of tomorrow, we can more fully enjoy today.

When a building is said to have "integrity," it means that its construction is sound, so it can stand firm and immoveable. The same could be said of Joseph. He allowed his future, which certainly looked nothing like he imagined at age seventeen, to be built on God's plan instead of his own. And look where it took him.

Your future is both in God's hands and your own. As you choose to live a life of integrity, you allow God's plans for you to unfold in wonderful ways—and His grace to flow through your life into the lives of those around you.

LEND A HAND

There is a friend who sticks closer than a brother.

PROVERBS 18:24 NASB

I t had really only been six weeks, but it seems like a lifetime since you focused your eye on that shimmering prom dress and waited for it to go on sale. Now that it has been marked down to a price you can comfortably afford, it does not look like you'll be buying it after all.

You just learned that your sister was laid off from her clerking job—something she has been too embarrassed to tell the family so soon after her husband and she separated. The bills are piling up, and a second mortgage payment is about to come due.

You love your sister and would do anything to help her. But to be able to buy that dress has almost become an obsession. Now that it is within reach, how can you possibly pass it up?

Because your sister needs your help.

As a Christian, you have been made into the image of God. That means you think like He thinks, act like He acts, and love like He loves.

Jesus Christ, who is love, never passed someone in need and refused to stop and help. Each time, that person's need became a priority for Him—so much so that He put aside whatever else He was doing, or delayed wherever He was going to provide assistance.

That's the same kind of love that makes you choose your sister over that gown, and causes you to be quick to ask: "What can I do to help?"

Laying aside your personal desires to help someone else in need is one of the strongest acts of love ever. It pleases God to see you respond that way.

GRACE FOR TODAY:

God sees our generous hearts and is proud to call us His own.

GIVING IS A WORK
OF HEART

If you are really eager to give, it isn't important how much you are able
to give. God wants you to give what you have, not what you don't have.

2 CORINTHIANS 8:12 NLT

A teenager visiting his biological father during the summer accompanied his dad
to church in a small farm community. As the pastor stood at the pulpit and
began his sermon, the teen thought, *This guy is the worst preacher I've ever heard. He isn't
funny or insightful like my pastor back home. And he doesn't have a very good speaking voice
either. Plus, he looks nervous and uncomfortable up there.*

The teen sat bored and discouraged for the next twenty minutes. At last, he sighed
with relief when he heard the words "And in conclusion. . . ."

Thank goodness that's over, the teen thought cynically. Then, he heard a faint snif-
fling sound and turned to a woman sitting next to him. She was sobbing quietly and
dabbing her eyes with a tattered tissue. "That was just what I needed to hear," she said,
her voice ringing with gratitude and sincerity.

The teen swallowed hard, feeling a bit guilty. But he learned a valuable lesson that
day: Through God's grace and provision, a message that might lack in style can still
speak to the hearts of listeners.

Have you ever been afraid to write a poem, draw a picture, or sing a song because
you think your talents aren't worthy of anyone's attention? If so, take heart. God does-
n't expect you to be polished and perfect in your endeavors. He's not going to compare
your efforts with someone else's. He just expects you to be sincere and faithful. And if
you simply do your best, your efforts can touch hearts.

GRACE FOR TODAY:

Sincerity of heart brings God's power on the scene.

A HELPING HAND

You enjoy your job waiting tables because it gives you an opportunity to meet people. But every now and then, you wish you could be on the other side of the fence—being served instead of always serving. You would feel better giving orders instead of following them, or sitting down and letting someone wait on you.

But if your goal is to be like Jesus, then service will be a top priority with you. The Bible is clear on how important God considered servitude. During Jesus' time on the earth, He walked in power and authority. Yet, when He was called upon to meet some personal need He never hesitated to stop and do whatever was asked of Him. At one point, Jesus took on the role of servant to His disciples by taking off His robe, kneeling down, and washing their feet.

GRACE FOR TODAY:

Some of God's greatest blessings are found in servitude.

Jesus set an example for them to follow. He said, "Now that I, your Lord and Teacher, have washed your feet, you also should wash one another's feet" (John 13:14).

Knowing that the Son of God humbled himself in such a way is a perfect example to follow. It does not mean that you should literally wash someone's feet, but find a way to serve others.

It's normal to want to be catered to—to have someone wait on you or give you what you want. But as a Christian, you are no longer controlled by selfish desires. Your desire is to love and put others before yourself.

You will experience joy when you share God's love as a servant.

Love others as well as you love yourself.

MATTHEW 22:39 MSG

HOPES FOR HAPPINESS

By John C. Maxwell

We have in our society a lot of false hopes for happiness. We have what I call destination disease. People think that when they arrive at a certain point, they'll be happy. When they retire, when they get rid of this job, when they take that trip, when they graduate, when they meet that goal—then they'll be happy.

There's another false hope for happiness that I call someone sickness. That's when you say, "If I could just meet that person; I'd be happy." But you are the only one who can make yourself happy. No one can bring happiness to someone who is miserable. When we begin to take responsibility for our own happiness and realize that it comes through growth and growing experiences—even though they may be painful—then we really can achieve happiness.

One last false hope for happiness is the problem-free plague. There are many people who want to live in a problem-free society, and they're plagued with that hope. They say, "Boy, if I just wouldn't have problems, I would be happy." No, no, no! Problems have nothing to do with your happiness. In fact, in your stretching periods you will probably have more problems than at any other time, and those will be the greatest times of your life.[46]

—⁕—

LORD GOD: I AM PLACING MY HOPE FOR HAPPINESS IN YOU AND ONLY YOU. THANK YOU FOR GIVING ME YOUR GRACE TO SEE MY PROBLEMS AS THE GREATEST TIMES OF MY LIFE. AMEN.

Hope does not disappoint, because the love of God has been poured out in our hearts by the Holy Spirit who was given to us.

ROMANS 5:5 NKJV

CONTROL FREAK

The steps of a good man are ordered by the LORD:
and he delighteth in his way.

PSALM 37:23 KJV

A re you a control freak? Do you like knowing what's going to happen in the future? Unfortunately, that's just not possible. While it would be really wonderful for all of us control freaks if we could know exactly how our lives would play out, it just doesn't happen that way.

But, we can take comfort in one thing—God knows how it all plays out, and if we're walking with Him, we're covered. The Bible says in Jeremiah 29:11 that He has a good plan for us, so we can take comfort in that, too. He loves us and wants the very best for us. So, when bad things happen that take you by surprise, just remember—they didn't catch God off guard. The Bible also says that He doesn't sleep or slumber, so He is always watching over us.

Start each day saying, "My steps are ordered of the Lord," and remind yourself of that truth several times throughout the day. Ask God to help keep you on the right path, and if you stray from the path a little bit— don't worry. God will find you. Walk with Him daily and listen for His cues. You probably won't hear a loud, booming audible voice, but you'll feel the urgings of the Holy Spirit, directing your choices every day.

So, you may not know the future, but you do know the One who does. That should comfort the control freak inside you. God is looking out for you, so cheer up! Your future is bright!

> GRACE FOR TODAY:
>
> When we know the Light of the World, our futures are bright!

HEARTFELT FANFARE

Come, let us bow down in worship,
let us kneel before the LORD our Maker.

PSALM 95:6

A s the lights begin to dim, the crowd erupts into a roar that would drown out the sound of a 747 landing onstage. But, what's coming into the auditorium is even bigger. It's the band-of-the-moment, playing the song that's been the hottest music video around for the last ten weeks. And you get to see it all live.

Everyone's up on their feet. There's screaming, clapping, whistling, hand raising, foot stomping, hooting, and hollering. The fan to the left of you is so excited she even begins to cry. And when the drummer speaks to a girl in the front row after the band finishes the first song, she can't even respond. She's speechless in the presence of a real teen idol.

That's what worship looks like. Well, idol worship, anyway. God has a lot to say about idols, whether they're made of wood or stone, or hold a guitar in their hands. That's because God doesn't want people to follow false leaders. He is the only one worthy of worship, because He is the only one who holds real power.

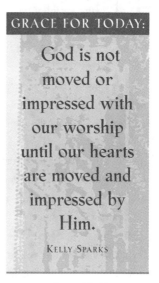

GRACE FOR TODAY:

God is not moved or impressed with our worship until our hearts are moved and impressed by Him.

KELLY SPARKS

The only power idols have is the power their fans or followers give them. God's power doesn't depend on anything other than the truth of who He is.

When you catch sight of how big and loving God really is, you can't help but worship Him. That worship may look like what you see at a concert. It may be expressed through the chorus of a simple song or in the words of a whispered prayer. It may also be visible through the way you honor God by giving to others—sharing your time, your money, your possessions, and your love.

You can worship God anytime, anywhere. How about right now?

TAKE THE BLAME

Confess to one another therefore your faults
(your slips, your false steps, your offenses, your sins).

JAMES 5:16 AMP

Have you ever done something wrong, and then tried to cover it up because you were afraid of what others might think or say? Maybe you broke something, and then tried to fix it before anyone noticed it had been broken. Or maybe you loaned out your brother's video game without asking and said nothing while he searched the house for it.

Trying to cover your tracks by lying and being dishonest is not the right way to handle any situation. That's how cowards respond when they aren't willing to face the consequences of their actions. They are afraid of what might happen to them.

Honesty is the best policy, no matter what the consequences are.

Unfortunately, admitting that you are at fault is not easy for most people. They would rather make excuses, or lie altogether.

People make mistakes all the time, and you are no different.

But as a Christian, you have to be different when it comes to how you handle correcting those mistakes. When you make a mistake, don't take the cowardly way out by trying to cover your tracks with lies. Do the honorable thing, and own up to your wrong. Admit your mistake, and get rid of the guilt. Then trust your loving Father God to help you to make it right. Confessing your wrong gives you peace in knowing you did the right thing.

GRACE FOR TODAY:

God will reward our honesty and integrity with forgiveness, and help make things right for us.

TOGETHER IS BETTER

Two can accomplish more than twice as much as one,
for the results can be much better.

ECCLESIASTES 4:9 TLB

The emperor penguins of Antarctica know the importance of teamwork. They huddle together by the thousands, sharing warmth that allows them to survive the brutal, freezing weather—which can make a steel screwdriver as brittle as a pretzel stick.

The penguins take turns monitoring the outside of their giant huddle, on the lookout for danger, or food. After one of the birds has finished its "perimeter duty," it moves to the inside of the group so it can get warm and sleep. The baby penguins stand on their moms' and dads' feet to protect themselves from the icy surface. If a penguin tried to survive alone, it wouldn't make it through one frozen winter night.

We can all learn from these penguins. Teamwork can equal survival. And the tougher the conditions, the more important it is for people to band together. You might not ever need to share physical warmth, unless your school heater goes out this winter, but you can share encouragement, empathy, and ideas.

You can share the workload on a huge assignment or be part of a study group for finals testing. And there's something else you can share: The sense of success and accomplishment that results from committed, unselfish teamwork.

GRACE FOR TODAY:

What an honor to realize that God
wants uson His team.

PROUD TO BE AN AMERICAN

B ackyard Fourth of July barbecues. Patriotic parades. Red, white, and blue Sno-cones. Fireworks at the park. Ahhhh . . . patriotism in America. Americans celebrate their freedom every Fourth of July, but since September 11, 2001, we have been celebrating America at every given opportunity. After that fateful day, people across the United States became much more patriotic. Even now, people have yellow ribbons on their cars, showing support for the troops overseas. And, you'll see many flags in yards across this nation.

That beautiful song by Lee Greenwood that says, "I'm proud to be an American," has become our anthem. Suddenly, every person sings the National Anthem with more passion. People recite "The Pledge of Allegiance" with much more heart. Aren't you thankful for your freedom today? Thank the Lord that you can worship freely here. Thank Him that you can grow up in a land governed by democracy. Thank Him that you live in the land of the free, home of the brave. Thank Him that you enjoy so many liberties here.

Take this moment to thank God for America, and pray for our leaders and the men and women who defend this country. Encourage your friends and family to pray along with you. Make it a habit to pray for America and those who lead this mighty land—not just today, but everyday. When you see a servicemen or women, go up and thank them. Write thank you letters to your leaders. Get involved in volunteer work that benefits our military personnel. Make a difference. Make every day the Fourth of July!

GRACE FOR TODAY:

By God's grace we live our lives in freedom.

If my people, who are called by my name, will humble themselves and pray and seek my face and turn from their wicked ways, then will I hear from heaven and will forgive their sin and will heal their land.

2 CHRONICLES 7:14

FOCUS YOUR VISION

By John C. Maxwell

There are four areas in which we need to fine-tune our vision. First, do I see myself correctly? How can we see ourselves accurately? Spend time in prayer and meditation. Notice what kinds of problems continually arise in your life and when they occur?

If your problems are similar in nature and they occur in the same types of situations, you've never really dealt with the cause. Ask yourself some questions: What kinds of circumstances cause me to show strong emotion, either positive or negative? What kind of people do I spend my time with? What spiritual gifts do I possess, and am I using them? How am I living in the light of my knowledge of God? If there are areas in which you're falling short, try to identify the reasons why.

The second thing we need to see is our inner desires. If you could be anything you wanted to be and do anything you wanted to do, what would you be or do? What would really bring joy to your life? If you can answer this question, you have identified your inner desires. Knowing this will help you reach your potential.

Third, we need to see our resources, both internal and external. What are your personal strengths? What can you draw on to help you possess the land? Do you surround yourself with supportive people? Do you use past experiences to your benefit? Do you take advantage of opportunities as they arise?

Fourth, we need to get a clear sight of our God. We need to see Him as the God "who is able to do far more abundantly beyond all that we ask or think, according to the power that works within us" (Ephesians 3:20 NASB).[47]

—∿—

DEAR FATHER: THANK YOU FOR PLACING A VISION IN MY HEART. BY YOUR GRACE, HELP ME TO FINE-TUNE IT AND MAKE IT PROFITABLE FOR YOUR KINGDOM. AMEN.

If people can't see what God is doing, they stumble all over themselves; but when they attend to what he reveals, they are most blessed.

PROVERBS 29:18 MSG

BE AN ANGEL

Go near and listen to all that the LORD our God says. . . .
We will listen and obey.

DEUTERONOMY 5:27

A s a man was leaving Wednesday night Bible study, he meditated on the pastor's message. Sitting in his car, he prayed, "God, if You still speak to people, speak to me. I will listen. I will do my best to obey." As he continued down the road, he had the strangest urge to buy a gallon of milk. He shook his head and asked, "God is that you?" He continued toward home, and once again felt that same yearning to buy milk. So, he stopped and bought milk.

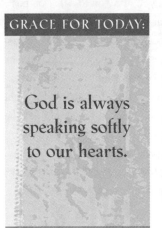

GRACE FOR TODAY:

God is always speaking softly to our hearts.

As he passed a certain street, he felt directed to turn down that street. "This is nuts," he thought, but he obeyed. He drove several more blocks when he felt that same urging to pull over. Again, he sensed God's urging to give the milk to the people inside the house across the street. He wrestled with this instruction, but he obeyed and rang the doorbell. Immediately, a man's voice yelled, "Who is it? What do you want?" Then the door opened. The young man handed the man the gallon of milk and said, "Here. I brought this for you."

The man took the milk and rushed down the hallway. He came back holding a baby. With tears streaming down his face, he said to the young man, "We were just praying. We had some big bills this month, and we ran out of money. We didn't have any milk for our baby."

His wife yelled from the kitchen, "I asked God to send an angel. Are you an angel?" The young man smiled and gave them what money he had with him. As he walked back to his car, he vowed to listen closely for God's voice from that moment on.

Maybe God would like to use you as an "angel" today. Perk up your ears and open your heart. He may be speaking right now.

STANDING TALL

**It's the person who acts rights who is right,
just as we see it lived out in our righteous Messiah.**

1 JOHN 3:7 MSG

H e was a hero without a name. Some say he was a student, others the son of a factory worker. Though his identity is still a mystery, what he did on June 5, 1989 will long be remembered. For several weeks students, workers, parents, and children had filled Tiananmen Square in the capital city of China. In a country where the power of the individual is very limited, more than a million people joined together to cry out for democracy. The government answered the protest on June 4th by randomly shooting hundreds of people in the Square.

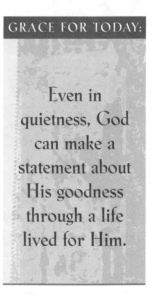

GRACE FOR TODAY:

Even in quietness, God can make a statement about His goodness through a life lived for Him.

The next morning, Tiananmen Square was empty and eerily quiet—until a line of tanks began to file into it. Out of the crowds on the outskirts, a young man walked across the nearly deserted square, stopping directly in the path of the oncoming tanks. When the first tank tried to turn left, the man moved to his right. When the tank veered right, the man moved to his left. Then, the young man climbed up onto the tank and spoke to the driver. His exact words, like his identity, are still unclear. But the tank didn't move any farther forward, as the young man climbed down and disappeared back into the crowd.

There were two heroes that day. The young man who stood up for what he believed and the driver of the tank who chose to do the right thing. It takes courage and conviction to do what you know is right, especially when those around you are pressuring you to compromise. But with God's help, you can be a modern-day hero. Even if no one remembers your name, the times you dare to do what's right help others see God's character in a visible way.

BENEATH THE SURFACE

People judge by outward appearance,
but the LORD looks at a person's thoughts and intentions.

1 SAMUEL 16:7 NLT

Oh no! A large red pimple seemed to appear on the tip of your nose overnight, and class photos are today. You are already angry and disappointed because you did not lose weight before tomorrow night's dance, and now this! What will your date say when you show up looking like a stuffed Rudolph the Red-Nosed Reindeer?

God, who runs the universe, loves you more than you know. He has all the time in the world to talk with you because what is important to you is important to Him. He knows your feelings and is ready to help you with this problem.

Also, consider that your date agreed to go with you to the prom because you are a wonderful person. Your looks only add to the great personality that God has given you. He does not want you stressing out because of what you look like.

People who really like you know that there is more to you than meets the eye. Deep inside, where God lives, is where your true attractiveness really begins.

So forget about it. Give it your best make-up fix, and put it out of your mind. Think instead about Christ who loved you so much that He was willing to die for you—blemishes and all! He is the one who sees your true beauty, and He's the one who can help your inner beauty shine brightly, in, around, and through even the most embarrassing facial flaws.

GRACE FOR TODAY:

God's love is more than skin deep. He loves you
through and through.

GIVING TEMPTATION THE COLD SHOULDER

I've banked your promises in the vault of my heart so I won't
sin myself bankrupt.

PSALM 119:11 MSG

R anchers have a saying that goes, "Once you're tromping through a cow pasture, it's a little late to worry about soiling your Sunday shoes."

This bit of sound advice carries far beyond the ranch fences. The key to avoiding danger and sin is determining—in advance—to stay far away from compromising situations.

Be aware, however, that sometimes trouble will reveal itself a little bit at a time. It can pique your curiosity, beckoning you to come closer, "just for a look." The next thing you know, you're up to your knees in it.

Right now, promise God, and yourself, that you will resist giving temptation even a passing glance. Don't allow yourself to fantasize about indulging in some kind of sin. As singer Steven Curtis Chapman puts it (in a song titled "Run Away"), "Don't even look in the direction of a thought you should not entertain."

Another key to avoiding trouble is to prayerfully decide ahead of time how you will handle various unavoidable temptations—the ones you don't see coming until they're upon you. What will you say if you're offered drugs? What will you do if you're at a friend's house and someone orders a pornographic movie via cable or a satellite service? How will you respond if you're given answers to an upcoming test?

To the best of your ability and knowledge, determine where the "cow pastures" are in your life, and decide how you're going to avoid them. There is trouble underfoot, so tread carefully. Don't step in something you shouldn't.

GRACE FOR TODAY:

When we pay attention, God is more than happy to order our steps.

BELIEVE THE UNBELIEVABLE

As a small child, you most likely experienced a desire for the invisible, imaginable, and hope against hope—the unbelievable. Like God, you were born with creativity and imagination. It is an element of faith. When you believed on Jesus as your Lord and Savior, your faith ignited—the substance of everything you dreamed could be, now with the power to make it happen.

Abraham, in spite of his old age, believed God would keep His word—His promise—and God did! He gave him a son. The Israelites expected a deliver, and Moses was born. He led them out of captivity. and they walked across the Red Sea on dry ground. Generation after generation dreamed of the Messiah, and Jesus came to set all men free forever.

God wants your passion for the supernatural, spiritual part of Him that lives in you to grow to maturity. Fully developed faith can bring every dream and desire He placed in your heart into reality.

Are you hoping today with earnest expectation? Do you dream and imagine fulfillment of the grand and wonderful plans God has for your life? He dreamed them first. Now your faith is the bridge that will take you to the place He's destined for you all along. Believe the unbelievable, and you will eventually see evidence of what you could only imagine.

> **GRACE FOR TODAY:**
>
> Fully developed faith can bring into reality every dream and desire God places in our hearts.

Jesus loudly declared, "the one who believes in Me does not [only] believe in and trust in and rely on Me, but [in believing in Me he believes] in Him Who sent Me."

JOHN 12:44 AMP

THE TROUBLE WITH RULES AND REGULATIONS

By Warren W. Wiersbe

The Bible says we are called to liberty. Christians are free—free from the guilt of sin because they have experienced God's forgiveness. Free from the penalty of sin because Christ died for them on the cross. And they are, through the Spirit, free from the power of sin in their daily lives. They are also free from the law with its demands and threats. Christ bore the curse of the law and ended its tyranny once and for all. We are "called unto liberty" because we are "called into the grace of Christ" (Galatians 1:6). Grace and liberty go together.

This, however, is the fear of all people who do not understand the true meaning of the grace of God. "If you do away with rules and regulations" they say, "you will create chaos and anarchy." Of course, that danger is real, not because God's grace fails, but because

men fail of the grace of God. (See Hebrews 12:15.) If there is a "true grace of God," then there is also a false grace of God; and there are false teachers who "change the grace of our God into a license for immorality" (1 Peter 5:12 and Jude 1:4). So, Paul's caution is a valid one. Christian liberty is not a license to sin but an opportunity to serve.

This leads to a commandment: "By love serve one another" (Galatians 5:13 KJV). The key word, of course, is love. The formula looks something like this:

Liberty + love = service to others; liberty − love = license (slavery to sin).[48]

—∽—

HEAVENLY FATHER: THANK YOU FOR THE FREEDOM YOUR GRACE HAS PURCHASED FOR ME. I LOOK TO YOU TO HELP ME LIVE IN IT, LOVING AND SERVING OTHERS. AMEN.

It is absolutely clear that God has called you to a free life. Just make sure that you don't use this freedom as an excuse to do whatever you want to do and destroy your freedom. Rather, use your freedom to serve one another in love; that's how freedom grows.

GALATIANS 5:13 MSG

PUNCTUALITY COUNTS

There is a time for everything, and a season for
every activity under heaven.

ECCLESIASTES 3:1

P unctuality. Just reading the word might be painful for you—especially if you're
one of those habitually late people. Are your friends constantly waiting on you?
Are you tardy for school several times a week? Being on time is a tough one for some
of us, but it's also very necessary.

If you have trouble being on time, think about this:
God is NEVER late! That's right—never! Not by one
day, one hour, one minute, one second. Sure we may
think He's late because He doesn't do things by our
schedules. But the truth is that He is always on time—
just in time to save us, just in time to help us, just in
time to heal us, just in time to bless us. After all, God
set the clock for the universe. All time and space
revolve around Him. His timing is always perfect.

GRACE FOR TODAY:

God is never
late, and He can
help us be on
time too.

That's good news, whether you are waiting for
something from God or learning to be more like Him.
His grace extends to both. If you struggle with punctuality, if you are always running late, God can help you
with that. He can help you honor others with the gift of punctuality just as He honors
us with His gift of timely encounters and interventions in our lives. As it says in 2
Corinthians 6:2: God says, "In the time of my favor I heard you, and in the day of salvation I helped you."

INNER OVERHAUL

Be known for the beauty that comes from within, the unfading beauty of a
gentle and quiet spirit, which is so precious to God.

1 PETER 3:4 NLT

I t's your sixteenth birthday, and your parents have given you the ultimate gift—your
own set of wheels. At first glance you can tell this isn't just any old junker off the
used car lot. It's a ruby red convertible with black leather interior, polished chrome
hubcaps, and stereo speakers the size of dinner plates.

Hardly able to contain your excitement, you get in
and turn the key. Nothing happens. No power, no
music, nothing. That's when your parents come clean.
They had to cut back on the budget to pay for your
braces. In other words, the only power this car has is
three hamsters running on a wheel under the hood—
which, unfortunately, your folks have forgotten to feed.
What good is a car that looks great on the outside but
has nothing of value under the hood?

GRACE FOR TODAY:

Extreme
makeovers
from God are
constructed
from the
inside out.

The same can be said about people. A lot of people spend time, money, and energy trying to look good
on the outside. They buy the right clothes, get the right
haircut, even have surgery to get just the "right" nose.
But none of these outward changes helps them become
more attractive on the inside, where it really counts.

God is in the business of extreme makeovers. However, He only helps beautify
what matters. He works from the inside out, changing your heart to become more like
His. As your heart becomes more attractive, you'll find people more attracted to you—
and to the God you love.

THE IN-CROWD

He will shield you with his wings . . . His faithful promises are your
armor and protection.

PSALM 91:4 NLT

As a freshman in high school, you welcomed the opportunity to hang out with
some of the school's most popular guys. But many of your friends warned you
not to hook up with that group because it could spell a lot of trouble.

Now that a couple of the guys in the group were in serious trouble after pulling a
prank that resulted in the elderly Mr. Bolton being hospitalized, you are glad you lis-
tened to your friends and said no when the guys asked you to join them.

Because God loves you, He will never let you walk into a dangerous situation
without first warning you. Sometimes, the warning sign might come through a friend
who knows more about a matter than you. He might urge you to back off so you won't
be deceived by appearances or enticing words.

At other times, the caution might come from your parents who have been assigned
by God to watch over and protect you. They walk closely with God and are sensitive
to His voice. When He shows them something, they are quick to point it out to you.

Then again, the warning could come through the Holy Spirit—God's Spirit on the
inside of you. He knows all about you—everything you do—and is always watching out
to help you not stumble into trouble. He is also always ready to strengthen you, and
give you courage to boldly say no to sin.

However the warnings come, thank God that He sends them. Thank Him also that
you are close enough to Him to know when He is talking to you.

GRACE FOR TODAY:

God will warn and protect us even when
we will not look out for ourselves.

THE SERIOUS BUSINESS OF LAUGHTER

A happy heart is good medicine.

PROVERBS 17:22 AMP

Nutritionist and author Pamela Smith takes laughter seriously. That's because she knows that 100 laughs a day provide a cardiovascular workout equal to about ten minutes of rowing or biking. And there's more happy news: Laughter stimulates stress release in the same way exercise does. Laughter, Smith notes, also helps fight infection by sending into the bloodstream some hormones that reduce the immune-system-weakening power of stress.

Proverbs 14:30 puts it this way: "A heart at peace gives life to the body."

As a teen, you face a variety of pressures—from school to work to extra-curricular activities to relationships with family and friends. And beyond this, you're flooded with more information—from a wider variety of sources—than any generation in history.

In other words, you might find your life becoming one giant pressure cooker. Laughter is the safety valve that lets the steam escape before there's an explosion. So, don't become so caught up in life's demands and stressors that you can't lighten up.

Loosen up once in a while. Laugh at life's absurdities, rather than letting them get under your skin. Seek out the comic relief provided by humorous books, TV shows, and other media. Look for the humor in various situations—and strive to be a source of laughter and good humor wherever you go. There's no denying it: Life is hard and stressful. But if you can maintain your sense of humor, you can have the last laugh.

GRACE FOR TODAY:

The book of Proverbs says that laughter "is good medicine." And, like all of God's gifts, it's available without a prescription.

WATCH YOUR WORDS

Words can be lethal weapons, did you know that? With our mouths, we can curse someone and do irreparable damage to them. On a daytime talk show not long ago, the topic for the program was titled, "You ruined my life." All of the guests who came onto that show shared heartbreaking stories of how someone had said horrible things to them, changing the entire course of their lives. Some of the show's guests had lived with the sting of those hurtful words for more than twenty years. That's a long time.

The guests who were the most messed up had internalized damaging words from their parents. Maybe you've been the victim of verbal abuse at your house. Maybe you've heard things like, "You are so stupid. You will never amount to anything." If so, those are very hurtful comments, and they are also very untrue. Though it's difficult, you have to speak good things over your life to counteract those damaging effects. When someone says, "You are stupid." You should say, "No, I am wise. The Bible says I have the mind of Christ, and He is all knowing!" (See 1 Corinthians 2:16.) When someone says, "You'll never amount to anything." You can come back with, "I can do all things through Christ Who gives me strength. I am well able to fulfill my destiny." (See Philippians 4:13.)

You should also be conscious of the things you speak to others. Take the time to encourage those around you. Say, "You've got what it takes! No weapon formed against you is going to prosper! I love you, and God loves you!" Use your words wisely. They hold the power of life and death.

> **GRACE FOR TODAY:**
>
> God framed His world with words and has given us the power to frame our worlds with our words.

No man can tame the tongue. It is a restless evil, full of deadly poison.

JAMES 3:8

WHAT WILL YOU CHOOSE?

By Luis Palau

Every Christian must choose, more than once, whether to live for self or for God. That choice makes all the difference. When I think of the life–long significance of choosing to please God, I think of George Beverly Shea.

Mr. Shea made the choice to live for God when he was a young man in New York City. He and a friend sold insurance during the week and sang at evangelistic street meetings on Sundays. A well–known producer heard them sing one evening and offered them a contract to perform on a television program. He also offered them a substantial amount of money, far more than they would earn selling insurance. They said they would pray about it.

Mr. Shea and his friend were very excited about the idea, but as they prayed, they didn't have peace about taking the job. Nothing was wrong with the program; it just didn't seem right. So Mr. Shea decided to continue singing at evangelistic meetings. He eventually began singing for WMBI, the Moody Bible Institute radio station in Chicago. And after Billy Graham heard him singing on that station, he invited Mr. Shea to join his evangelistic team. As a result of his commitment, George Beverly Shea has ministered to millions of people around the world and has sold millions of records. What an influence he has had on the world because he chose to live for Christ.

When we live to please Him, the life of Christ keeps flowing through us— giving us compassion for the lost and the fear of the Lord that compels us to persuade others to follow Him.[49]

—⁂—

FATHER: BY YOUR GRACE, I CHOOSE TO LIVE FOR YOU. TAKE MY TALENTS AND POINT ME TO THE PATH YOU HAVE PREPARED FOR ME. AMEN.

Our steps are made firm by the LORD, when he delights in our way; though we stumble, we shall not fall headlong, for the LORD holds us by the hand.

PSALM 37:23–24 NRSV

POSITIVE THINKING

Whatever is true, whatever is noble, whatever is right, whatever is pure, whatever is lovely, whatever is admirable—if anything is excellent or praiseworthy—think about such things.

PHILIPPIANS 4:8

It has been estimated that the average human being has approximately 50,000 thoughts per day. Now, that's a lot of thinking. In fact, when we're awake, we're practically thinking all the time. That's why our thought lives are so important. We need to do just as the Bible advises—think on good things.

GRACE FOR TODAY:

When we ask for His help, God shows us how to change our thoughts.

Think on positive things. Of course, out of 50,000 thoughts, you're going to have some negative thoughts. It's only normal. However, what you do with those negative thoughts—that's what matters. The Bible tells us to take every thought captive. In other words, don't let your thoughts run out of control. If you have a fight with your parents and exchange some angry words, don't dwell on that all day. Say you're sorry, and move on. Take control of your thoughts. If you don't, worry, guilt, condemnation, and all of their ugly friends will dominate your thought life.

Practice ignoring your negative thoughts. You can choose which thoughts you allow to fill your mind, so choose wisely. Meditate on good things. Memorize scriptures so you can think on those when situations arise. Think about the goodness of God. And, if you can't quit thinking of negative things, speak it out. Cast out those thoughts by using your mouth to speak positive things. With God's help, you can turn it around. Once you become a Christian, the Bible says you have the mind of Christ. That means you can control your thought life. God will help you. All you have to do is ask.

WE'VE GOT SPIRIT, YES WE DO!

Don't you know that your body is the temple of the Holy Spirit, who lives in you?

1 CORINTHIANS 6:19 NLT

God's Spirit is often misunderstood. At one time, He was commonly referred to as the Holy Ghost, leading some people to believe that when they began a relationship with God, something resembling Casper would begin to inhabit their body. But the Holy Spirit is Someone, not something. He is as much God as the Father and the Son. And He is alive and doing great things in you.

Jesus referred to the Holy Spirit as a comforter and counselor, but He's also a translator. For those who don't know God personally, God's words and ways often don't make sense. But when you want to know God, when you reach out to draw closer to Him, the Holy Spirit helps you hear God more clearly. He helps you better understand which way God wants you to go. He even helps your prayers become more "fluent" in God's own language. When you don't know what to pray, the Holy Spirit helps provide the right words.

Knowing God's Spirit is actually living inside you changes the way you look at yourself. It motivates you to give God a more desirable place to live. That means keeping your body and your mind pure. It's also a reminder that you are a visible expression of an invisible God. As you give the Holy Spirit more freedom to work in you, you'll find that God's image will shine more clearly through you.

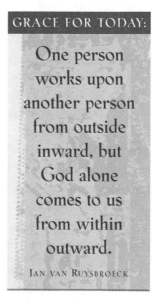

GRACE FOR TODAY:

One person works upon another person from outside inward, but God alone comes to us from within outward.

JAN VAN RUYSBROECK

When you need a comforter, translator, or friend, God's Spirit is always there. As you learn to depend more closely on Him, He'll help you become a translator to those around you, helping them better understand the God that's alive in you.

THE RIGHT WAY

The integrity of the upright will guide them.

PROVERBS 11:3 NASB

Initially, you wanted to say no when you were asked to participate in the weekend clean-up project. Your school schedule was already heavy enough with several after school activities, not to mention the two-hour tutoring sessions you conduct on Thursdays to help younger students with their math.

But remembering how God was there for you—how He provided someone to help you through a troubled time in your life—was all the motivation you needed to offer your assistance. Now, you are trusting God to give you strength as you fulfill your commitment.

Everyone gets tired after awhile and would like to give up doing a few things—especially the ones that are taking up too much time. But keeping your word is important. Not only does it help you to maintain a good reputation; it honors God.

When you make a commitment, you make a promise. You are telling others they can depend on you—that you are trustworthy. If you break that promise, you send a message that your word is no good and that you are not dependable.

Always consider other things that require your time before you make a commitment. While your intentions are good, the Bible says it is better not to make a promise than to give your word and then not keep it. That is the same as telling a lie.

Before you make a commitment that you might end up regretting, take time to pray and ask God what you should do. He wants you to help others, but it is also important to Him that you be trustworthy. Asking God for wisdom in setting priorities will help you keep your promises—and your integrity.

GRACE FOR TODAY:

God honors His Word, and He will help us to honor ours.

A GOD WHO UNDERSTANDS

He will rescue the poor when they cry to him; he will help the
oppressed, who have no one to defend them. . . . for their lives
are precious to him.

PSALM 72:12, 14 NLT

When they hear the word "God," some people think of the Red Sea–parting,
earthquake–shaking, raising–the–dead power behind the universe. And
this is certainly part of who God is.

But God also revealed himself in the form of a helpless baby boy, born in a barn
more than 2,000 years ago. The next time you hold a baby in your arms, just imagine
the Ruler of the universe cooing with delight, crying in hunger, or shivering from the
cold.

God could have come to earth as a full–grown man or an invincible super–human
hero. But He deliberately chose to begin his life as an infant and go through all the
stages of growth to adulthood. Yes, Jesus even went through puberty. He knows first-
hand what it's like to be baby, a child, a teen. God the Son probably endured His share
of nightmares, bruises and scrapes, harassment from bullies, misunderstandings with
His earthly parents, social isolation, and betrayal by so–called friends.

No wonder the Bible is full of passages about how much God loves the younger
members of His creation. He knows how hard it is to be young. Jesus empathizes with
youth culture so much that He taught, "Whoever welcomes one of these little children
in my name welcomes me; and whoever welcomes me does not welcome me but the
one who sent me" (Mark 9:37).

Isn't it a comfort that God understands, from experience, what it's like to be your
age?

GRACE FOR TODAY:

When the Lord says He feels our pain, He means it.

DIRECT LINE TO HEAVEN

D id you know that you don't have to call a prayer line to get an answer to prayer? Maybe your church has a "Church Hotline" phone list. Every other night, your parents might get an urgent call from someone else on the prayer line, relaying another prayer request within the church. That's how it works.

Maybe this has led you to believe if you have a really urgent prayer request, you need to call the local body of prayer warriors, or perhaps call a prayer line listed at the bottom of a Christian program on television. Maybe you even believe they have a better chance of reaching heaven than you do, but that's simply not true. Prayer lines and prayer chains all serve a powerful purpose, but you have a direct line to the Father. All you have to do is call on His name, and you're immediately hooked up. You can reach heaven all by yourself, but agreement in prayer with someone else is a very powerful force.

GRACE FOR TODAY:

God's line is never busy.

According to this verse in Matthew, if ANY two agree on something and ask the Father, it will be done. Well, I've got good news—we qualify as ANY! So, the next time you have an urgent prayer request, grab your best friends and ask them to agree with you as you lift up your request to heaven. Maybe you could even ask your best friend to be your "prayer partner." You two could have your own little prayer line. Remember, your prayers availeth much!

Again, I tell you that if two of you on earth agree about anything you ask for, it will be done for you by my Father in heaven.

MATTHEW 18:19

WE ARE AMBASSADORS

By Luis Palau

Have you ever seen an ambassador in action? When I was at Cardiff Castle in Wales, I saw the Japanese ambassador arrive for a meeting with British officials. What an impressive sight! A band played near the entrance to the castle. Banners and flags waved in the breeze. As we watched, a long, black limousine with flags mounted on its front fenders pulled up to the entrance. We were pushed aside as the ambassador stepped out of the limousine. All the officials of the city, who were dressed in their proper historical costumes, greeted the ambassador and ushered him into the castle.

An ambassador is treated with respect because, although he is a foreigner in a strange land, he represents his government. The Bible says that every believer is an ambassador for Christ. In light of our eternal home, we are foreigners in the world; yet God has given us the responsibility and authority to be ambassadors of His kingdom. No matter what our background, status, or natural sphere of influence, we are ambassadors of God. He has given us power and authority to "make His appeal through us"—to persuade others to come to Christ.

As ambassadors of Jesus Christ, we don't do whatever we please. We aren't ambassadors to serve our own egos. We are ambassadors for God—who speaks through us. We are to speak with His authority and reveal His glory. People aren't going to listen to us very long or pay much attention to what we say if we're just ordinary human beings. But when we speak in the power of the Holy Spirit, truth and authority fill our words.[50]

—∞—

DEAR FATHER: POUR OUT YOUR GRACE ON ME AND MAKE ME A WORTHY AMBASSADOR FOR YOU. AMEN.

We are ambassadors for Christ, since God is making his appeal through us; we entreat you on behalf of Christ, be reconciled to God. For our sake he made him to be sin who knew no sin, so that in him we might become the righteousness of God.

2 CORINTHIANS 5:20-21 NRSV

DO UNTO OTHERS . . .

The entire law is summed up in a single command:
"Love your neighbor as yourself."

GALATIANS 5:14

D o you feel like you're always going the extra mile and being taken advantage of? It's difficult to walk in love on a daily basis, especially when others think of themselves first. Abraham probably found it hard to walk in love when Lot chose the best piece of land.

Abraham followed God's leading and gathered all of his family, traveling for months before finally arriving to the new land. But after being there only a short while, they discovered there wasn't enough land and water to support all of the people and flocks. So, Abraham told Lot, "We're going to have to separate. Choose whichever piece of land you want, and I'll take whatever is left over." Lot looked around and chose the beautiful green, lush valley, leaving Abraham an old dry field.

GRACE FOR TODAY:

Honor others because God honors us.

Don't you imagine that Abraham felt used and unappreciated? But, that's not where the story ends. God saw Abraham's selfless act and rewarded him accordingly. He told Abraham to climb the highest mountain and look in every direction. Then He said, "As far as you can see, I'll give it all to you." That's the kind of God we serve. (See Genesis 13:5-18.)

When you're good to people, God will make sure you come out on top. God sees you putting others first. Nothing that you do goes unnoticed by Almighty God. That doesn't mean that you have to be a doormat, but you should "do unto others as you would have them do unto you." In other words, you don't have to let others walk over you in order to walk in love.

A BRIDGE BETWEEN TWO HEARTS

A friend loves at all times.

PROVERBS 17:17

A lice and Mary had been friends for seventy-two years—before they met face-to-face. They became pen pals in the ninth grade, back in 1932. Long before e-mail and cell phones, they learned a lot about each other just by exchanging letters back and forth. Alice Melby lived in the United States. Mary Popova lived in Bulgaria.

Mary shared how the communist government took her family's possessions and how they struggled just to get by. Alice responded not only with words, but with gifts of coffee, sugar, and gelatin. In turn, Mary sent gifts of wise and loving words that encouraged Alice spiritually. At the ages of eighty-five and eighty-six, Alice and Mary finally got to hold in their arms the one they had held in their hearts for so many years and across so many miles.

Friendship builds a bridge between two people that can span any distance. Though every "bridge" between friends differs a little from every other, every true friendship shares a common foundation—loving another person the way God loves you. Even those who haven't yet gotten acquainted with God unknowingly follow in His footsteps every time they reach out unselfishly to someone else.

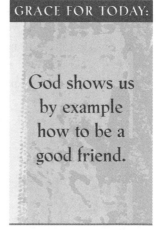

GRACE FOR TODAY:

God shows us by example how to be a good friend.

Consider how you can share more of God's love with your circle of friends. A phone call, a funny card, a flower left in a locker, or a prayer offered to the Father for someone you care about can help strengthen a friend-ship—whether your friend lives right next door or around the world. Friendship is one of God's most valuable gifts. And the funny thing is, the more you give it to others the more you'll find you receive.

WITH APPRECIATION

So speak encouraging words to one another. . . .
Overwhelm them with appreciation and love!

1 THESSALONIANS 5:11,13 MSG

As a young child, you were probably taught to say "Thank you" when someone paid you a compliment or gave you a gift. Busy lifestyles today offer little time to demonstrate our admiration, gratitude, and thankfulness as often as we should.

Perhaps that is why when someone does offer little words of encouragement, approval, or acceptance; we are so captivated by their thoughtful gifts to us—someone buys your lunch, someone returns your lost keys, another compliments you on the colors of your clothing or your new shades. It can be a smile, a wave, or a simple little e-card that lets you know you were in their thoughts today.

Do you really have to go the extra mile and make room for that moment of appreciation? If it's difficult for you to express thanks, start with someone easy to go to—your heavenly Father. It can be as simple as telling Him how much you enjoyed the sunrise this morning or the rainfall that allowed you to sleep in. As you share your gratefulness with Him, your heart will fill with His goodness and joy that comes from spending time with Him.

Then it will be easy for you to add a drop of thankfulness into the lives of those around you. Offer a smile or cheerful hello. Surprise someone in the hall with a genuine greeting—just glad to see ya! It can become contagious. You might be surprised who catches a taste of God's goodness from you.

GRACE FOR TODAY:

Fill up with appreciation for God and His goodness
will spill out into the lives of others.

GETTING PERSONAL WITH GOD

See how very much our heavenly Father loves us,
for he allows us to be called his children.

1 JOHN 3:1 NLT

A huge gap, a Grand Canyon, stands between knowing about God and truly knowing Him. For many of us, God is like a movie; we've read the reviews, seen the previews. We can summarize the plot, even quote a line or two of dialogue. We can even form a thumbs-up or thumbs-down opinion. But we haven't seen the film ourselves.

God is your loving Creator, and He wants you to experience Him firsthand. So read His book. Listen to His music. Hear His modern-day prophets (pastors, youth pastors, singers, authors, and musicians).

Take time to simply be still in God's presence, and ask Him to fill your head and your heart with His love. Let your prayers become conversations with Him.

To have a close, rewarding relationship with God, you don't have to be perfect. But you do need to be genuinely committed to the relationship. Just as a person can't be "mostly married" or "somewhat pregnant," you cannot have a "sort of" relationship with God. A relationship with the all-loving, all-powerful God of the universe just doesn't work that way. Being close to God includes spending time with Him at His house, with His people. Making time to worship. Time to praise. Time to support and be supported by other believers.

If you avoid church or let your Bible gather dust on a shelf, will God still love you? Of course. He loved you long before you were even aware of Him. He loved you before the first church was built or the first word of the Bible was penned. But if you truly want to grow close to God, to return even a portion of the love He has showered on you, you need to spend time with Him.

GRACE FOR TODAY:

God loved us before the first church was built or the first word of the Bible was penned.

SUCCESS BOUND!

In the early 1950s, Lillian Vernon spent $500 on her first advertisement, offering monogrammed belts and handbags. At the end of the first round of sales, she had made $32,000 profit! Fifty years later, Lillian Vernon is still selling gift items and personalized goodies through a very successful catalogue sales program. In fact, her company now generates more than $250 million in sales every year.

During an interview about her success, she said, "There were naysayers along the way, but I couldn't be defeated. Because all it really takes is commonsense intelligence and hard work."

You might say Lillian Vernon is driven. She knew in her heart that she would succeed, and she did. With determination and hard work, you can accomplish much. But, with determination, hard work, and God; you can accomplish more than you ever imagined!

God has placed a dream in your heart, and no matter how big it is—you can do it! Ask God to help you see your future through His eyes. Ask Him to grow that seed of a dream in your heart until if fills you up and spills over.

As you are constantly asked, "What are you going to be? Where are you going to go to college? What are you going to major in at college?" don't get overwhelmed or stressed out. Let God lead you down the path to success. Soon, we'll be sharing your success story!

> **GRACE FOR TODAY:**
> God's road may not prove easy, but following Him assures us success.

[Jesus said,] "Again, I tell you that if two of you on earth agree about anything you ask for, it will be done for you by my Father in heaven."

MATTHEW 18:19

SEVEN PROMISES

By Luis Palau

Seven promises are listed in 2 Corinthians 6:16–18—promises that God will fulfill when we live holy lives through the power of the Indwelling Christ.

The first promise is that God dwells within us—He lives with us wherever we are.

The second promise is that God lives and walks among us. This is plural, referring to the church—the body of Christ.

The third promise is that God will be our God. When we separate ourselves from what is improper and unrighteous, God will reveal himself to us. We will feel and enjoy His presence.

The fourth promise is that we will be God's people. We aren't like the masses of the world; we are the people of God, the family of God.

The fifth promise is preceded by God's call. He calls us to separate ourselves from past sins and everything in our lives that is unclean, improper, or sinful. Then He promises to receive us. What a promise! How beautiful it is to know that God receives us into His presence with open arms.

The sixth promise is that God will be a Father to us, an absolutely perfect Father. He will care for us, protect us, and love us. What more could He do for us?

The seventh promise is that God will confess us to the world as His sons and daughters. There can be no greater honor than to stand before multitudes while God proclaims us His sons and daughters![51]

—⁓—

HEAVENLY FATHER: THANK YOU FOR THE WONDERFUL PROMISES YOU'VE GIVEN ME IN YOUR WORD. COVER ME WITH YOUR GRACE AS I DETERMINE TO LIVE A LIFE OF HOLINESS, PUTTING YOU FIRST IN EVERYTHING I DO AND SAY. AMEN.

Let's make a clean break with everything that defiles or distracts us, both within and without. Let's make our entire lives fit and holy temples for the worship of God.

2 CORINTHIANS 7:1 MSG

Topical Index

Author Index

Endnotes

1. *Found: God's Will* by John MacArthur Jr. Copyright 1973 SP Publications, Inc. Published by Cook Communications Ministries. All rights reserved. Page 26.
2. *Be All You Can Be* by John C. Maxwell. Copyright 2002. Published by Cook Communications Ministries. All rights reserved. Pages 13–14.
3. *Found: God's Will*. Pages 28–29.
4. *Stop Pretending* by Luis Palau. Copyright 1985, 2003 by Luis Palau. Published by Cook Communications Ministries. All rights reserved. Pages 39–41.
5. *Anxiety Attacked* by John MacArthur Jr. Copyright 1995 by John MacArthur Jr. Published by Cook Communications Ministries. All rights reserved. Pages 15–16.
6. *Be All You Can Be* by John C. Maxwell. Copyright 2002. Published by Cook Communications Ministries. All rights reserved. Pages 52–53.
7. *Stop Pretending*. Pages 33–34.
8. *Anxiety Attacked*. Pages 28–29.
9. *A Journey into Spiritual Growth*. Copyright 1999 by Evelyn Christenson. Published by Chariot Victor Publishing, a division of Cook Communications. All rights reserved. Pages 35–36.
10. Ibid. Pages 175–176.
11. *Be a People Person* by John C. Maxwell. Copyright 2004, 1994, 1989 by Cook Communications Ministries. Published by Cook Communications Ministries. All rights reserved. Page 43.
12. Ibid. Page 61.
13. Ibid. Pages 50–51.
14. Ibid. Pages 144–145.
15. *Found: God's Will*. Pages 14–15.
16. Ibid. Pages 20–21.
17. *Stop Pretending*. Pages 31–32.
18. *Be Free* by Warren W. Wiersbe. Copyright 1975 by SP Publications, Inc. Published by Cook Communications Ministries. All rights reserved. Page 121.
19. Ibid. Page 117.
20. *A Journey into Spiritual Growth*. Pages 207–208.
21. *Found: God's Will*. Pages 23–24.
22. *A Journey into Spiritual Growth*. Pages 43–44.
23. *Found: God's Will*. Pages 32–33.
24. *Handle with Prayer* by Charles Stanley. Copyright 1982, 1992 by SP Publications, Inc. Published by Cook Communications Ministries. All rights reserved. Page 53.
25. Ibid. Pages 11–12.
26. *Encouraging One Another* by Gene Getz. Copyright 1981, 1997, 2002 by Gene Getz. Published by Cook Communications Ministries. All Rights reserved. Pages 129–130.
27. *Found: God's Will*. Pages 33, 35–36.
28. *Found: God's Will*. Page 30.
29. Taken from a 1740 sermon by John Wesley.
30. *The Adequate Man: Paul in Philippians* by Paul S. Rees (Westwood, N.J.: Revell, 1959). Page 106.
31. *Anxiety Attacked*. Page 34.
32. *Eating Disorders Throughout the Life Span*, Field and Domangue, p.31, 1987.
33. *Handle with Prayer*. Page 79.
34. Charles Spurgeon, Sermon No. 229, Love, 1858.
35. John Wesley, Sermon LXVII, On Divine Providence, 1786.
36. Thomas Watson, "The Lord's Prayer," *A Body of Practical Divinity*, 1692. Page 34.
37. Charles Spurgeon, *Morning and Evening Daily Readings*, "November 4 AM," Grand Rapids, MI: Christian Classics Ethereal Library.
38. Dwight L. Moody, *D. L. Moody's Select Works*, "The Way to God," Chapter 7: Repentance and Restitution; (Whitby, ON: J. S. Robertson & Bros.), c. 1890.
39. Thomas á Kempis, *Imitation of Christ*, Book 1, Seventh Chapter, public domain.
40. Francis de Sales, *Introduction to the Devout Life* (Grand Rapids, MI: Christian Classics Ethereal Library, 2002) (public domain). Pages 32–33.
41. Charles Spurgeon, *New Park Street Pulpit*, Sermon No. 246, "Mr. Fearing Comfort."
42. Charles Spurgeon, Sermon No. 80, *God Alone the Salvation of His People*, 1856.
43. *Handle with Prayer*. Page 75.
44. *Be All You Can Be*. Page 45.
45. *Be All You Can Be*. Page 93.
46. *Be Free*. Page 127.
47. *Stop Pretending*. Pages 130–131.
48. *Stop Pretending*. Pages 138–139.
49. *Stop Pretending*. Page 150.

Additional copies of this and other
Honor Books products are available
from your local bookseller.

The following titles are also available from Honor Books:
God's Devotional Book for Teens
Connect2God
Glimpses of an Invisible God for Teens
God's Hand on My Shoulder for Teens

If you have enjoyed this book,
or if it has had an impact on your life,
we would like to hear from you.

Please contact us at:
Honor Books, Dept. 201
4050 Lee Vance View
Colorado Springs, CO 80918
Or visit our Web site:
www.cookministries.com

HONOR HB BOOKS
Inspiration and Motivation for the Seasons of Life